Greenhill Books

HANNIBAL

VOLUME II

Also by Theodore Ayrault Dodge

ALEXANDER
A History of the Origin and Growth
of the Art of War from the earliest
times to the Battle of Ipsus, 301 BC,
with a detailed account of the
Campaigns of the Great Macedonian
Volume I: 375 pages. ISBN 1-85367-148-7
Volume II: 360 pages. ISBN 1-85367-153-3

With 237 charts, maps, plans of battles and
tactical manoeuvres, cuts of armour,
uniforms, siege devices and portraits.

HANNIBAL

A HISTORY OF THE ART OF WAR AMONG
THE CARTHAGINIANS AND ROMANS
DOWN TO THE BATTLE OF PYDNA, 168 BC,
WITH A DETAILED ACCOUNT OF
THE SECOND PUNIC WAR

By Theodore Ayrault Dodge

WITH 227 CHARTS, MAPS, PLANS OF BATTLES
AND TACTICAL MANOEUVRES,
CUTS OF ARMOUR, WEAPONS AND UNIFORMS

VOLUME II

Greenhill Books, London

This edition of *Hannibal* first published 1993 by
Greenhill Books, Lionel Leventhal Limited
Park House, 1 Russell Gardens, London NW11 9NN

British Library Cataloguing in Publication Data
A catalogue record for this book is available
from the British Library

ISBN 1-85367-152-5

*Library of Congress
Cataloging-in-Publication Data available*

Publishing History
Hannibal was first published in 1891 (Houghton Mifflin
Company) and is reproduced now exactly as the original
edition, complete and unabridged, in two volumes.

Printed and bound in India

TABLE OF CONTENTS.

LIST OF ILLUSTRATIONS.

HANNIBAL.

XXV.

MINUCIUS. FALL, 217 B. C.

HANNIBAL had had wonderful military success, but the fidelity of the Roman allies had prevented his making any substantial gain. The Romans had suffered grievous defeats, but they had not lost ground; for the integrity of the Latin confederacy held good. The dissatisfaction of senate and people at Fabius' policy grew apace. Fabius was called to Rome, and left Minucius in command, with orders to pursue the same course. For a while Minucius obeyed orders, but soon he descended to the plain, intent on trying conclusions with Hannibal. The latter was forced daily to send out two thirds of his men as foragers, for he was accumulating victual for the winter. On one of these occasions Minucius attacked his camp and came near winning a success; but some of the foragers returned and Hannibal drove the Romans off. This action, reported at Rome, gave Minucius a great repute, and he was made equal in power with the dictator. When Fabius arrived, Minucius took half the troops and moved to a new camp. Here Hannibal managed to lure him into an ambuscade, and would have utterly destroyed his army, had not Fabius opportunely appeared on the scene. Minucius, after this check, was satisfied to work under Fabius' orders; and Fabius recovered his standing with senate and people. Both armies went into winter-quarters.

THE allies were in a pitiable condition. The vaunted power of Rome had failed to be of any protection to them. The barbarians had for months ravaged their lands, and no one had dared lift a hand against them in aggressive defense. The feeling against Fabius and his policy grew apace and waxed bitter. The summer of 217 B. C. was gone. Hannibal had marched throughout the length and breadth of Italy. He had won brilliant victories. He had shown that the Romans were unable to cope with him in open battle. This was a sad military record for Rome. On the other hand, not one of the Italian confederates had proven traitor; not one of their cities had voluntarily opened its gates to the invader, — a wonderful political record.

This fidelity was far from what Hannibal had counted on. He had had reason to believe that the Roman allies would yield him their support so soon as he proved his ability to help them ; but it was not so. Hannibal had too well-balanced a mind not to know that this strong fealty foreboded evil; that he and his army alone could not accomplish all he must, if he would not fail ; and though his character was such as to lead him to wait patiently for results, he must have comprehended that he was no whit further advanced than when he descended from the Alps upon the Po. Still he was not discouraged. He knew that time works wonders, and he hoped that the successes which he felt certain that he could win when the next year's campaign should come, might still change the current of opinion. He had taken up his winter-quarters for B. C. 217–216 in the richest part of Apulia ; had accumulated stores enough for a number of months, and immense booty, and had established his magazines and hospitals and quartered his troops in a position which he could afford for a while to hold, till he could again try to disaffect the allies. With this he was fain to be content.

Fabius, on the other hand, not cast down despite his humiliating want of success and apparent lack of stomach, — his playing the part of " Hannibal's lackey," as it were, — never wavered in his belief that his policy was the only one by which to cope with this subtlest of adversaries. He too could be patient and wily, even if not on a par with his great opponent. But being shortly after called to Rome on public business, — to make certain annual sacrifices, and probably to satisfy the senate as to what he had done, as well as to still complaints, — he was compelled to leave the command in the hands of Minucius, which he did with orders to continue his system, and by no means to risk a general engagement.

As is almost invariable in such cases, there was a show of reason in the dissatisfaction with Fabius' non-fighting strategy. The Romans called him Hannibal's pedagogue, since he did nothing but follow him up and down, and wait upon him, says Plutarch. Still more, there were several circumstances which told against him. Hannibal, no doubt with a sincere admiration of his opponent (for what soldier has not generous impulses?), had ordered that certain estates belonging to Fabius should be excepted from the general devastation. This gave immediate rise to a cry of treason among the citizens of Rome. Livy charges Hannibal with deceit in this matter; but the Carthaginian showed repeatedly, by scrupulously observing the funeral rites of his fallen adversaries and by other acts of good feeling, that he possessed the soldier's warm heart, and Livy is unsupported in his slur. Again, Fabius had concluded a convention with Hannibal for the exchange of prisoners, in which any excess of men was to be paid for by either side, at a certain rate in money. For such a treaty Fabius had a clear precedent in the First Punic War. Fabius had received two hundred and forty-seven extra men. For these the senate refused to pay, declaring his convention void. Hereupon, Fabius sold the estates saved harmless by Hannibal and paid the ransom himself. But even so public-spirited an act as this could find those to misrepresent it. Fabius' stay in Rome was prolonged for many days.

Minucius had for a while ridden to orders, but, urged on by his own ambitious courage, as well as by the advice of his friends, he finally determined to cross swords with his antagonist, and Hannibal discovered the indications of this purpose with evident satisfaction.

Left to his own devices, Minucius had lost no time in approaching the Carthaginian army, and after keeping to the hills for a few days, had descended to the plain and camped

within five miles (A) of it. Hannibal had been in the daily
habit of sending out two thirds of his force into the surrounding country as foragers, keeping the small balance on hand

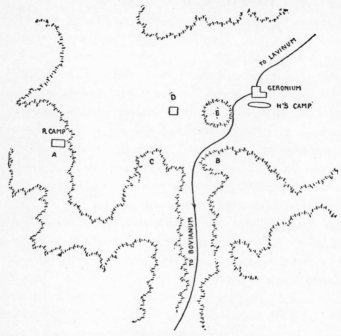

Operations at Geronium.

to protect the camp. When the Roman army came nearer,
these foraging parties for a while were cut down to a much
smaller limit, in the expectation that Minucius would show
signs of fighting; but as Hannibal was busy accumulating
winter stores, which, having so much cavalry, he must make
very ample if he would keep his horse in good condition, he
was soon again compelled to resume foraging on the old
scale.

The country about Geronium was rolling but open. Aware
of Fabius' departure, Hannibal doubted not that Minucius,

whose excessive ardor he well knew, would before long essay to attack him. Nothing loath, and with the purpose of fostering such an attack, he left Geronium and moved his camp to an eminence (B) some two miles from his camp at the town, and somewhat nearer the Romans, where he could better observe their movements and keep them from attacking his foragers. Then throwing forward by night a force of two thousand Numidians, he occupied a hill (C) between the two camps, as an outpost which should be a direct threat to the Roman camp. This small detachment, which had not intrenched itself, Minucius next morning early attacked with a superior force and drove away, establishing his own camp in the place it had been holding. This brought the two camps into close proximity.

Hannibal expected and hoped for a general engagement; but Minucius was wary and could not be drawn out. For several days Hannibal had kept all but his whole force in camp, anticipating that he could taunt Minucius into risking a battle, but when he saw that he could not bring it about, he was constrained himself to resort to Fabian tactics, and again to send out the bulk of his men as foragers day by day; for he had a goodly number of herds to graze, and must not consume the vast stores accumulated for the winter, if he expected to keep his men in good stomach for the spring campaign.

Minucius was not slow to profit by Hannibal's thus weakening the force in camp. He sent out his cavalry to cut off the foragers and herdsmen, ordering them to take no prisoners. A very large number of these men were intercepted and killed. He himself led his infantry in order of battle against the Carthaginian camp. Hannibal, thus taken at a disadvantage, — for he had but a third of his force in camp, — was neither strong enough to leave his intrenchments nor yet to afford aid to his foragers; the Roman infantry was eager to wrest a present advantage from the enemy, and advanced so gallantly that the legionaries had begun to pull out the palisades of which the stockade at the top of the Carthaginian wall was made; and it was with great personal exertions that Hannibal was able to hold his own till a body of four thousand foragers, who had sought refuge from Minucius' horse in the camp at Geronium, was collected and brought to his assistance by Hasdrubal. He then drove away the assailants and drew up in order of battle before his camp, ready to chance the day upon an equal fight, but the Roman general deemed it prudent to retire. The Carthaginian losses had, however, been large, both at camp and among foragers. Livy says they were reported to be five thousand Romans and six thousand Carthaginians, and Minucius might congratulate himself on a successful diversion. If he had made his best attack on the supply-camp at Geronium, and a lighter one on the military camp occupied by Hannibal, he would very likely have been able to capture the former and to destroy a large part of Hannibal's winter rations; for it was held in but small force, — an evident lapse on the part of the usually very careful Carthaginian, who perhaps took too many chances on Minucius' lack of enterprise. Livy sums up the affair by saying that Minucius conducted an enterprise " rather joyful than successful," so that we may assume that the Roman gain was not great, nor Hannibal's check severe.

Hannibal appreciated the danger he had run, and feared that Minucius, who had shown himself both bold and able, might some day attempt to interpose a force to cut him off from his camp at Geronium, or to surprise the town, which was but illy fortified, while his foraging forces were absent. He decided to return to his former camp. Minucius at once occupied the hill he had yielded, and camped in the very spot he had just left (B).

The test of military skill is, unfortunately, often made to consist only of success. While this is, within its bounds, an excellent rule, it must be remembered that temporary success may not mean eventual gain. The Romans were tired of Fabius' prudence, which, in their very natural and characteristic manner, they termed mere timidity. Minucius' slight gain, to which Hannibal probably gave little thought as a matter of success, was magnified into a wonderful performance, particularly as Hannibal foraged thereafter with more caution, and the Roman soldiers began to breathe more freely. Minucius not only became the hero of the hour, but as magister equitum he was made by the senate the equal in rank of Fabius the dictator, a thing never before known in Rome, and now only brought about by an excited condition of the public mind. It had been almost impossible for Fabius to justify his conduct in the eyes of the senate ; and the fickle populace — through the tribune of the people, Metillius — took open sides against him. Fabius, however, maintained his equipoise, and set out to rejoin the army. Few characters in history have exhibited so great continence under trying circumstances.

It will not do to elevate Fabius into one of the great generals of the world. He has not earned that rank. Able to a degree and possessing noble qualities, he was, perhaps, more the creation of circumstances than the creator of a new method. He was brought to the front as a foil to the idiotic foolhardiness of such men as Sempronius and Flaminius, and naturally of a hypercautious nature, he was, for the moment, the very man for the place. But it was Roman grit and political soundness, not Fabius, that saved the republic. An indefinite course of such a policy as his would have ruined the cause. The Roman generals of the Second Punic War were Marcellus and Nero and Scipio. It is honor enough for Fabius to rank beside them.

In order to enjoy the authority his elevation gave him, Minucius proposed to Fabius (or, as Polybius has it, Fabius proposed to Minucius, when he saw that Minucius was bound

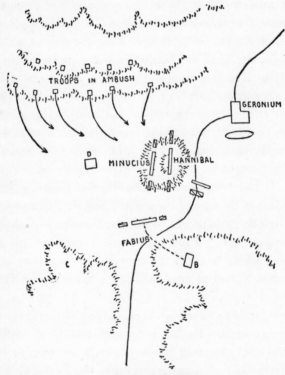

Battle of Geronium.

to be rash) to command on alternate days, or to divide the army, each taking two legions and a fair proportion of other troops. Fabius saw less danger in the latter proposal, as Minucius could in that case jeopardize but half the army in case he should undertake a dangerous offensive, and accepted this arrangement. Minucius at once withdrew his two legions from the old quarters, and camped, a mile and a half away,

well forward in the plain (D), so that the three camps stood
not far from equidistant from each other.

Hannibal was entirely satisfied with this change, which he
soon perceived from the division of the camp, from his scouts
and from deserters who, Livy says, went over to him, and at
once based a plan of action upon it. Between the two camps
stood a hill (E), commanding either. Hannibal determined
to take advantage of Minucius' evident desire to fight to lure
him if possible into an ambuscade. He accordingly, one
morning just at daybreak, sent a small force to occupy the
hill, with orders to demonstrate sufficiently to draw on the
Romans to an attack, and to hold the hill only for a short
time when the Romans should have advanced. Meanwhile,
in some ravines and behind some accidents in the ground,
which Minucius had not perceived because the ground was to
all appearances devoid of obstacles, Hannibal had concealed
during the night about five thousand infantry and a body of
five hundred Numidian horse, in such detachments of two
hundred and three hundred each, and such positions that
they would fall upon the Romans' flanks and rear when the
latter should move against the force on the hill. And that
their presence might not be discovered by the Roman scouts,
he kept the Roman line busy by the activity of the skirmishing detachment.

Nothing is easier, with proper precautions, than to hide
behind even slight undulations of ground a considerable force
of men. Any one familiar with our prairie country is well
aware of this.

No sooner did day open than Minucius, perceiving that
Hannibal had occupied the hill, sent some light troops, followed by a column of cavalry, to dislodge the Carthaginians
and take possession of it. Hannibal kept on supporting his
men on the hill by small reinforcements, so as to induce

Minucius to bring his entire force into action. After a while, irritated at the opposition of the enemy, and too much annoyed to perceive any other thing, Minucius ranged his legions in order of battle and advanced in full force against the height. Hannibal on his side threw in his own heavy troops. The velites, thus overmatched, were hustled back on the Roman line, and threw it into considerable confusion; but this was soon corrected, and the legions advanced in tolerable order. By the time the sun was up the combat had become general. At the proper moment, on a given signal, the hidden bands emerged from ambush upon the flank and rear of the Romans. Instant and perilous panic was the result. The Roman legions turned to flee, and the Carthaginians began pursuit. The rout of the Trebia seemed imminent, when Fabius, who had held his troops well in hand and ready for battle, anticipating that he might be needed to come to Minucius' rescue, appeared upon the scene, moved sharply forward to sustain Minucius' broken ranks, and reëstablished the failing fortunes of his colleague.

Fabius at this moment stood ready to offer Hannibal battle in earnest with his whole force, and made bold front; but the latter, satisfied with what he had gained, and never caring for action unless he could have it on his own terms, his men being, moreover, somewhat dispersed with the pursuit, deemed it wiser to decline, and retired to his camp. "Did I not tell you," said Hannibal jestingly, "that this cloud, which always hovered upon the mountains, would, at some time or other, come down with a storm upon us?"

The Roman losses were very heavy, especially in the bravest of the legionaries, and the velites were all cut up. Minucius, humbled at his ill-success, was sensible enough to see, and man enough to acknowledge, his own folly and the wisdom of Fabius. He openly declared to the troops that the fault was solely his, laid down his equality in command, and offered thereafter to act strictly under Fabius' orders. From this time he abode by the discreet advice of the dictator.

These incidents at once turned the current again in Fabius' favor, and every voice in Rome and the army was raised to yield him thanks for his skillful and magnanimous conduct.

Hannibal fortified the hill where the battle had taken place, occupied it with a strong force, drew a line of intrenchments from the hill to his camp and went into winter-quarters.

The term of Fabius as dictator was about to expire, and the command of the army devolved on the consuls Servilius and Atilius, who had succeeded Flaminius, until new consuls should be elected and take command. The Roman army retired to its old location on the slopes of Mt. Calene, near by, to winter.

Servilius, at sea, had not had much good fortune. He had made a descent on the African coast, but had been beaten off. On the other hand, the Spanish fleet under Hasdrubal had also suffered a complete defeat at the hands of Cnæus Scipio, near the mouth of the Iberus; and the latter had driven back to Carthage a fleet which was to land reinforcements for Hannibal at Pisa. The Romans had made a decided gain at sea. We have seen what Cnæus Scipio's success had been in 218 B. C. on the Spanish mainland, and that P. Cornelius Scipio, his brother, had joined him with eight thousand reinforcements in 217 B. C. Thus encouraged by substantial aid, as well as the moral effect of the naval victories, the two made bold to advance, and soon reached Saguntum and strongly established themselves near that city. By their military skill and judicious policy, they made large conquests among the allies of Hasdrubal, thus weakening the Carthaginian cause in Spain. Hannibal was not happy in the lieutenants he had left behind him.

XXVI.

ÆMILIUS PAULUS AND VARRO. SPRING, 216 B. C.

In 216 B. C., Æmilius Paulus and Terentius Varro were consuls, and Rome had nearly one hundred thousand men in the field. Æmilius was a man of the highest character; Varro was of low birth and without those qualities we most esteem. Hannibal and the Roman army lay facing each other at Geronium until May. He had tried to lure the consuls into an ambuscade, or to battle, without success. The Romans were gaining in ability; and the number of veterans in their ranks was now considerable. The vicinity of Geronium had been eaten out; Hannibal must move to new quarters, for he had not the aid of the population to bring him supplies. There was a great depot of bread-stuffs at Cannæ, south of him, on the Aufidus, which the Romans were care-lessly guarding. By a secret and clever march, Hannibal seized on Cannæ. The consuls were at a loss what to do. Cannæ was in the Apulian plain, where Hannibal could make efficient use of his cavalry. But the senate advised another battle, if it could be had on equal terms; and the consuls marched to Canusium, south of the Aufidus, and camped six miles from the Carthaginian. Here, a few days after, Varro crossed swords with Hannibal, and won a certain advantage. This whetted his appetite for a pitched battle, much to Hannibal's delight. The Romans had eighty thousand foot and seven thousand horse to Hannibal's forty thousand foot and ten thousand horse. They had also established a small camp on the north bank, to protect their foragers. Both sides prepared for battle.

NEXT year, B. C. 216, C. Terentius Varro and L. Æmilius Paulus were consuls. Varro was the popular, Æmilius the senate's candidate. As prætors, Pomponius Matho, Publius Furius, M. Claudius Marcellus and L. Postumius were chosen; and the two latter were respectively assigned to Sicily and Gaul. The senate made unusual exertions to raise troops, and put nine Roman and nine allied legions, each of five thousand foot, into the field, making with the horse ninety-eight thousand men, a much larger force than Rome had so far reached in the Second Punic War. Still the cavalry was less than Hannibal's and vastly inferior to it, and cavalry was the winning arm. The Scipios in Spain were continued in command, and an expedition against Africa from Syracuse was planned. One of the new legions was assigned to the prætor L. Postumius, whose orders on leaving for Gaul were to create such a diversion as might result in the Gallic auxiliaries in Hannibal's command being recalled to the defense of their own country. The proconsul Servilius was ordered by Æmilius to undertake no operations in force against Hannibal, but to exercise his men in slight skirmishes and exchanges with the Carthaginians, so as to lend them confidence and aplomb, — a duty which Servilius apparently performed with skill and success. The troops this year all took a new oath " never to fly from the enemy, never to leave the ranks except to get weapons or palisades, to kill an enemy or save a fellow-citizen." Rome was now in earnest if ever.

The new consuls were the antipodes of each other. Æmilius was an aristocrat, a man of noble character and fine bearing, and a good soldier, courageous but discreet, who, as consul three years before, had commanded with credit in Illyria, and brought that war to a successful issue. He had intelligence enough to approve the Fabian policy. Varro was a plebeian, son of a butcher, and is generally represented as a brutal and common demagogue. Polybius calls him base and worthless. But the historians are apt to be partial to the patricians, and Varro had given, and later on gave again, signs of ability, though no doubt he was open to the gravest criticism and, according to some, to the charge of lacking stomach to fight to the bitter end.

Hannibal remained in his camp at Geronium until May, the Roman army still encamped where it had been all winter in his front, backing on the foothills for protection from the

Numidian cavalry. The recklessness bred of Minucius' success had been quite dissipated by Minucius' later failure. But under Servilius the condition of the Roman soldiery had constantly improved.

Why Hannibal remained at this point so long, as well as many other interesting circumstances, are left without explanation by the historians, who only speak of waiting for the crops to yield forage and rations. Contrasting the Carthaginian's long period of rest in winter-quarters with Alexander's abnormal activity, which knew no seasons, no obstacles, no difficulties, these apparent delays appear strange in a man whom we know to possess no less real energy than the great Macedonian, and to whom at first blush we assume time to have been of the essence of success. His army had now enjoyed a long respite from work, and he must himself have been anxious for action. During the winter and spring there had been frequent outpost combats, but nothing of which the historians make more than casual mention. But in these combats the Roman legionaries gradually acquired experience and hardihood. They were transforming themselves from raw levies to seasoned troops, and the number of men who had seen service was fast increasing. We can only guess that Hannibal's time had been taken up in negotiating with the Roman allies of southern Italy, and that he was waiting developments. Nothing shows the extraordinary force of character of the man better than the fact that, with such heterogeneous elements as those of which his army was composed, he experienced no difficulty in keeping his troops in heart and health during the winter, — a season which is always prejudicial to discipline, owing to the enforced idleness, to the impossibility of finding work for the men to do.

While in this vicinity, Hannibal tried one or two more stratagems to gain an advantage over the Romans. After a certain affair of the outposts, in the spring of 216 B. C., in which he may have suffered somewhat more loss than the enemy, though probably not seventeen hundred killed to the Romans one hundred, as Livy states, Hannibal withdrew from camp during the night, the men bearing naught but their weapons, and leaving the tents and equipage in disorder, as if the Carthaginians had suddenly retired in a panic. Moving off to a distance, he concealed his infantry in the cover of some hills, his cavalry near by and his baggage-train beyond. He hoped that the Romans would plunder his camp, and that he might take advantage of the disorder thus engendered. He had left the camp-fires burning, in order to lead the Romans to believe that he had intended to persuade them that he was still in camp, so that he might retreat to a greater distance before they caught up with him. The Roman generals came dangerously close to falling into the trap. The army had been ordered into line; but the consuls were restrained partly by fear of a ruse, partly by the bad appearance of the sacrificial victims. For once these annoying omens proved of use. As a rule, unless in the hands of a man like Alexander, who could turn the priests to good account and lead the oracles by his own better judgment, they were an unmitigated nuisance, a hindrance to all military operations. In this instance, before the legions actually advanced, news was brought in from the front that the Carthaginians were lying in ambush beyond the hills.

Such a stratagem appears to us trivial indeed; but ancient history is full of such, — both successes and failures. And when we consider, for example, how Hannibal escaped from the Falernian plain by his stratagem of the oxen, and what the conditions of ancient warfare were, the originality of such proceedings, and their not infrequent singular success, excites our admiration. Even in modern war, less good ruses have lain at the foundation of great victories.

One word about Livy, whose statements with regard to Hannibal are often manifestly inexact, like the one above quoted, namely, that the Carthaginians, in a combat having no serious consequences for them, lost seventeen hundred men to the Roman one hundred. Much of what Livy says it is impossible to accept without reading between the lines for explanation. That what this arch-enemy of Hannibal's tells us about him makes him out one of the greatest of men, in spite of all his slurs and charges, should be praise enough. Cornelius Nepos all but overdraws the picture when he says that " as long as he continued in Italy, none made a stand against him in a regular engagement, none, after the battle of Cannæ, pitched a camp against him in the field ; " but he is far more near the truth than Livy in his attempts to underrate his work. And yet it is on Livy, after Cannæ, that we must rely for our facts. Polybius' history exists only in fragments after 216 B. C. We shall construe Livy as we go along, usually by his own statement.

Advancing spring had brought to a low ebb the stores which Hannibal had accumulated for the winter ; and the neighborhood had been completely drained by the presence of both the armies. The Roman senate, moreover, had ordered all farmers to bring their grain into the fortified cities. The Carthaginians found that they must make a change of location for mere subsistence ; and it had also become certain that Hannibal must win some signal success to encourage his own and intimidate the enemy's troops. He was in a position which demanded constant success. A single bad failure meant destruction. The Romans had the whole population at their service for victualing, as well as many large depots of provisions and munitions of war, which enabled them to remain wherever they chose ; while Hannibal, regardless of strategic reasons, was compelled to move from place to place for the mere purpose of feeding his army. For the inhabitants were still generally hostile. He was compelled to detach considerable forces of foragers, thus at all times weakening his own main body, and affording the Romans the additional chance of falling upon these detached parties. It was essential for him to lay hold of some large town for a storehouse for the approaching campaign, and this in a region as yet unexhausted by the presence of an army.

The Romans had created a magazine of stores at Cannæ, in Apulia, on the Aufidus, from which they were rationing the army in Hannibal's front. The northern portion of Apulia is an immense plain, — the largest south of the valley of the Po. It is not far from fifty miles from northwest to southeast, and half as wide. Small parts of this prairie land are to-day bare and unproductive; for the most part it is rich, and produces largely all kinds of grain and much good wine. Cannæ occupied a position on the southerly boundary of the region, and, as Polybius says, commanded the whole country, — probably meaning as a town which was fairly well fortified, and was the principal grain mart of the section. By very gross mismanagement, this depot, though garrisoned, had not been so well provided with defenses as to be placed in security against capture out of hand by a large force. These facts Hannibal had fully ascertained by the use of constant spies. The time of the early harvest had arrived, and there was plenty of forage for the beasts and grain for the men, — everywhere except in the region which had been eaten out during the winter by both the armies. The vicinity of Cannæ, a big plain, afforded the Carthaginian chances for manœuvring which he had not in his position near Geronium. Everything spoke in favor of a change of location.

To reach the Aufidus, Hannibal must turn the Roman position unobserved. This, by skillful and well-concealed

movements and forced marches, he managed to do, reached
Cannæ and seized it, with its abundant supplies. To judge
by the topography and the roads then probably existing, he

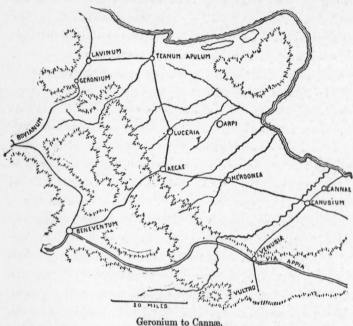

Geronium to Cannæ.

left his camp-fires burning at his camp near Geronium, and
retired rapidly on Larinum, whence by Teanum Apulum, Luceria, his old stronghold, Æcæ and Herdonia, he reached
Canusium and Cannæ. It is probable that there was a road
along the coast, but this required the building of too many
bridges for a rapid march. The Romans must pass by Bovianum and Beneventum to reach Æcæ; or from Beneventum the Via Appia would take them to Venusia, whence there
was a road to Canusium. Once on the march, Hannibal's
cavalry could easily have prevented the Romans from interfering with his progress, even if they had tried. And

after they discovered his departure, they did not guess his objective.

Not only had Hannibal provided himself with a storehouse full of victuals, but he had robbed the Romans of a fine town and magazine, in a section of country of great importance to whomever held it; and he had also placed himself between the Romans and much of the grain-giving section of Apulia, where the wheat earliest came to maturity. This afforded him every hope of compelling the enemy to give him battle.

The proconsuls, who appear to have still been in command until the new consuls should join, had been negligent indeed. They could readily have kept a sufficient garrison in the citadel of Cannæ, but this, little anticipating Hannibal's turning march, they had not done. They could have kept watch on Hannibal, but so illy did they do this that they were scarcely aware of his breaking camp, and knew absolutely nothing of his direction, until they heard of the fall of Cannæ. No Roman could keep track of Hannibal. His marches were too rapid and secret. Thus suddenly deprived of their largest magazine, the proconsuls sent helplessly to the senate for orders, saying that they could not avoid battle if they followed up Hannibal, for he was in a level country, where they would be at the mercy of his cavalry.

It was Hannibal's cavalry which so far had been his right arm in battle, his means of gathering rations. Without his cavalry he would have starved. Like Alexander, the Punic captain understood and utilized this arm as it deserved. It must not be forgotten that the dangerous zone of the weapons of the heavy foot was not over twenty yards from its front, and that cavalry could thus charge close up to a line of battle; while the farther carrying missiles of the velites were far from deadly to well-armed men. Small wonder that the enemy's cavalry was the dread of the Romans, who had nothing wherewith to match it.

The proconsuls were instructed by the senate to await the arrival of the new consuls, for special reliance was placed on Æmilius Paulus, who had orders to try conclusions with Hannibal in another general engagement, if it could be done on even terms. The consuls, arrived on the ground in early summer, themselves readily saw that they must either leave Hannibal in possession of Apulia, or follow him up and harass him as Fabius had done, or settle the matter by fighting; and that the latter should be done soon was the evident sentiment of the conscript fathers. They had eight Roman legions and the accompanying allies. The Roman legions had been purposely raised from four thousand foot and two hundred horse to five thousand foot and three hundred horse, and the allied legions had the same number of foot and twice the horse per legion. The whole consular army was thus eighty thousand infantry and seven thousand two hundred cavalry, against Hannibal's forty thousand infantry and ten thousand cavalry.

The assembling of this enormous army for one duty showed the anxiety Rome was beginning to feel as to her ability to cope in any way with the Carthaginian. The Roman numerical superiority was vast. It brings Frederick to mind, whose battles were all but invariably fought against odds as great or greater.

But there were other factors in the problem. A leaven of Hannibal's troops were his old and tried soldiers, accustomed to victory and not liable to panic; the Romans were many of them young and inexperienced in actual war; and though there was, perhaps, as large a percentage of veteran material, that is, soldiers of several campaigns, in the Roman army, it was not beyond the chance of losing heart in any unforeseen

contingency. Even the raw Roman legionary was capable of
dying where he stood, with face undaunted towards the foe.
He had shown this valor many times. But demoralization
is an element impossible to foresee, difficult to arrest. And
the Roman, brave as he was, must have looked with some
dread at the coming conflict, though eager to punish this
ruthless destroyer of his farms, his hearth-stones and his
household gods. Punic craft was an uncertain danger which
he could not forecast or provide against. It was really a
question of leaders more than armies. In this the invaders
had the distinct advantage. Again, divided authority reigned
in the Roman camp; there was but one will in the Punic
forces. One of the consuls was a headstrong leader; we know
what Hannibal was. In these last factors lay the chief advantage of the Carthaginians as against the Roman vast
numerical superiority.

It was highly dangerous for the Romans to leave Hannibal
in Apulia. One more campaign such as the last might detach
the Apulian confederates from the Roman alliance. A Fabian policy on these broad plains was far from an easy problem, and perhaps had long enough obtained. The consuls
had received instructions from Rome to bring Hannibal to
battle. They broke camp and marched to Canusium, which
they reached in two days, and took up a position between five
and six miles from Hannibal's, who had established himself
in a strongly intrenched camp near the town of Cannæ.
The camps backed respectively on Canusium and Cannæ,
which were about seven miles apart.

The country is a huge prairie. From his quarters at
Cannæ, Hannibal could look northwest forty odd miles to the
long range which divided Samnium from Apulia; on his right
lay the sea; on his left rose the distant peak of Vultro; at
his back the ranges of southern Apulia. In his immediate

front were the sinuous windings of the Aufidus, emerging from
the hills on the west and flowing a bare half mile from both
Canusium and Cannæ. Between him and the mountains on

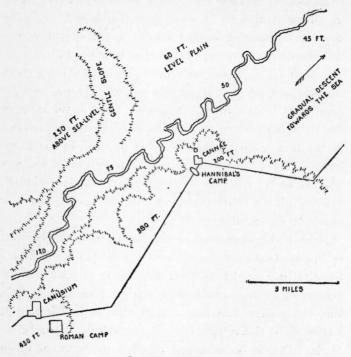

Canusium and Cannæ.

the northwest lay a flat alluvial plain of great extent, hemmed
in between these mountains and the sea; behind him was a
rolling country. The ground towards Canusium and beyond
was clear, with a gradual rise and slightly accentuated surface.

The Aufidus is the only river of Italy which breaks through
the Apennines. Its general course is northeast. Just before
reaching Cannæ, it emerges into the perfectly flat plain of
which we have just spoken.

The consuls, it will be remembered, commanded on alternate

days. Varro desired at once to attack. Æmilius feared lest
a battle on a plain, where Hannibal could use his confessedly
superior cavalry, might again be fatal, and desired to lead the
Carthaginians to a spot where the infantry would have the
most of the fighting. Varro characterized Æmilius' policy as
Fabian; Æmilius reminded Varro of the fate of Sempronius
and Flaminius. Such dissension foreboded no good.

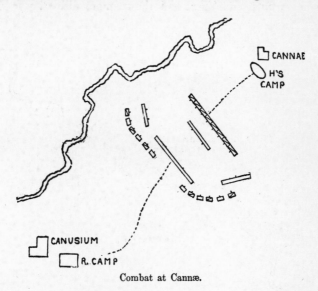

Combat at Cannæ.

The next day after the arrival of the army at Canusium,
being one on which Varro's turn to command came, he marched
out from camp and offered battle on the ground between the
two camps. Hannibal accepted the gage, and at once attacked
the Roman van of heavy troops with eight thousand light infantry and all his cavalry, and threw the Romans into some
confusion. But Varro had cleverly supported his line with
cavalry, among whose turmæ he had interspersed some velites
and a few legionary cohorts, says Polybius; and, moreover, he
had a considerable preponderance of force in line. He fought

his men well, and though Hannibal kept up the action till
evening, using apparently every effort to overcome the Roman legions, the Carthaginians had decidedly the worst of
this first encounter.   The Romans kept the battle-field.
Losses are not given.

Hannibal retired to his camp at Cannæ.   If these are all
the facts, he had made a mistake in not ordering up some of
his heavy foot, and Varro had shown more discretion in his

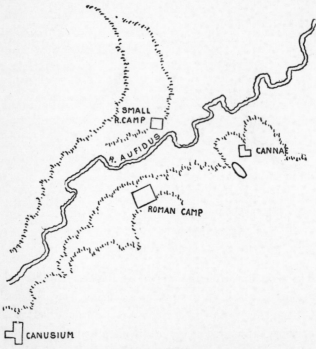

Camps at Cannæ.

management.   But Hannibal was probably the gainer in that
Varro's appetite had been whetted for further action, a thing
most earnestly desired by the Carthaginian.   It seems to be
a question whether Hannibal did not purposely allow Varro

this success. He did not put in his whole force, as he would have done had he desired a battle *à outrance*. When he fought, he wanted different conditions. The Roman camp was advanced to the location of the battle-field.

On the evening of this day, after their successful combat, the Romans lay encamped on the south side of the Aufidus, three miles only from the town of Cannæ. Next morning, Æmilius took command. He was badly placed in the open field, where, despite his numerical superiority, he could not well resist the tactics of Hannibal's cavalry. Neither wishing to remain where he was, nor to try to follow up Varro's success of yesterday, nor to withdraw to better ground, lest this movement to the rear should dishearten his men, he took an aimless course, for that reason a weak one. His foragers and watering parties were being harassed by the Carthaginian scouting detachments on the other side. He sent one third of his force across to the northern bank of the Aufidus, which at this season is everywhere fordable, to a place a trifle down-stream, where he had a number of foragers, partly to sustain these and partly to form a secondary camp, from which he might annoy the enemy's parties which were roaming all over the plain in quest of corn. This smaller camp was nearly a mile from the main camp and a trifle farther from Hannibal's.

Hannibal saw this uncertainty in manœuvres with satisfaction. He divined that the moment had arrived for which he had longed for months; that it was about to come once more to the arbitrament of battle, this time, perhaps, a final one. He had probably heard that the Romans had decided on a more vigorous policy, and he knew that Varro was precipitate, and that Æmilius would be necessarily drawn into active measures. Both commanders made stirring addresses to their armies, Hannibal promising certain victory, and

Æmilius showing the Roman soldiers, by the experience of yesterday's success, that the Carthaginians were not invincible.

Polybius and Livy both give the harangue of Æmilius to the consular, and that of Hannibal to his own army. The latter bears the true ring of the great captain. Whether fanciful, or preserved by tradition, or otherwise recorded, it is what we can well imagine this soldier to have said to his soldiers. Thus ended his glowing words: " Tell me, warriors, could you have asked of the gods more than to bring the enemy to action on such a ground, where our cavalry is sure to overwhelm him ? Thank ye the gods for bringing us certain victory ! Thank me, your general, for bringing the enemy where he cannot decline to fight ! By your former combats ye have gained the open country of the Roman ! By to-day's victory ye shall have his cities, his treasures, his power ! Let us hasten into action ! I promise you victory, and, the gods willing, I will make my promise good ! "

Hannibal bade his troops prepare their weapons and strengthen themselves with rest and food ; and, on the second day after, he left the camp and formed his army in line of battle with the right leaning on the Aufidus, and invited Æmilius to join battle, having probably made his tactical calculations with care ; but the latter, not liking the flat terrain, and knowing that lack of forage for his enormous number of beasts would sooner or later constrain Hannibal to move his quarters, contented himself with strengthening both his camps, reinforcing his outposts and the communications between the camps, and hoping that Hannibal might attack him in this position. Not caring to run so great a risk, Hannibal, after standing in line all day, was compelled to forfeit whatever dispositions he had made. He returned to camp, but sent out his Numidians to the other side of the river to attack the Roman foragers, and to prevent their seizing the banks so as to cut off a proper water supply, or if possible to prevent their watering their own horses. This latter the Numidians did to good effect, marching up even to the gates of the Roman camp.

Knowing that on the next day Varro would be in command, and that he would be burning to avenge the taunt of battle offered and declined, Hannibal made up his mind to again seek battle; and he made arrangements to do so with his entire forces, leaving eight thousand men to guard his camp.

Carthaginian Coin.

XXVII.

THE BATTLE OF CANNÆ. JUNE, 216 B. C.

HANNIBAL had sent his Numidians across the river to attack the smaller camp. Varro next day crossed to protect it, and Hannibal also crossed and offered battle. The Romans faced southerly, the Carthaginians northerly. Varro had sixty-six thousand foot and seven thousand two hundred horse in line to Hannibal's thirty-two thousand foot and ten thousand horse. Hannibal backed on the river to prevent his flanks from being overlapped. Varro crowded his maniples together so as to strengthen his line and be more certain to crush his opponent; but he was really losing his mobility and giving his men a feeling of uncertainty in this new formation. Hannibal put his Spaniards and Gauls in the centre, and his Africans on the flanks of this infantry; eight thousand horse on the left and two thousand Numidians on the right. He advanced his centre in a salient, so as to take the first shock of the Roman onset, purposing to withdraw it gradually, and then if the Romans followed it to have his Africans wheel in upon their flanks. So it happened. The Carthaginian horse defeated the Roman and allied horse and drove it from the field, pursued by the Numidians. The Roman foot broke in the central salient of Hannibal, but when they followed it up, crowding in their eagerness out of all formation, the Africans wheeled in on their flanks, and the cavalry rode down on their rear. The entire Roman army was destroyed; Hannibal lost but six thousand men. The defeat was due to Varro's blundering tactics and Hannibal's superb manœuvring. There is no victory in history which was more fairly won.

THERE has been much discussion as to which bank of the Aufidus the battle of Cannæ was fought on. There has been still more discussion as to just how the armies faced, whether at right angles to the river, or parallel to it. An intimate knowledge of the field makes both matters plain. Polybius clearly states that Varro crossed the river from the main camp, that is, to the north bank, and, reinforcing his legions from the little camp, drew up in line in such a way as to face south. This statement is fully confirmed by Livy, who evidently copied from Polybius, as he uses substantially the same words. He had no evidence to conflict with the Greek historian. Moreover, both state (Livy again copying) that the sun, *when it had risen*, was inconvenient to neither, facing, as they did, northerly and southerly. The hour of opening the engagement was probably sunrise, and in June the sun rises in the northeast. Hannibal is also said by these authors, and by Appian and Plutarch, to have had his back to the wind Vulturnus, or southeast wind, which blows now, as it did then, in the June harvest-time. Both authors state that the Roman cavalry on the right leaned on the river; but they do not state that this remained so throughout the battle. Such a position, according to one theory of the battle, would conflict with the other statements and the topography, and if we were to throw out anything, the assumption that the Romans fought with their right on the river is the one which we can best dispense with. But this does not seem necessary to be done, as will be seen. The tactical manœuvres are all clearly ascertained, and these form the chief interest of the battle.

Reading these positive statements in connection with a knowledge of the topography of the region, derived from personal examination, makes it seem incontestable that both commanders crossed to the north bank. There was reason for it. Hannibal did so not only because the ground was there quite level and better suited to his cavalry, but also because he felt sure that the danger to their new camp would make the Romans anxious to accept battle. Varro did so to protect the new camp, and because he thought he could back up against a slight rise in the ground just above this camp, — at that day considered a decided advantage. So when he crossed, left in front, he first began to form line, facing east, "placing his cavalry in the right wing, which was next the river," where it stood with its rear to the small camp which

Hannibal's men had attacked the day before, and might attack again. But when Varro saw Hannibal's formation backing on the river, his natural ardor, and the fact that he so

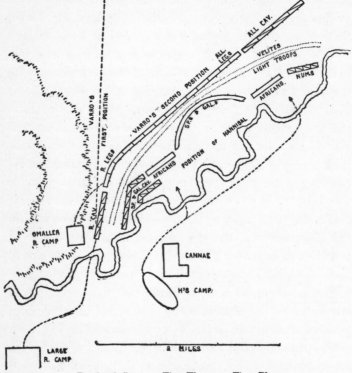

Battle of Cannæ.   First Theory — First Phase.

largely outnumbered the Carthaginians, induced him to accept
Hannibal's offer of battle, and either to pivot on his right-
centre and swing round his centre and left opposite to Hannibal, or to move his whole army into one straight line, " facing
southerly," actually southeast. The former theory satisfies
all the statements of Polybius and Livy, and no other does.
The second one satisfies all these statements, except the one
that the Roman right was on the river.

Arnold has read the histories to mean that the Carthaginians were on the south side and had their left flank on the river, while the Romans had their back to the sea, in other words, that their positions were reversed. It is scarcely probable that the Romans would purposely cut themselves off from Canusium and Venusia. The habit of fighting with the camp in the rear of an army was all but universal at that day, and particularly the rule among the Romans; that they would manœuvre so as to back up against the enemy's camp before engaging battle seems inadmissible.

Swinburne tells us that the Aufidus, after having flowed straight east for some time, makes a sharp elbow towards the south, and thus describes a very wide semicircle, precisely opposite the position where was the Carthaginian camp, and that it was in this part of the plain that the principal effort of the battle occurred. Niebuhr has adopted this theory of the terrain and position of the rival armies, and Colonel McDougall, in his admirable volume on Hannibal, has followed their statements. The theory of the left bank and the northerly and southerly facing of the armies is without doubt the best. It accords with the historians' record, and satisfactorily elucidates the manœuvres. But there are some topographical errors in Swinburne, Niebuhr, and McDougall, which are apparent to any one who has studied the battle on the field itself.

The general course of the Aufidus between Canusium and Cannæ is exactly northeast. The river is full of windings; but there is not now, nor is there any appearance of there ever having been, a southerly bend of the river two or three miles wide. Standing to-day on the slight elevation, crowned by several hillocks which hide the relics of the ancient town of Cannæ, perhaps one hundred and fifty feet above the plain, and looking out towards the Aufidus, one's eye is at once caught by a marked southerly sweep of the river. To any one who has not seen an army of fifty thousand men in line, this sweep would appear large. This is probably what Swinburne saw and described. But it is in reality less than one half mile wide; and to locate the battle of Cannæ within this sweep is to seek to fit the foot of Gargantua into the slipper of Cinderella. The length of the Roman and Carthaginian lines must have been at least three miles.

Historical as well as topographical errors are easily propagated; the author fell into this one before studying the battle on the field. The mistake is now rectified. The accompanying charts give the correct topography of the region, and it is thought the true location of the troops. They certainly fit both the authorities and the terrain; and no other plan will do so. The only statement to be rejected, and this only if we accept the second theory, is that Varro leaned his right — the Roman cavalry — on the river; and this is met by the probability that he did so on first crossing, and afterward changed his mind. It is much more probable that, with his great superabundance of forces, he threw his cavalry around in a crotchet or circle to reach the river or to lean on the small camp, which being itself near the river, would amount to the same thing. This first theory is to be preferred. It accords entirely with the authorities and best with their clearly described course of the battle.

The disposition of the troops adopted by many historians, including Mommsen, to the effect that the armies crossed to the north bank, and that the Carthaginian left and Roman right leaned on the river, each backing in the direction of his own camp on the other side, disregards the positive statements that the Romans faced southerly, and the Carthaginians northerly and with their backs to the wind Vulturnus. In such a position, if they stood at right angles to the river, the

Carthaginians would be facing all but south, and the Romans all but north, the very reverse of what both Polybius and Livy tell us; and, moreover, Hannibal would be unapt to attack uphill, as this position, in addition to leaving his right flank in the air, would make him do. Had his right flank been thus misplaced, he would have been apt to make it stronger than he did by merely posting his two thousand Numidians there. If we intend to be governed by what Polybius and Livy tell us, we must accept the positions as laid down.

Varro had made up his mind to fight. He could not stomach the insult put upon the Roman army. Before daylight on the morning succeeding the attack of the Numidians on the lesser camp, all his preparations had been completed, and without consulting his colleague, he put his troops under arms, and, leaving eleven thousand men — perhaps two legions, perhaps extraordinarii and other supernumeraries — in the larger camp, with orders to attack Hannibal's camp during the battle, he crossed the river, left in front, and joining the bulk of the forces of the lesser camp to his own, prepared to offer battle. Polybius and Livy both state that Varro crossed first; but it is probable that Hannibal had either left some skirmishers on the farther side, or had shown him some other indication that he would give battle on that bank.

Hannibal on his side forded the stream in two columns and drew up his army so that it backed on the river. His front he had previously covered with archers and slingers in such a manner as to hide his tactical formation from the Roman generals as well as to shield his crossing. The Roman line, by its greater extent and number, could readily overlap his own, and thus endanger his flanks. But by backing on the river, he could, if desirable, so manœuvre his cavalry, which was on the flanks, as to throw it back at a slight angle to the river bank, and thus save his infantry from being taken in reverse.

Seeing Hannibal's general position, the Roman consul, already over, concluded to draw up in the plain opposite the Carthaginians. He was burning to have it out with this arch-enemy of Rome. No doubt every soldier in the ranks was equally ardent. But Varro held fast to the smaller camp and the river.

This theory of the battle may be thought to be weak in that it makes Hannibal fight with a river at his back. But at this distance from the sea the Aufidus is everywhere fordable at the early harvest-season, so that the river was practically not a danger; or at least a lesser one than being overlapped, and in any event a decisive defeat now would be the end of Hannibal's career. This he well knew, and he proposed to make his men fight out the battle to the bitter end. The river helped to do this.

Varro also threw out his light troops in advance. He saw that it would not avail him to extend his line beyond that of Hannibal, as the troops on the flanks would, owing to the Carthaginian position, have nothing in their front and be unable to take part in the battle; but in order to make his line the heavier he changed the formation of his legions, so that, as Polybius tells us, "the maniples were nearer each other, or the intervals were decreased more than usual, and the maniples showed more depth than front." This is construed by some modern authorities to mean that Varro made his maniples sixteen deep and ten front, instead of ten deep and sixteen front as usual. Such a change would decrease his front to near that of Hannibal's. There is nothing to show just what the change was.

Whatever the change, it was a great error. The men were unused to the formation, and the mass was so dense that it could not act. Varro had sixty-six thousand infantry in line, that is, out of his eighty thousand men he had left eleven thousand in the larger and three thousand in the lesser camp. Had he left the formation as it was, and put twenty thousand of this infantry in reserve, this body might have changed the entire result — called on at the proper moment to act. They could have fallen on the flanks of the Africans when these troops wheeled in to encompass the packed masses of the Roman legionaries.

The infantry was in the usual three lines, — fourteen legions in all, if two were left in camp. Varro seemed intent on as many changes as could be made. Instead of giving the Roman legions the centre, as usual, he placed them on the right, the allied on the left. The Roman cavalry, twenty-four hundred strong, was on the right flank. The allied cavalry, forty-eight hundred strong, was on the left. It would have been better to place all the cavalry on one wing and make its use a decisive one. If all the horse in one body on the left could have succeeded in breaking Hannibal's right when the centre fell back, it would have gone far to produce a victory. But the one adopted was the only formation known at that day, and was almost uniformly adhered to. Æmilius commanded the right, Varro the left wing, — the proconsuls, Atilius and Servilius, the centre.

Hannibal had placed on his left, opposite the Roman cavalry, his heavy Spanish and Gallic horse, eight thousand strong, leaning on the river, two thirds in a first and one third in a second line, all under command of Hasdrubal; and on his right, facing the allied horse, his two thousand Numidians, also leaning on the river. The cavalry on the left could not only probably crush the opposing cavalry, but could cut off the retreat of the infantry to its camps, if he beat it. No doubt this heavy body was placed here with this in view, another instance of Hannibal's appreciation of what the enemy's strategic flank means. Of the infantry, the

Spaniards, in their purple-bordered white tunics, and the
Gauls, naked from the waist up, were in the centre, in alternate bodies. His best troops, the Africans, which he had
armed Roman fashion from the weapons captured at the
Trebia and Trasimene, he placed in the usual order, on either
flank of the Spanish and Gallic foot. The cavalry and the

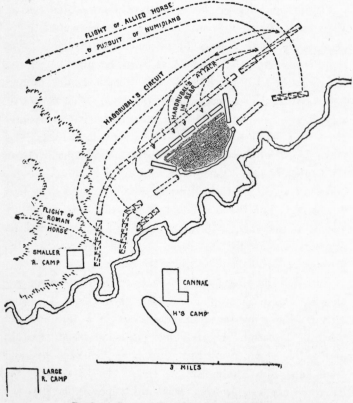

Battle of Cannæ.   First Theory — Final Phase.

Africans he hoped might leaven the whole lump. His infantry we suppose to have been drawn up in the Greek manner, in phalangial taxes, each of one thousand and twenty-

four men. The African infantry was in sixteen ranks, as usual; the Spaniards and Gauls were reduced to ten ranks. He had in all some thirty-two thousand infantry in line, that is, his total foot was forty thousand, and he had left eight thousand in camp.

Hannibal had been obliged to make his centre thin to cover the ground he was to occupy, but he had seething in his brain a manœuvre from which he proposed to snatch an advantage from this very weakness, even though the Romans had made their own centre heavier. He had no difficulty in predicating the general position of the Roman troops in line, and he had no doubt matured his manœuvre, and impressed it on his lieutenants. Hannibal commanded the centre in person, with dashing Mago to help him; Hanno had charge of the right; and, as we have seen, Hasdrubal commanded the cavalry on the left. It could not be in better hands. Maharbal is stated by Livy to have been on the right. Likely enough the difficult problem of the Numidians was committed to his charge.

In making his left-wing cavalry strong, Hannibal had in mind the fear that Varro might again mix foot with his horse upon the right and that he might need a solid body to defeat this mixed array. He had no doubt that Hasdrubal with his eight thousand men would beat the Roman horse, however sustained, and if necessary be able to go to the aid of his own right, where but two thousand Numidians were placed. These were to play a skirmishing game, to which their temperament and tactics were peculiarly suited. The cavalry problem settled, came the question of infantry. Hannibal was as familiar with the tactics of Marathon as any man alive; and he had at the Trebia seen how the Roman centre had pierced his own and escaped the general slaughter. Acting on both ideas, Hannibal proposed to advance his centre and then gradually allow it to withdraw, under the weight of the heavy Roman legions, to such a distance as should enable his wings to wheel in upon them and take the advancing centre in flank. But it was a dangerous evolution, unless carried out with the greatest exactitude, and unless the advance of the Roman centre was checked at the proper time. This checking would be aided by the knowledge of the men that the river was in their rear; but particularly by the fact that the centre had been fully prepared for the proposed manœuvre, and that Hannibal himself was to be the ruling spirit of the work.

The Carthaginians, remember, faced northerly, the Romans southerly. The rising sun was on the flank of either. The wind was southerly, — Florus says from the east, in reality southeasterly, — and blew the sand and dust into the faces of the Romans. The light troops of both sides opened the action, which lasted with alternate success for some time and was very fiercely contested by each line. Hannibal had rehearsed the details of this new manœuvre with all his subordinates, hoping that the Romans would be lured into aiding its execution. He had a way of making his purpose clear to his lieutenants, and himself proposed to see personally to its being properly done. During the preliminary fighting of the light troops he advanced his centre — the Spanish and Gallic infantry — in a salient or convex order from the general line, the phalanxes of alternate Spaniards and Gauls on the right and left of the central one, probably advancing *en échelon* thereto; but when the fighting began the whole assumed one huge convex line of more or less regularity. The space occupied by these troops must have made a crescent of nearly a mile and a half. The wings where the African infantry was posted kept their position on the original line.

While this was being done, Hannibal ordered Hasdrubal,

with the eight thousand heavy cavalry on his left flank, to
charge down upon the twenty-four hundred Roman horse
opposed to them.   This they did with their accustomed gal-

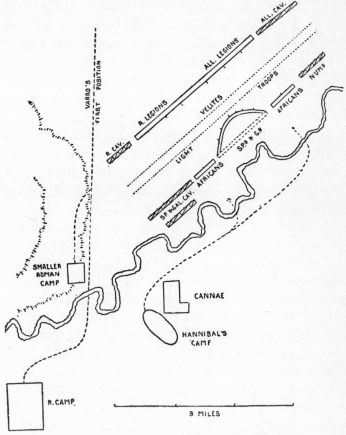

Battle of Cannæ.   Second Theory — First Phase.

lantry.   The shock was tremendous, but handsomely maintained by the Roman knights, who contested every inch with
the greatest obstinacy, and, when dismounted, fought on foot
to the last.   Many purposely dismounted in order not to be

driven from the place by sheer momentum of horses. When word was brought to Hannibal by a staff officer that the Roman cavalry had largely dismounted, " This pleases me better than if they had been delivered to me bound hand and foot," said he. The combat was not carried on by successive shocks, as usual in cavalry engagements; but by stubborn hand-to-hand fighting with the white weapon, like that of Alexander at the crossing of the Granicus. But the weight and experience of the well-trained Carthaginians was far too great. They rode down the whole body of Roman horse, and soon had crushed it beyond reorganization. Æmilius himself was wounded, but he escaped the ensuing massacre and joined the infantry of the centre, hoping yet to turn the tide of victory. It is probable that the infantry of the Roman right was placed *hors de combat* by this victory of Hannibal's heavy squadrons, and thrust back in disorder, or else pushed in on the centre. It could not have maintained itself against the weight of eight thousand heavy cavalry on its flank.

The Numidians, opposed to the allied cavalry on the Roman left, had orders to skirmish with it, but not to bring about serious work for the time being. Livy relates that a party of five hundred Numidians, hiding their swords under their cloaks, pretended to desert to the Romans, and being received and placed in the rear, later fell upon the Romans from behind. Appian places this incident in the infantry, and narrates remarkable feats which the five hundred men were able to perform. All this we may relegate to the domain of pleasant fable. The Numidians as a body skillfully accomplished their purpose by riding in squadrons round and round the Roman left flank, and by their peculiar tactics held their foes from serious attack until the Carthaginian heavy horse, having utterly destroyed the Roman cavalry and swept it from the field (a bare handful escaping up river),

made, under the inspired leadership of Hasdrubal, a circuit
by the rear of the Roman army, and rode down upon the
allied cavalry from behind. Then the Numidians, seeing their
opportunity, attacked sharply in front, and, between these two
bodies of veteran horse, there was speedily left not a single
Roman or allied horseman on the field, except the dead and
wounded. The Numidians were then put in pursuit of all who
fled, while Hasdrubal, with the heavy cavalry, turned to sustain the African foot.

During the cavalry fight, but long before the Carthaginian
horse had finished its first work on the Roman right, the light

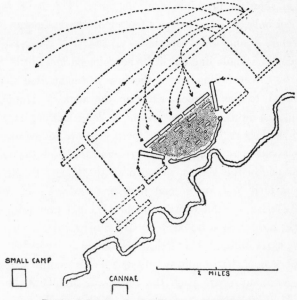

SMALL CAMP

CANNAE

2 MILES

Battle of Cannæ.   Second Theory — Final Phase.

troops of both sides had been withdrawn through the intervals, and had taken place in second line behind the Carthaginian army, and in rear of or in line with the Roman triarii.

Each had been ordered to form where they could act as reserve, to fill gaps in the lines of heavy infantry, or to furnish fresh weapons.

Varro had committed error upon error. In endeavoring to make his line so strong as to be, apparently, irresistible, he had ordered the maniples of principes to advance into the intervals between the maniples of hastati, instead of remaining in second line, as usual; or else he had drawn the maniples of each line together, so as almost to obliterate the intervals, thus preventing the principes from advancing through the hastati to sustain the combat when needed. The relations are not entirely clear; but the words of Polybius, above quoted, show the principle of his changes. This novel formation not only gave the troops a feeling of uncertainty as being irregular, — and this especially to the new troops, — but crowded the whole line out of its accustomed mobility. Still, with its never failing spirit, the heavy Roman line sharply advanced to the charge. Striking the apex of Hannibal's salient, the fighting at once became as fierce as the fury which filled the breasts of each; and Varro, eager to follow up what he felt sure was an approaching victory, ordered the triarii, sustained by the velites, to move up to support the already overcrowded first and second lines, and to drive back the obstinate Carthaginian centre, which Hannibal now reinforced by his light troops, to keep up the spirits of the men and better carry through his tactical manœuvre.

The legionaries fought stoutly and soon accomplished their purpose; they drove back the Spaniards and Gauls, but to the perdition of the Roman army. Varro saw sure signs of victory by breaking Hannibal's salient, and now depleted his wings to strengthen the already overcrowded centre. His every act was playing into Hannibal's hands. For as the Roman line, three in one, pressed on, the ranks became crowded out of all shape, and the one feature of the legion, its great elasticity of movement, was cast to the winds. Still the Roman soldiers, individually and in groups, though fast losing their maniple formation, fought their way into the enemy's line, step by step. The Carthaginian salient was steadily thrust back, and back, and farther back, until from a salient it straightened to a line of battle, and then, yet farther yielding, it began to assume the form of a reëntering angle. Into this breach the Roman infantry now poured, shouting their cry of victory.

They were met, not by a flying foe, but by the fatal consequence of overaudacity. So closely had their lines been formed and so sharply had they become pressed in that the soldiers had no room left to wield their weapons. The five feet square of the Roman legionary had been crowded down by more than half. Still the mere weight of the mass of men with their knobbed shields kept pushing back the Carthaginian centre, which Hannibal in person was handling in the thickest of the fray, and which, by his skillful dispositions, he kept in astonishingly good order and without a symptom of demoralization. Wherever he appeared, was cheerful confidence and courage. The Carthaginian infantry wings, as the Roman centre pushed forward, also advanced steadily and in admirable order, thus all the more crowding the Roman line, which itself had now assumed the form of a wedge and had begun to lose all semblance of its maniple structure. Plutarch and Appian state that the southeast wind blew with such violence as to all but blind the Romans with the sand which flew in their faces, and seriously to hamper their movements.

The decisive moment had come. Hannibal, seizing it with the instinct of the born commander, gave the anticipated order to his African infantry on the wings. These, pre-

viously prepared, wheeled round in perfect order to the right
and left and closed in upon the flanks of the Roman masses,
whose ardor had now huddled them together in shapeless
masses and quite destroyed their ability to manœuvre as well
as fight. Not until this moment had Varro's legionaries seen
that their hoped-for victory was ruin. But soldiers quickly
seize the meaning of what transpires around them. The Romans grasped their peril, but were Romans still. They fought
as bravely as for a triumph, but soon the last ray of hope
was gone. The consul in command had already fled with the
allied cavalry, while his brave colleague, Æmilius Paulus, had
been manfully struggling to rehabilitate the disorder of the
maniples, exposing his person with the utmost recklessness,
but in vain.

At this moment the heavy cavalry under Hasdrubal, having destroyed the Roman and allied horse, returned to the
field and rode down upon the Roman rear like a thunder-
cloud. Breaking into small detachments, it rode into their
midst and sabred the legionaries right and left. Parts of the
cavalry made their way through the intervals of the African
foot-phalanxes, and aided in the butchery of the Roman
soldiery on the flanks. The battle was ended, but not the
massacre. No quarter was asked or given. The legionaries
died with their faces to the foe, as so many Romans had done
before them. The bloody work continued till but a small
group of prisoners was left alive.

Livy and Polybius variously put the killed at from forty
thousand to seventy thousand men. Mommsen credits the
larger figures. Varro, who early escaped from the fray with
the cavalry of the Roman left, managed to turn up with a
squad of seventy men at Venusia; Æmilius Paulus fell in the
midst of his legions covered with wounds, in the vain effort to
retrieve the disaster. Servilius, Atilius, Minucius, two quæs-

tors, twenty-one military tribunes, a number of ex-consuls, prætors and ædiles and eighty senators perished with the army. In all certainly over forty thousand foot and four thousand horse remained upon the field.

During the battle, the eleven thousand men who had been left behind by Varro to attack Hannibal's camp carried out their orders; but Hannibal had been wise enough to leave the camp well provided against them. The Romans were driven back with a loss of two thousand men. Some seven thousand Roman infantry cut their way out from the battlefield and reached the small camp on the north side. Another body of ten thousand crossed the river and rejoined the large camp. Some six or eight thousand prisoners were made; ten thousand to twelve thousand men escaped into the country; and a body of four thousand men — no doubt the bravest — left the camp at night, eluded the Carthaginian scouting parties and marched to Canusium. Next day those who remained in the camps surrendered at discretion. They were allowed to purchase their freedom at the rate of three hundred denarii for a Roman, two hundred for an ally, one hundred for a slave, and to depart with one garment.

The splendid Roman army of eighty-seven thousand men had vanished as if swallowed up in an earthquake. Among the men who reached Canusium were Sempronius, four military tribunes, Scipio (later Africanus Senior) Appius Claudius and Fabius, son of the dictator. These officers found a small force of forty-three hundred men, and at once organized means of holding the place. Shortly after they learned that Varro had reached Venusia, a score of miles westerly from Canusium, with four thousand men. Sending to him for orders and reporting their condition, Varro shortly joined the forces at Canusium, and out of the fourteen thousand men who gradually assembled there began the nucleus of a new army.

Hannibal's loss had been barely six thousand men, of whom two thirds were Celts. Few were merely wounded. A wounded man had no chance in that fight. Hasdrubal, in command of the cavalry, had shown himself a *beau sabreur* of the highest order by the vigor of his charges and by returning to the battle-field in lieu of pursuing to a distance. His feat was like Cœnus' ride by the rear of Porus' army at the Hydaspes. It was the fine handling of the cavalry which permitted the infantry to carry out its programme.

This victory, it is seen, was largely due not only to the handling but to the excellence of the Carthaginian horse. It is hard to explain why the Romans should have been so persistently careless in improving this arm. There is no question that Hannibal owed his marching and foraging capacity, and certainly his success on the battle-field, more to his skill in using this arm than to any other one thing. At this period, when projectiles were cast to no great distance, cavalry could hover in the immediate vicinity of infantry, ready to fall upon it at any moment. The march of infantry on a plain in the presence of cavalry was difficult and dangerous. There was no reason whatsoever why the Romans should not have raised and disciplined a large force, as able to cope with Hannibal's as the infantry. They did so later, but it took them several years to discover the secret. In 1861 and 1862 our cavalry stood in the same position; but it took a short time for us to improve it into the gorgeous body of ten thousand horse commanded by Sheridan.

Few battles of ancient times are more marked by ability on the one side and crude management on the other than the battle of Cannæ. The position was such as to place every advantage on Hannibal's side. The manner in which the far from perfect Spanish and Gallic foot was advanced in a wedge in echelon and under the most vehement of attacks by the

Roman legions, was first held there and then withdrawn step by step, until it had reached the converse position of a re-entering angle, and was then held in place by ordering up the light troops, — all being done under the eye of Hannibal himself, — is a simple masterpiece of battle tactics. The advance at the proper moment of the African infantry, and its wheel right and left upon the flanks of the disordered and crowded Roman legionaries, is far beyond praise. The whole battle, from the Carthaginian standpoint, is a consummate piece of art, having no superior, few equal, examples in the history of war.

In direct contrast to this was the bad management of Varro. The errors he committed have already been pointed out. He robbed his army of all its mobility, — the one quality in which the legion was supreme, — first by deepening ranks, and then by crowding in more men where were already more than the space would allow. He undertook with new troops to make alterations to which they were unaccustomed. He left the command of his legions to subordinates, nor when his centre began to show signs of confusion was he on hand to correct it. Æmilius Paulus, wounded, essayed to do the work which Varro should himself have done. Varro intended, to judge from his assuming command of the left, to undertake some decided manœuvre with the cavalry of that wing; but he failed to make any marked demonstration against the Numidians, and fled from the battle-field — as is claimed — before the battle was absolutely lost. He failed to steady the cavalry of the right wing with foot, an advantage which he had learned by the success of but a day or two before. Altogether his conduct is checkered by errors, and stamped by the ugly seal of having survived the disaster due to his blunders. Æmilius Paulus is the Roman hero of Cannæ. And Hannibal, after the action, recognized this fact by a persistent search for his body and by paying the highest honors to his remains in the burial of the slain.

The news of the disaster of Cannæ, unequaled in Roman annals, was not to be the end of the disasters for this year. It was later followed by the intelligence that the prætorian army on the Po had been destroyed by the Gauls. It is hard to say whether political or social distress was uppermost in Rome. Few things show how drained of its better element the country already was more than the fact that the normal number of the senate — three hundred — had dwindled to one hundred and twenty-three. No less than one hundred and seventy-seven new senators had to be elected to fill the body.

It is here that we are compelled to take leave of Polybius as a constant companion. His work exists only in fragments after this battle. We cannot be so sure of our facts, or of doing as ample justice to the great Carthaginian as he deserves.

The relations of these campaigns by the ancient historians are so full of gaps, and often so contradictory, that it is impossible to always explain the movements or delays. Why Hannibal, after the battle of Cannæ, did not at once seize Canusium, which had but ten thousand defenders, is one of the questions we must ask and leave unanswered. He doubtless had some prevailing reason; we cannot allege one, but we may assume the existence of a convincing one to him. Again, shortly after the battle, Marcellus was able to reinforce this garrison with another legion. How Hannibal, alive to all his chances as he was, could have allowed Marcellus to do this is inexplicable. It would seem that some of the facts essential to a correct judgment must have been omitted in the narration, or have perished with the missing volumes of Polybius.

XXVIII.

AFTER CANNÆ. SUMMER. 216 B. C.

HISTORIANS often blame Hannibal for not marching on Rome immediately after Cannæ. That he did not, is one of the most decided proofs of his ability. A Pyrrhus could do so reckless a thing; but not a Hannibal. Rome was twelve days' march away. She had over forty thousand men to defend her strong walls. How could Hannibal, with his less than forty thousand men and no siege machinery, expect to take Rome, when allied forces, numbering hundreds of thousands, would certainly assemble in his rear? Hannibal was bold beyond any one in history in invading Italy, but he was not rash. He would have been insanely rash to march on Rome. He had two things to count upon, — help from home, and the disaffection of the socii. Without the first he must soon succumb. Without the last he could never conquer Rome. What he now did was to seek to influence the socii to join his cause. As a soldier alone, with his limited forces, he could not win the peace he aimed at. A great part of his time must be devoted to the political side of his problem. He now lay on his arms, with a military record unequaled in Roman annals, and sought to win his end by a persuasive policy. He looked farther into his problem than those who would have him do a foolhardy thing because it was brilliant. Rome rose to the occasion as never before. Not for an instant did she dream of peace, compromise, or anything but resistance to the last man. If Hannibal had marched on Rome, he would have ended the war, perhaps, but by the destruction of his own army.

IT is related by Livy that after the battle of Cannæ Maharbal asked permission to follow up the advantage gained with the horse and light troops, promising Hannibal that in four days he should sup in the Capitol; and that on Hannibal's declining this proposal, Maharbal exclaimed: "Thou knowest indeed, Hannibal, how to win a victory, but thou knowest not how to use one!"

It is not unusual for historians to blame Hannibal for not

at once marching on Rome. Let us see what his chances were. We have no hint of what he himself thought, of what his reasons were for not so doing; we must content ourselves with collecting a few guess-work facts and endeavoring to argue as he did.

Two facts are peculiarly prominent in Hannibal's campaign in Italy. First, he had opposed to him the troops of the strongest and most intelligent military power of the world, — some of which were, to be sure, comparatively raw in active duty, but yet trained to war from their youth, mixed with legionaries of many campaigns, and instinct with the courage of fighting for their own soil. It will not do to claim that Hannibal's troops were veterans, — the Romans levies of a day. During the first three years this was partly true, and defeat, no doubt, somewhat drew the temper of the Roman blade, but during the rest of Hannibal's campaigns the Roman army was much superior to his own in all but one quality, — that strange influence which a great general exercises over the soldier. It will be noticed, that whenever the fighting was on equal terms, from the beginning the Roman soldier gave a good account of himself. But Hannibal's victories were won by tactical genius and his skillful use of his cavalry arm, not by mere fighting. In the latter, the legionary was always equal, if not superior, to the phalangite. So that one cannot compare the task of any other great captain to Hannibal's, with any show of fairness.

Secondly, Hannibal had calculated absolutely upon being able to detach some of the allies and colonies from their fealty to Rome, to break up the Italian confederacy. We cannot imagine him to have set out on his marvelous expedition without having made this the prime factor in his calculations. Hannibal was no madman, as some authorities have tried to make Alexander out to be; he was a keen, close calculator.

But he would have been insane indeed if he had ventured into Italy without a reasonable basis for this expectation. He was well justified in calculating on such defection. There had always been a good deal of opposition to high-handed Rome among all her allies and colonies, and it was a fair assumption that many, if not most of them, would be glad to free themselves and humble their conqueror and mistress. In this expectation Hannibal had been entirely disappointed. He had gone as far towards breaking up the confederacy as it was possible to go. If Cannæ would not weaken the allegiance of the allies, only force would do it, for success and terror had reached the highest notch. Despite which, none of the allies — the socii who had made equal alliances with Rome — had shown any disposition to meet him other than with the sword; none of the colonies, except in distant Gaul, had met him even half-way. He had captured towns and territory, and had garrisoned citadels. But the aid he received was not that aid which enables a conqueror to hold what he takes, except with the strong hand. And without just such aid Hannibal could not only not win; he could not be otherwise than defeated in his contest with mighty Rome. To assume that Hannibal did not see all this, and that he was not fighting against hope almost from the second year, is to underrate this man's intellectual ability. No one probably knew all Hannibal's thoughts. He was so singularly reticent that Roman historians called him treacherous, because no one could from his face or conduct gauge either his thought or intention, or calculate upon his acts. He had no Hephæstion, as had Alexander. We learn nothing of his inner thoughts or motives. But no doubt he was keenly alive to the failure, so far, of his calculation on the disaffection of the allies.

And now, after the overwhelming victory of Cannæ, he had to weigh, not only the strategic and tactical difficulties, but the still more serious political ones. Indeed, Livy hints that he was busy about just this. If the allies — or a good part of them — could be induced to join his cause, Rome would fall sooner or later. If not, he could never take Rome, or permanently injure the Roman cause.

Hannibal was fighting, not to conquer Italy, but to win such a peace as should insure to Carthage the possession of Sicily, Spain, Sardinia, Corsica, and put Rome on her good behavior. To capture Rome was but a means towards an end. The chances were, in a military sense, all against his seizing Rome by a *coup de main.* If he failed, the game was lost. It was far wiser for him to still seek to influence the allies, which he could now do with a record of wonderful victories, such as the Roman world had not yet seen. Hannibal was not a military gambler. He never risked his all on a bare chance, as some other soldiers have done. He sifted and analyzed his facts with scrupulous care. And every reason prompted him not to risk the loss of his all on the chances of a brilliant march on the enemy's capital, twelve days' distant, which had only its boldness to commend it, and every military reason, as well as the stanch Roman heart, to promise failure as its result. For there was no obsequious satrap to open its gates and welcome the conquering hero. If Hannibal marched on Rome, he must be prepared to besiege the city, and we have already shown how impossible this was. "Modern campaigns are decided on the battlefield. Of old, a fortress might neutralize the greatest victory. After the landing of Regulus, Carthage was in vastly greater danger than Rome ever was; and yet the weak and vacillating senate of Carthage made a stand and won."

Hannibal probably at this time harbored the hope that after this fourth and overwhelming defeat of the Romans, the allies would finally see that their interests lay with him, and the time which he now spent in the vicinity of his late battle-field was no doubt devoted to political questions, the favorable solution of which could be better brought about by not for the moment risking his present unquestioned military suprem-acy. He was negotiating with the larger cities, and it was but a short time before Capua, the second city of Italy, cast in her lot with him. Such a triumph had much more value than the destruction of another consular army. Hannibal knew the fact and worked hard for this very end.

Hannibal had two things to hope for : reinforcements from Spain and the disaffection of the allies. The first had been rendered largely nugatory by the successes of the Scipios, and the other seemed unattainable. Carthage had done something to aid Hannibal, but he was not to expect much. This he had known from the beginning, though he had placed entire reliance on aid from Spain. Carthaginian fleets were busy threatening the Italian coast and keeping Roman fleets away from Africa. There was as yet no port of disembarkation for Carthage in Italy. For many years the Barcine generals had made war in Spain self-supporting, and Carthage would expect the same now in Italy. Hannibal's resources, though well husbanded, had begun to dwindle, his veterans grew fewer, his men failed to get their pay. But Cannæ stirred up the Carthaginian senate, which resolved to aid the war both in Spain and Italy.

A treaty was made with Macedon to land an army in Italy, Philip hoping by such means to regain Epirus; and Hiero of Syracuse being dead, the new king joined the Carthaginian cause.

Now was the chance for Carthage if ever. If she could have looked at the matter broadly, and not through the eyes of political envy; if she could have concentrated in southern Italy the easily raised thousands of good African foot and horse; if she could have forgotten Spain for a bare year, and aided Hannibal instead; if she could have utilized Macedonia and the promised resources of Sicily, there is no doubt that such a peace could have been dictated to Rome as would have given the Punic power the upper hand in the western Mediterranean for many generations. But Carthage was blind and indolent, and the splendid work done by Hannibal with the Army of Italy was wasted.

The institutions and laws which gave Rome strength never demonstrated her greatness so well as now. The people which had created these institutions, which had made these laws, never rose superior to disaster, never exhibited the strength of character of which the whole world bears the impress, so well as now. The horrible disaster to both state and society — for there was not a house in which there was not one dead — by no means changed the determination of the Roman people, however horrified the cool-headed, however frightened the many. Not that among the ignorant there was not fear and trembling, but it was not the ignorant who made up Rome. The more intelligent and courageous element spoke with a single voice. The prætors at once called the senate together to devise ways and means. Fabius advised first to send out a portion of the cavalry to ascertain the situation of Varro and Hannibal, which was done. The senate remained in constant session. All Rome was in affliction, but this must not interfere with the necessity of saving the commonwealth — and courage must be outward as well as in the heart. The word "peace" was forbidden to be pronounced in the city. Mourning was limited to thirty days. Tears were prohibited to women in public. New energies were at once put at work. In view of the alarming circumstances and the impossibility of carrying out the requirements of the law, the senate itself made M. Junius Pera dictator, who chose Tiberius Sempronius Gracchus as master of cavalry. The entire male population above seventeen years of age was enrolled. Four new legions and one thousand horse were thus added to the city's garrison. All mechanics were set to work to make and repair weapons. Old spoils hung in the temples were taken down for use. The walls were already in a state of excellent defense. The senate purchased and armed eight thousand slaves and four thousand debtors or criminals, with promise of freedom or pardon. This is the first such instance in Roman history. Naught but stubborn resistance to the last man was thought of.

Rome could count on for the immediate defense of the city : —

Two urban legions	10,600 men.
At least among the old soldiers over age . .	10,000 men.
Slaves and freedmen	12,000 men.
With Marcellus at Ostia, two legions . . .	10,600 men.
Total	43,200 men.

This was a larger force than Hannibal commanded.

Finally, Varro was heard from. He announced that he had rallied the wreck of the army at Canusium, and that Hannibal showed no intention of marching on Rome. A moment's breathing spell was had. But the list of disasters was not yet filled. The rumor of two Carthaginian descents upon Sicily at the same moment came to the ears of the senate. That part of the coast which was the territory of Hiero, king of Syracuse, a Roman ally, who had recently supplied arms and men to the army at Cannæ, was being ravaged, and another fleet was threatening Lilybæum and a portion of the island subject to Rome. Speedy help must be had if the Sicilian possessions were not to be forfeited. But much help could not be afforded. All the men who could be spared from the fleet at Ostia were of necessity called to

Rome, and the commander, Marcellus, was ordered to Canusium with a legion to add to the troops to oppose Hannibal, while Varro was recalled to Rome to give in his report. Thus depleted, the fleet was sent to Sicily.

When one considers the immense resources of Rome and the comparatively small number of men commanded or procurable by Hannibal, when one looks at the dauntless front presented by the freedom-nurtured republic, it is all the more apparent that there could be but one end to the conflict. Rome still numbered her possible levies by the hundreds of thousands. Hannibal's force was only that with which he had so far made his conquests, plus a number of local recruits, and he looked forward with uncertainty to any further outside help. The anxiety of the most stout-hearted, the terror of the weak in Rome, was justified, but Hannibal himself saw the outcome as it must be, — unless the allies could be persuaded to join him, — and bent all his resources to this end, neglecting, perhaps, his military scheme for the greater political necessity.

That there was grave demoralization among all but the strongest hearts, even in the army at Canusium (and at the front demoralization is always less marked than at the rear), nothing demonstrates more than the fact that a number of young nobles, headed by Lucius Cæcilius Metellus, who were at this place, seriously proposed to leave the Roman army and seek to establish a colony in some other part of the world, or to offer their services to some king, as Livy says, deeming the days of the supremacy of Rome to be numbered. A defection like this would have been fatal, for from such an origin it would have spread like wildfire on all sides. It is related that Appius Claudius and Publius Scipio, when informed of this conspiracy, at once visited the chief projectors, and sword in hand forced them to swear never to desert the republic while in danger. Thus was this most threatening of all the clouds dissipated.

Some allege that Varro put down the outbreak. But after this had been done and he had brought the army to a state of decent discipline, on the arrival of Marcellus, who was placed in command, Varro returned to Rome, to submit himself to the mercies of the people and senate, bearing with him the responsibility for the most grievous disaster Rome had ever suffered. If it was really Varro who restrained the defection above mentioned, and calmed the panic of his troops to the extent of again making them reliable, this would show him to have been a man of uncommon character, however faulty as a soldier or unworthy in a social aspect. And his returning to Rome to bow to the will of the people, acknowledging the entire blame to be his own, shows a certain nobility of character which we cannot but weigh highly in estimating him. He was employed in one or other military capacity till the end of the war.

The dignity of the senate maintained itself in receiving Varro. Though full of his bitter political enemies, though he had been the cause of the death of the nearest relatives of each and all, though he had brought about the gravest danger Rome had ever seen, this noble body, in lieu of punishing Varro for his defeat, thanked him publicly "for that he had not despaired of the republic." Much has been said in denunciation of Varro. But that the Roman senate, in this hour of peril and grief, should have so acted seems to show that there still was a good side to this man, which history does not bring to the fore, as of necessity it must his weakness and want of skill. How much of the condonation by this public body was due to the chastening influence of such an overshadowing disaster as Cannæ cannot be said. But the fact does not remain without significance.

XXIX.

MARCELLUS. FALL, 216 B. C.

HANNIBAL gave all his Italian prisoners their freedom, and placed a ranson on the Romans; but the senate refused to allow their families to enrich the Carthaginian by paying this ransom. A large number of cities in southern Italy joined Hannibal, but the socii clove to Rome. The confederacy was like a Cyclopæan wall. Hannibal moved to Campania. He aimed to get a seaport in this province as a base for further operations, but he was unable to lay hold of one. Capua, the second city of Italy, joined him, and he won several smaller towns, among them Casilinum; but at Nola, Marcellus, who was the coming Roman general, checked him in an attempt on the place, with heavy loss. The Hanno party in Carthage was voted down, and reinforcements were ordered from Spain to Italy; but the Scipios defeated Hasdrubal Barca, and prevented their leaving the peninsula. Cannæ had been a great gain for Hannibal, but it had not brought him that support which would enable him to win. The cities which joined him did so because they looked on him as a new master, and not from approval of his course; in many instances from hatred of Rome. The structure which Rome had erected in Italy was sound enough to stand every test. Hannibal went into winter-quarters in Capua.

THOUGH in need of money, Hannibal, after the battle of Cannæ, sent his Italian prisoners home without ransom, as a bid for the support of the confederates against Rome. Having fixed a ransom upon the Roman prisoners, he sent a deputation of these prisoners, accompanied by Carthalo, a noble Carthaginian and commander of the light horse, to Rome, with authority to treat with the senate or else with the families of each. The deputation made a good showing to the senate, but this body, with the wonderful self-confidence which always characterized its actions, refused to allow Hannibal to be enriched in this manner, either from the state or from private funds, declined to treat with Carthalo, and

ordered him forthwith to leave Roman territory. Pliny
states that Hannibal avenged this insult in a terrible manner
upon his Roman prisoners. Livy and Polybius do not mention the fact, as the former would assuredly have done had
there been any truth in the report; and unnecessary cruelty
was foreign to Hannibal's character or intent. Such an
act would have made his future battles harder to win, for no

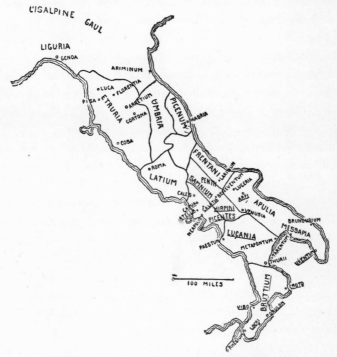

Hannibal's Allies after Cannæ.   (His allies underscored.)

Roman soldier would thenceforth have surrendered. History
shows only too well what fighting capacity such a spirit in an
army breeds. Policy was Hannibal's strongest characteristic,
and reprisals upon the persons of his prisoners would have
been in the highest degree impolitic. He would scarcely
have invoked such a weapon against himself.

These last wonderful successes of Hannibal, coupled to his generosity to the Italian prisoners, proved too much for the fidelity of some of the Roman dependencies. Livy tells us that there joined Hannibal: Arpi in Apulia, and Uxentum in Messapia; all the Bruttian towns, — of which, however, some few had to be besieged; most of the Lucanians; the Salernian Picentes; the Hirpini; the Samnites except the Pentii; and Capua, which, it is said, could raise thirty thousand foot and four thousand horse, with the neighboring towns of Atella and Calatia. The aristocrats in all the cities unwillingly joined or openly opposed Hannibal. The South-Italians held to Rome, having many Roman garrisons, and because Rome had been gentle to the Greeks in Italy. Neapolis, Rhegium, Thurii, Metapontum, Tarentum resisted Hannibal. Croton and Locri were stormed. Brundisium, Venusia, Pæstum, Cosa and Cales, Latin colonies, that is, Roman fortresses, remained faithful. If Hannibal restored Italian liberties they would suffer. "Not one Roman citizen nor one Latin community had joined Hannibal." "This groundwork of the Roman power could only be broken up, like the Cyclopæan walls, stone by stone," says Mommsen.

Still Hannibal may have seen in what had occurred the beginning of real success, and have devoted himself to following up this political gain. It must be noted that the Roman colonies which joined Hannibal scarcely did so of their own free will. They felt that they were conquered, and were but accepting a new master for an old one. Beside this fact, a chain of Roman fortresses still covered the land and kept these new allies restless. What Hannibal had gained was not hearty support, but uncertain submission.

Hannibal, after plundering and destroying the two Roman camps near Cannæ, marched up the Aufidus and into Samnium to the land of the Hirpinians, and here he possessed himself of Compsa by the treachery of a strong party which had embraced his cause. This place he made a depot of stores and booty, leaving his brother Mago to seduce other towns in the district. Later he sent him into Bruttium with a strong division to help forward the cause, and Hanno to Lucania on a similar mission; while he himself, with the bulk of his army, moved into Campania. Reaching Neapolis, he tried to seize an entrance into the city by ruse, and came very close to succeeding, but failed at the last moment; and as the Romans had thrown a garrison into the place, and it was very well fortified, he could not undertake a siege. In fact, he scarcely had time, in view of all the conditions surrounding him, to sit down in front of any strong place, unless of the greatest importance.

In addition to Neapolis, Nuceria and Cumæ, the latter on the coast, from which he might have had easy communication with Carthage by sea, — and Hannibal much needed a seaport, — proved too strong for him to gain; but Capua, which for some time had looked on Hannibal as the eventual conqueror of Rome, and therefore deemed it politic to be among the first to play into his hands, — though the Romans had endeavored to cajole her by the offer of a leading share in the struggle, — concluded an alliance with him and received his army. This was a first and most distinct triumph, though Capua made some marked reservations in her compact with Hannibal, such as that he should have no right to compulsory service of the population of Campania, nor to interfere with the city laws. Atella and Calatia, near by, followed the lead of Capua.

Cannæ, says Mommsen, was the direct result of the mutual suspicions and jealousies of the senate and the citizens of Rome. The first consequence of this was the appointment

of such men as Flaminius and Varro. Demagogism had
seized the reins. What the Scipios in Spain had done was
due to their being good men beyond interference. Even Fabius was not above acting on political prejudices in what he
did. His cunctatory policy was in part a protest to the insane combativeness of Flaminius and Varro. It was the present reconcilement of senate and people which gave back to
Rome her strength. She had been taught by bitter experience that she could not successfully conduct war with political quarrels at home. She put her best men in command,
and kept them on the duty they showed they could perform.

Marcellus, who was the coming man, had received his
training, and a good one, against Hamilcar in Spain, and had
conducted the late wars against the Celts, in which he slew

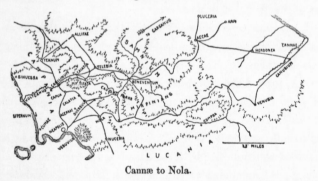

Cannæ to Nola.

with his own hand Britomartus, the king of the enemy, and
took his spoils. He was noted for strong military common-
sense as well as personal prowess. He had erected a temple
in Rome to Honor and Valor, of which he himself was the
embodiment. No man deserved better of the republic. Still,
splendid a character as Marcellus was, it was not he who res-
cued Rome. It was the Roman citizen. Marcellus was but
the most useful of the citizens, and the most brilliant. He
was the first Roman who combined boldness with caution.

His method in dealing with Hannibal was far beyond that of Fabius. He was the father of the system which eventually drove the Carthaginians out of Italy.

While Hannibal was endeavoring to add to his list of allies, Marcellus had been withdrawn from Canusium, and had marched by way of Beneventum and Allifæ with two legions, the wreck of Cannæ, to Teanum Sidicinum, where reinforcements from Rome and Ostia reached him, and thence to Casilinum to cover the line of the Vulturnus. The dictator, M. Junius, had been able, out of the two legions raised in Rome and the slaves and debtors, to leave a suitable garrison in the capital and to advance with twenty-five thousand men to the same locality. Here were armies exceeding in numerical strength those under command of Hannibal.

Mago, after his work in Bruttium, embarked for Carthage to make his chief's report and ask for reinforcements. Neither Carthage nor Rome was at this moment undisputed mistress of the sea; for Carthage had made some strides in her naval growth, and troops could at any time be debarked in Bruttium without all too grave risk. It was the salvation of Rome that Hannibal's worst enemies were in Carthage, among the supporters of Hanno, and that the reinforcements which ill-success made it essential to send to Spain constantly proved the excuse for denying triumphant Hannibal that which might have enabled him to conquer a glorious peace in Italy.

As showing what the rock was on which Hannibal's success was wrecked, the answer of Hanno in the Carthaginian senate to the message of Mago may well be quoted from Livy. "This, then," said he, "is what you say: 'I have slain the armies of the enemy; send me soldiers.' What else would you ask if you were conquered? 'I have captured two of the enemy's camps, full of booty and provisions; supply me with corn and money.' What else would you ask if plundered or stripped of your own camp? Since, as you say," he continued, "the battle of Cannæ annihilated the Roman power and it is a fact that all Italy is in a state of revolt, in the first place, has any one people of the Latin confederacy come over to us? In the next place, has any individual of the five and thirty tribes deserted to Hannibal?" When Mago had answered both these questions in the negative, he continued: "There remains, then, still too large a body of the enemy. But I should be glad to know what degree of spirit and hope that body possesses." Mago declaring that he did not know, " Nothing," said he, " is easier to be known. Have the Romans sent any ambassadors to Hannibal to treat of peace? Have you, in short, ever heard that any mention has been made of peace at Rome?" On his answering these questions also in the negative, " We have upon our hands, then," said he, " a war as entire as we had on the day on which Hannibal crossed over into Italy." And on this theme, whose basis was clear truth, he opposed all sending of aid to Hannibal. His premises were correct, — but only literally correct, actually wanting in breadth of view; his conclusion was therefore absolutely wrong, — in a military sense, at least. The man who showed he could command success should have been sustained, even if all Iberia fell under Roman sway. Conquer a peace at the gates of Rome, and the evacuation of Spain could be demanded as a condition. This simple fact Carthage never could comprehend. She aided Hannibal, but in a stingy manner.

The Carthaginian senate, unwilling to listen to Hanno, voted that four thousand Numidians, four hundred elephants and much money should be sent to Hannibal, and that twenty thousand foot and four thousand horse should go to him from Spain. But all this was done with the sloth bred of success and of lack of common purpose.

The integrity of Rome and the opposition of Hanno wrecked Hannibal's wonderful work.

The surrender by Capua of her Roman fealty was followed by the similar action of a number of other Italian cities. Excepting that some cities with Roman garrisons could not be reduced, Hannibal had gained all southern Italy below a line extending from the mouth of the Vulturnus to the promontory of Mons Garganus.

Nola, east from Neapolis, had a Roman garrison, but the popular party offered to open the gates to Hannibal. Marcellus, who was near Casilinum, was warned by the Roman party in Nola in season, and, anticipating Hannibal's seizure of the town, marched up the Vulturnus to Caiatia, crossed and, passing along the east slope of the mountains back of Suessula, threw himself into the town and prevented the Carthaginian from taking advantage of this offer. Hannibal then made another attempt to take Neapolis, but this too failed, on account of recent reinforcements under Silanus, sent to the city by the Romans. Nuceria, however, he took in a short siege by starvation, and, giving the inhabitants their lives, plundered the town and razed it to the ground. He then marched back to Nola.

It is extremely difficult in many cases to ascertain the roads by which Hannibal or the Roman generals marched. The authorities are not always in accord, nor do we know just where there were practicable roads. But careful comparison of authors and topography usually results in coming close to the truth. In this case, we know that Marcellus marched back of Suessula; and as there is but one valley through which he could march, except by a very extensive circuit, it is assumed that a country road led along this valley in his age, as there does to-day.

Marcellus was himself in a difficult position in Nola, having only the senate of the town in his favor. He began by winning over to his side the leader of the Hannibal faction, Bantius, a young man whom, wounded at Cannæ, Hannibal had generously cared for and sent back to his native town loaded with favors, and who' had headed the scheme for going over to the enemy. Deprived of Bantius, the popular party was more easily controlled. Still danger from this quarter was not put aside, for it was reported to Marcellus that other leaders of this party had agreed with Hannibal, that when Marcellus should make a sortie from the town or draw up for battle outside, they would plunder the baggage and close the gates upon him.

Hannibal was encamped before the town, and there were daily skirmishes between the contending outposts and light troops.

Not feeling that he could long hold on under such conditions, Marcellus made up his mind to risk an attack on Hannibal, and thus cut the knot of the difficulty. It was a bold step. His plans were matured with masterly skill. He quietly drew up his line inside the walls, opposite three gates on the side where Hannibal was observing the town. He armed the walls with invalids and noncombatants, and parked his baggage-train in one place, with a sufficient guard of extraordinarii to prevent plunder, if attempted. Opposite the middle gate he drew up the Roman cavalry and old legions; at the other gates the allied legions and cavalry, and the light foot under Valerius Flaccus and C. Aurelius. He forbade any of the inhabitants to approach the walls, under threat of summary penalties.

Hannibal had been drawn up all this day in battle order, in front of his own camp, anticipating an attack by Marcellus or the usual skirmishes. He wondered that the Roman army did not emerge from the gates, and, seeing no garrison on the walls, naturally concluded that Marcellus had discovered his connection with the popular party, and did not dare to come out, lest he should be betrayed. He imagined that if he attacked he would be able to take advantage of the commotion

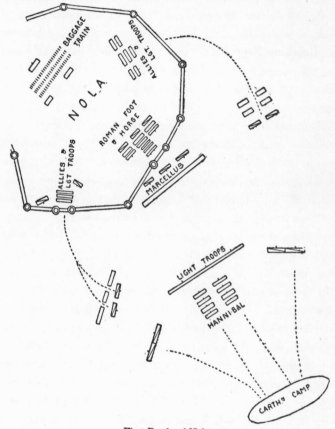

First Battle of Nola.

and indecision which would ensue. Arguing thus, he fell into Marcellus' trap, — he, the master of stratagem, — and though the day was far spent, at once made arrangements to attack the town. Sending the light troops forward, he ordered the

phalangites to provide themselves with ladders and whatever
machines, useful in an assault, happened to be at hand, and
to advance in column on the town.   The horse followed after.

The head of column had scarcely reached the wall, — it was
not in the strictest order, laden as it was with all manner of
tools, in addition to arms, and far from anticipating an attack, — when the gates were thrown open and, with a tremendous onslaught, Marcellus rushed forth, personally leading the centre, formed of the survivors of Cannæ, in two lines
of cohorts, and followed by the cavalry.   The Carthaginian
light troops were at once hustled back, and a formidable assault immediately made on Hannibal's phalanx.   Every man,
including noncombatants in the rear, had been ordered to
join in the battle-cry, to simulate numbers.   The allied horse
at the same time charged out of the side gates, hoping to take
the phalanx in flank ; but Hannibal, though surprised, was
far from losing his head, and had at the opening of the attack ordered up his own mounted troops on his either wing.
The suddenness and stoutness of the onset made a distinct
impression on the Carthaginians, and inflicted much loss.
But these veterans were not to be easily demoralized.   In a
short period, Hannibal, by his personal efforts among his
men, reëstablished the battle, and was about to turn the tide
of action, when the second line of the Roman wings charged
out of the side gates, and again took the Carthaginians on
both flanks.   The whole affair had been so admirably managed by Marcellus that Hannibal gave up trying to rescue
the day, and retired, in entire good order, but having suffered heavily in casualties.

Just now, such a success was a hearty encouragement to
the Romans.   They had fairly beaten Hannibal at his own
game — ruse.   As Livy says, " not to be vanquished by Hannibal then was a more difficult task to the victorious troops

than to conquer him afterwards." To Marcellus belonged the entire credit. He had shown himself worthy to lead Roman soldiers.

Marcellus punished the ringleaders of the popular party in Nola with death, garrisoned the town so as to put it beyond capture out of hand, and moved to a position above Suessula, where he intrenched himself.

Hannibal gave up hope of capturing Nola, and retired to a camp near Acerræ, not far from Suessula. He attempted to take the town by siege; but the inhabitants managed by a sortie to break through the line of circumvallation before it was finished, and escaped. Hannibal then destroyed the town.

Marcellus was both brave and discreet. Though he had once checked Hannibal under favorable conditions, he by no means flattered himself that he could cope with his great antagonist. He could play a Fabian game when it was useful; he would risk nothing needlessly; and he now held his fortified heights, whence he could watch Nola and Neapolis, and at the same time keep open his road of communication along the hills with the dictator, who was at Teanum.

The dictator, M. Junius, with his twenty-five thousand men, was reaching out towards Casilinum. Hannibal learned the fact. He was anxious to capture this place, — an important strategic centre, built, as it was, astride of the Vulturnus. He had had reason to hope that Casilinum might yield itself, as so many of the Italian cities had done. But when he marched against the town, he found that he was mistaken. It had a garrison of about fifteen hundred men, of whom some Prænestians appear to have been the controlling spirit. They had extinguished the pro-Hannibal party by executing many of them for treason, and had retired into that part of the city which lay on the north bank, where they made a most stubborn defense in the citadel. It seems as if Hannibal was compelled to operate against the town within a very limited space where he could use but few troops. As at Saguntum, numbers were not of much avail. The bend in the river obliged the garrison to defend but a very small part of their wall. The first Punic assault was headed by Isalca, a

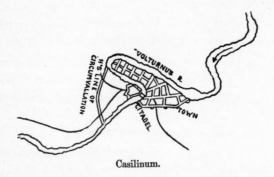

Casilinum.

Gætulian, and being partial only, and met by a sharp sortie, had no chance of success. Then a general assault, under Maharbal, was ordered, but, though this officer was wont to do good work, he too was repulsed by the plucky garrison in a sudden rush from the gates. Hannibal had underrated his enemy. Even reproaches addressed to the conquerors of Saguntum, says Livy, and the promise of a mural crown, did not provoke a stout enough assault to capture the citadel. He was driven to besiege it. He employed vineæ and mines ; but both were met by bulwarks and counter-mines by the garrison. Every effort he could make seemed to be set at naught by the excellent situation of the place. Leaving a portion of his troops to hold the lines of circumvallation he had made so as to keep it blockaded, he withdrew with the others to Capua, where he prepared to go into winter-quarters for the winter of B. C., 216–215. From Capua he controlled the south side of the river.

On finding that the Carthaginians had surrounded Casilinum with works, and that the blockade was not readily to be
broken, M. Junius returned to Teanum. Marcellus appears
to have remained in his camp on the hills back of Suessula.

During the year B. C. 216 the two Scipios made still further progress in Spain. They badly defeated Hanno and
Hasdrubal Barca, and drove them back of the Ebro. This
not only seriously cooled the ardor of the Spanish allies
of Carthage, but the situation in Iberia was made a pretext
by the Hanno party in Carthage to prevent the sending of
reinforcements to Hannibal. In the effervescence produced
by Cannæ, Hasdrubal had received orders to march to Italy
to join Hannibal, and Himilco had been sent to Spain to
succeed him; but the defeat of his army by the Scipios,
which occurred in the attempt to carry out his orders, and
the consequent desertion of his Spanish allied troops, so
entirely crippled him in strength that the programme could
not be carried out. The Scipios commanded the sea, the
Pyrenees and the Ebro, and through the Massiliots, Gaul.
Spain was severed from Italy. Thus Hannibal was left to
his own resources.

All this was fatal to success in Italy. Sicily was kept under Roman alliance or control; but Sardinia revolted. And
we have seen that the prætor and consul-elect, Posthumius,
in the course of this year, was ambushed and killed, and his
army utterly destroyed by the Boii in cisalpine Gaul. Under
these conditions all northern Italy was ripe for a fresh rebellion. Even small forces under experienced Carthaginian officers might have not only seized Sardinia and Corsica, but
again raised all Gaul into active hostility, a condition which
would have been of vast assistance to Hannibal, and might
have eventuated in inducing the Etruscans and Umbrians to
join the coalition against Rome. Such a situation would

have been a brilliant one for the Carthaginians. But the management of armies by politicians is as old as the world, and fraught with failure. While the soldier must always be the servant of the statesman, it behooves the statesman to study well into the requirements of the military problem. Spain was no doubt important; but it could not weigh in the balance against the campaign in Italy. Success here secured Spain; success in Spain might not affect the general result.

Towards the end of the winter, Casilinum was beginning to be much reduced by famine. Many men cast themselves from the walls, and others courted death by exposing themselves on the walls to escape the pangs of hunger. M. Junius had been called to Rome. His magister equitum, Sempronius, at Teanum, whom he had forbidden to engage in battle with Hannibal, was afraid to bring the garrison relief. But holding the upper river, he was able to send down by night casks filled with provisions, which the garrison intercepted. This continued until the Carthaginians discovered the trick. Then he floated down the stream huge quantities of nuts, which were caught by screens. At the other end of the line Marcellus kept close in his camp commanding Nola, its inhabitants fearing an attack by Capua, in case his army should leave, nor took any steps to act in concert with the army of the dictator. Under these circumstances, and being reduced down to eating the leather thongs from off their shields and equipments, mice and such roots as they could dig, the garrison of Casilinum was obliged to treat with Hannibal, who finally saw fit to accept its capitulation at a ransom of seven ounces of gold per man, and allowed it to depart to Cumæ on payment of the sum. This brought to an end a difficult operation and put into Hannibal's hands a valuable town, for Casilinum, situated astride of the Vulturnus, controlled the most essential bridge of the vicinity, over which passed the Appian Way. After its capture, Hannibal turned it over to the Capuans, but placed a Carthaginian garrison of seven hundred men in it, and made it an outpost to Capua, on the road to Rome.

Soldier's Cloak.

XXX.

CAMPANIA. 215 B. C.

"THE debauch of Capua" is purely hypothetical. It is true that up to the winter of 216–215 B. C. Hannibal won great victories, that afterwards he won fewer; but it had nothing to do with Capua. That Hannibal's army lost fighting capacity was due to two causes: the disappearance of his veterans, who were replaced by a poor element, and the fact that the Roman gain in skill and quality reduced Hannibal's status proportionately. That he assumed a defensive rôle was due to the political conditions and to his numerical weakness; to the fact, moreover, that the Romans now refrained from accepting battle, conscious of Hannibal's ability, and worked on the theory of tiring him out by a systematic small-war, — in other words, of starving him out of Italy. The Carthaginian army was between forty and fifty thousand strong. The Romans had this year one hundred and forty thousand men under the colors, of whom eighty thousand faced Hannibal, not counting garrisons. Capua induced Hannibal to remain in Campania, where, too, he still desired to make a base by securing a good seaport. The Capuans endeavored to aid in the scheme, but their efforts were weak. Meanwhile Hanno, in Lucania, was badly defeated; and Marcellus raided into Samnium among the new Punic allies. On the other hand, a small reinforcement from Carthage reached Hannibal. Making a second attempt on Nola, he was again thrust back, much as before, but the ensuing battle was drawn. Finally Hannibal retired to Apulia to winter. In Spain the Scipios once more beat Hasdrubal, and prevented his bringing aid to Italy; and the home senate gave Hannibal no further support.

THAT history repeats itself is true in more than one sense. A statement made by one historian is apt to get carried down the course of ages by mere repetition, without examination of its truth or falsity. It was said by Livy that the laxity of discipline in winter-quarters at Capua in B. C. 216–215 was the means of so entirely weakening the morale of Hannibal's army that thenceforth it was no longer able to win the great victories of yore. But this is not true.

"The debauch of Capua" is purely hypothetical. Hannibal's army, for a dozen years more, on Livy's own showing, continued to be the terror of Rome, all of whose generals and armies were in the highest degree shy of attacking it. The pride of the Romans had been so lowered by the Carthaginian successes that one can scarcely blame Livy for the hard things he has said of Hannibal. The winter-quarters at Capua may have been characterized by conduct very natural as a relief from the severity of the three years' strain of incessant campaigning, which had entailed trial, fatigue, hunger, exposure, danger and deprivation such as few armies ever undergo. It would have been strange if such had not been the case. But the army was not essentially weakened by its Capuan winter. So good a disciplinarian as Hannibal must have guarded against this. We have abundant proof of his exceptional ability in organization, and the facts prove that the army, after this winter in Capua, was practically in as good condition as before. It would be astonishing if winter-quarters in a gay city like Capua should not in some measure affect the discipline of an army which for several years had camped in the open field; but the injury was not permanent.

Hannibal had doubtless lost in fighting ability, but it was in one sense a proportionate loss only, for the Romans were growing in ability to manœuvre as well as fight; and so far as actual loss of fighting ability is concerned, it came from the disappearance of his veteran element, — of the larger part of the men who had come with him across the Alps, and from the necessity under which he stood of placing in their stead any and all sorts of material ready to his hand, no part of which could in any manner compare with even the raw levies of Rome.

That Hannibal's star from this year on seemed to pale;

that he seemed henceforth to resist defeat rather than win another succession of victories like the Trebia, Trasimene and Cannæ, is due more to the fact that other men than Sempronius, Flaminius and Varro were put into the field to lead the Roman troops; that the Romans were gradually learning the trade of war, and that Hannibal was outnumbered much more than he had previously been; in other words, that the Romans themselves had been taught a series of lessons from which they were beginning to profit.

And it must not be forgotten that Hannibal's problem, after Cannæ, was completely changed. We shall see how and why he shifted from the sharp offensive to a purely defensive rôle. It was not because his army had been debauched by Capuan orgies.

The defeat at Cannæ had borne the best of fruit to the Romans. Such a lesson, hard as it was, had been necessary to rouse that in the nation which always came out in times of grave political peril and rehabilitated the fortunes of the city. They had learned not only that they must put aside their internal quarrels and join hands in the common effort, but they saw that in pure, open warfare they had no one who could match Hannibal. They had learned that in the long run, with a mixture of Fabian and aggressive policy, they would certainly exhaust his resources and beat him. They had seen the folly of Varro, the wisdom of Fabius, the boldness of Marcellus; to this they added the ever-present Roman courage, discipline and fidelity; and they knew that the Roman organization was more durable than any which Hannibal could maintain on Italian soil.

The war had begun as an offensive one on the part of Hannibal, and had been met with a defensive — into which they had been forced against their normal habit — by the Romans. From now on, each party waged the war on what is called an offensive-defensive plan. Great battles in the open field gave way to camps strongly fortified in naturally good strategic centres, to manœuvring on the communications or about the flanks of the enemy, to an intelligent effort to seize upon important points. And when combats and battles came about, they were not called forth by a mere desire to win victories or to destroy armies, but by the desire to obtain a better defined advantage in a strategic sense. All this makes the last twelve years of the war of much greater interest to the student, though to the casual reader less brilliant, than the first few years. Hannibal's genius shines forth in threefold effulgence from this time on.

The loss of the army sent in 216 B. C. to cisalpine Gaul, already referred to, occurred after this fashion. Posthumius was marching through a wood, where the Gauls had laid an ambush for him. They had sawed a large number of trees nearly through, so that by a slight shock they would go down like a row of dominoes. Entering the wood, Posthumius and his twenty-five thousand men were caught in this snare, and either crushed to death or killed by the ambushed Gauls. The stratagem was ably conceived and executed, and the barbarians had relied on the well-known carelessness of the Roman armies on the march.

After the news of this defeat had been received, it was resolved by the Roman senate to give up any attempt for this year to carry on war in cisalpine Gaul, but merely to keep an observation army there.

Rome had her full share of troubles. The pro-prætors, Otacilius from Sicily, and Cornelius Mammula from Sardinia, complained of want of funds to pay and corn to feed their troops. But opportune succor was forthcoming. Fortune aided Rome as she aided herself. Hiero of Syracuse helped Otacilius, and the population of Sardinia put Cornelius Mammula out of his difficulties.

One of the consuls of the succeeding year, B. C. 215, was Posthumius. On his death he was succeeded by Marcellus, who declined on account of omens, and then by Fabius, the old dictator. His colleague was Tiberius Sempronius Gracchus. Rome made an extraordinary effort to place a force and generals a-field able in some sense to cope with Hannibal. Defeat and disaster had been harsh, but admirable teachers. Varro and Cannæ was the last bad error of Rome. Wisdom and strength now came to the fore, showing up doubly marked against the querulous and weak conduct of the Carthaginian senate. And fortune after Cannæ leaned towards her. The three army-commanders who opposed Hannibal were tried men: Marcellus, proconsul, and Fabius and Sempronius, consuls.

After some preliminary changes, followed by the casting of lots for the legions, to Fabius was given the command of the army, now at Cales, which had been under the late dictator at Teanum, and which consisted of two Roman legions with the usual complement of other troops; to Gracchus' lot fell that of the levies of volunteer slaves, and twenty-five thousand allies, says Livy. He assembled at Sinuessa, from which place he advanced to Liternum to protect Cumæ and Neapolis. Marcellus, as proconsul, retained the command of two legions at his eyrie back of Suessula, overlooking and protecting Nola. All the Cannæ fugitives were sent to Sicily for service, as a punishment for breaking their oath in that battle; these were joined by the less good material from Junius' army; and the two legions which had been in Sicily were brought back to Rome. Otacilius commanded the fleet in Sicily.

The Roman senate thus made good its threat to punish those who at Cannæ had failed to do their duty. The knights were dismounted and sent as foot to serve in various parts of Italy, and other degradations, including loss of pay, followed.

Varro was the sole and only exception. One is fain to feel that Varro was the most guilty of all the soldiers who escaped from this disastrous field. But the manifest fact that the senate honored him on his return, for that he had not despaired of the republic, and that they now exempted him from penalties, — and the Roman senate, despite the bitterness of politics, was a body of men whose superior has rarely been seen in history, — seems to indicate that there were excuses for his conduct which we do not now understand, and which the historians do not give us.

Marcus Valerius, the prætor, was ordered to the command of Varro's late legions in Apulia, and with the legions which returned from Sicily and twenty-five ships, was to protect the lower coast about Tarentum and Brundisium. There were also given the prætor Fulvius twenty-five ships to protect the coast near Rome. There were two legions in Sicily, — the Cannæ survivors, — one in Sardinia, one in Tarentum and two in Spain. This made a force of eight legions to oppose Hannibal, and six on outside operations, a total, including the excess of Gracchus, of over one hundred and fifty thousand men. Though the army destroyed in cisalpine Gaul was not replaced, Varro was sent to Picenum to head off any reinforcements which might come thence to Hannibal by way of the coast, Picenum being Varro's native province.

Imports and taxes were doubled to pay for these troops and material. A small-war by the Italian cities which remained faithful to Rome was organized against their deserting brethren. In Apulia, Brundisium, Luceria and Venusia; in Lucania, Pæstum; in Samnium, Beneventum, were Roman strongholds in the midst of these revolted provinces; and Cumæ and Neapolis remained true.

The plan of the Roman senate was to surround and watch Hannibal on all sides. It would not again stake its all on one cast. The defeat of a single army should not again bring the republic to the verge of ruin. A policy of counteracting what Hannibal had accomplished in acquiring control of so many Italian cities, it was thought would still further weaken him. This system was certainly not in accord with what might be called brilliant grand-strategy; for once Rome had found more than her match; but it was well adapted to the singular conditions under which Rome was struggling against her dangerous opponent, and worked well in the long run.

The force which Hannibal could command can only be estimated. The substantial Carthaginian reinforcements intended for him were diverted to other purposes. Mago was sent to Spain and Hasdrubal to Sardinia with what had been originally voted, and should certainly have been sent to Hannibal. After Cannæ there remained some thirty-four thousand infantry and nine thousand horse. Of this force, two divisions — how strong we do not know — were detached to Bruttium and Lucania, and these had much pains in holding head against the three Roman legions of Apulia and the partisans of the Italian cities. The meagre reinforcements which eventually reached him were only in cavalry and elephants. Hannibal, to offset this, had recruited a goodly number of men in Samnium and the Capuan territory. This had given him a considerable numerical force, but not of the quality of his daily dwindling veterans. It is not improbable that the detachments he had to make were offset by these levies, and that he had immediately under him thirty-five thousand foot and ten thousand cavalry, or perhaps as much as fifty thousand effective. For a man like Hannibal this was still a respectable army. But he had a vast work to do with this limited force.

From abroad he received some encouragement. Philip,

King of Macedon, under an arrangement with Carthage, sent him ambassadors, who, on the plea of a mission to Rome, managed to reach his headquarters, and concluded with the Carthaginians an alliance offensive and defensive, which was to include the landing of a Macedonian army in Italy. Hannibal had reason to hope that Tarentum, where he had many friends, would finally fall into his hands and thus give him the much desired important seaport, by which relations with Carthage and Macedon could be maintained. Carthage had likewise made an alliance with Hieronymus, the new king of Syracuse, from which Hannibal hoped for some advantageous results.

Forces in Campania, 215 B. C.

So soon as the season opened, Hannibal took up a position and intrenched on Mt. Tifata, a height commanding Capua. Over seventy-five thousand men at Cales, Sinuessa and Liternum, and Nola surrounded him. But his position was strong and central, and controlled the entrance to valleys where he could pasture his herds, and which furnished excellent and healthful camps for his men. He decided not to undertake the offensive, but awaited events, ready to act in whatever direction he might be called, preferring to lie in wait for some error on the part of the Roman generals of which he could take advantage, than to initiate operations. He was counting on Macedon, help from home, and additional allies in Italy. He could not force the fighting; he had not men enough; he must wait for openings, not create them. The Roman armies were all strongly intrenched. He had been compelled to turn over a new leaf.

Neither party moved. Hannibal busied himself with negotiations. Fabius clung to his old tactics of harassing the enemy, and interfering with his foraging, but without risking anything which might bring on a decisive conflict. The other generals bided their time. No attack on Hannibal was attempted. Nothing is more interesting than the manner in which this extraordinary man's personality imposed upon his adversaries. Even those who least lacked ability and aggressiveness were unwilling to meet him on equal terms. The scrupulous care they constantly exercised to keep well away from a battle in the open is a wonderful tribute to the skill and fighting capacity of this captain. And this wariness lasted till the end.

The Roman senate, among its other laws passed for this occasion, and in order to prevent Hannibal from victualing his troops, decreed that the inhabitants of the district where the rival armies were manœuvring should harvest the early crops, and carry the grain to the fortified towns before summer opened, under pain of having their homes devastated and being themselves sold into slavery. Everything was done to hamper Hannibal's movements, to neutralize his capacity for assuming the offensive. But no step was taken towards driving him from the land by force of arms. This was too big a task.

One of the early events of the new campaign was an attempt by the Capuans to seize upon Cumæ, whose citizens they had vainly sought to engage in revolt against Rome. Unable to make headway by such means, they resorted to the stratagem of inviting the leading nobles and officials to a conference at Hamæ, where there was a solemn sacrifice at this time, intending to seize upon the city during the solemnities. The Cumæans suspected something of this kind, and informed Gracchus of the facts. This officer had recently moved from Sinuessa to Liternum, on the coast above Cumæ. The Capuans had put fourteen thousand men in hiding near Hamæ, which was about three miles from Cumæ, with orders, after midnight, when the celebration should be at its height, to fall upon and seize Cumæ. But the scheme did not prosper. Gracchus arrived at the camp of the Capuan detachment before they set out, and falling unawares upon the force, cut out and killed some two thousand men of them, with a loss to himself of but one hundred; plundered their camp, and himself quickly occupied Cumæ, lest Hannibal, who was near by, on Mt. Tifata, should move out against him at Hamæ, which was an open place. In fact, Hannibal sought to do this very thing, hoping to catch Gracchus unawares; but reached Hamæ to find the Romans gone.

On the following day, Hannibal appeared again before Cumæ, and blockaded the place. As he had been unable to get Neapolis, he would have much liked Cumæ as a seaport. Both parties prepared for vigorous work. A tower was erected by Hannibal from which to mount the wall, and a corresponding one by Gracchus to defend it. Gracchus was fortunate enough to succeed in setting fire to the Carthaginian tower, and, in the flurry connected with this incident, made so sharp a sortie as to inflict, says Livy, a loss of thirteen hundred men killed and fifty-nine prisoners on the besiegers. Hannibal next day essayed to draw Gracchus out to fight in the open, but the wily Roman was not to be taken at a disadvantage, and the Carthaginian was fain to retire to his mountain stronghold, neither he nor his allies, the Capuans, having accomplished their purpose. Hannibal's poor success with nearly all his sieges in Italy shows that he was illy equipped for this work, and, like Frederick, he had perhaps not the patience, nor the aptitude for engineering which he possessed for every other branch of the military art. Fabius at Cales was detained by bad omens from helping Gracchus. " Nor," says Livy, " dared the other consul, Fabius, who was encamped at Cales, lead his troops across the Vulturnus, being employed in taking new auspices." This was Fabian tactics with a vengeance, when he had the chance of falling on Hannibal's flank at Cumæ.

This was not the only disappointment of these times. Hannibal was henceforth destined to possess his soul in patience under many a hard blow of fortune. His lieutenant, Hanno, met Sempronius Longus, a legate of Marcellus, at Grumentum in Lucania, and suffered a galling defeat and a loss of two thousand men, beating a hasty retreat to Bruttium. And Valerius made an inroad from Luceria into the Hirpinian domain about Beneventum, took three cities and one thousand prisoners, punished with death some of Hannibal's chief allies, and made good his retreat. This year was a sad one for Carthaginian luck.

Fabius finally got his auspices fixed, and was ready to advance beyond Cales with the purpose of joining hands with Marcellus and Gracchus, in the vicinity of Suessula. As Hannibal held Casilinum, he followed the same route as Marcellus, passed the Vulturnus near Caiatia, and under

cover of the hills, well back of Mt. Tifata, marched towards
the proconsul unopposed. In coöperation with Gracchus,
he took several towns (Compulteria, Trebula, and Saticula)
which had admitted Carthaginian garrisons, made many
prisoners, and punished the leaders of the Hannibal party.
Nola having still a very considerable popular party which
favored Hannibal, Fabius sent Marcellus back to that city,
of which he had some fears, while he himself took possession
of Marcellus' camp on the heights. It is not, however, probable that cautious Fabius was guilty of such an act of foolhardiness as to march his army between Capua and Mt.
Tifata, where Hannibal lay encamped, as Livy relates, especially when there was nothing to be gained by it.

Gracchus, from his camp at Cumæ, at the same time made
an advance towards Capua, which brought the three Roman
armies near enough to mutually sustain each other. Hannibal was practically hemmed in and robbed of his ability to
act in Campania, by this large Roman force so systematically
distributed. There was no army between him and Rome, but
the reasons for his not marching on the capital we already
know. Each Roman army lay in its intrenched camp or
walled city, showing no inclination to fight; and it must be
borne in mind that a battle could not be forced against a
camp any more than against a fortress. Very exceptional
circumstances only brought about the attack of a camp.
Hannibal could not afford to assault either without a special
gain in so doing. In the open country he would not have
hesitated a moment to attack the total forces if he had room
to manœuvre. But the Fabian tactics were bearing fruit.
The Romans preferred to wear Hannibal out by safer operations than fighting. They were holding the bulk of the Campanian plain against him. The three armies knew that
sooner or later hunger would drive him away, and leave

Capua to their mercy. They were covering the country on which he must rely for bread.

Hannibal's position had many difficulties. He could not desert Capua. This important ally must not be left to the mercy of Rome. But he had watched over the city until it had been able to harvest the crops ; it was strongly fortified, and he hoped would be able to hold its own, — at least for a while. He desired to aid his friends in Nola by advancing towards that town. Certain Carthaginian reinforcements of cavalry and elephants, under Bomilcar, had reached Locri in Bruttium, and Hannibal feared they might be intercepted by Fabius, as Appius Claudius, from Sicily, had vainly attempted to do. A multitude of cares called for his attention. He was in demand everywhere. The enemy could afford a policy of inaction, albeit with abundant means to carry on a vigorous campaign ; not so he, though he had but a fraction of what was essential to do his work. He must constantly keep in action. For want of success was starvation to this bold intruder on the territory of Rome.

Marcellus, from Nola, in connection with the prætorian army under M. Valerius, at Luceria, had made some raids into the land of the Hirpinians, Lucanians, and Caudine Samnites, and had played Hannibal's own game at devastation by fire and sword. These poor peoples, between the upper and nether millstone, cried for help to their new ally. Hannibal, to withdraw Marcellus from his quarry, left his fastness on Mt. Tifata well garrisoned, and marched on Nola, hoping to take by escalade this to him important town. But Marcellus, who was both intrepid and vigilant, had already returned and was ready to meet him. Marcellus was as cautious as Fabius, while not afraid of a sharp offensive. In the raids he had made we are told that he systematically reconnoitred his ground and carefully secured his retreat. He had acted in Hannibal's absence as if his enemy were near at hand. He had profited by the misfortunes of his predecessors in command.

Near Nola, Hanno joined his chief with a part of the four thousand recruits and elephants from Carthage, — a much needed reinforcement, and one which, however small, sensibly cheered the veterans of the harassed Punic army.

Hannibal first tried to gain Nola by treachery, but failed. This town seemed to be a stumbling-block to him. As on the first occasion, when he advanced to the assault, expecting nothing less than the repetition of the counter-attack of some months previous, Marcellus, watching the opportune moment, rushed from the gates with such vehemence that he drove in the head of Hannibal's column at the first shock. Hannibal got the men, however, speedily in hand. The fight was sharp but undecided. A heavy thunder-storm put an end to it this day, and Hannibal sat down before the town.

Three days after, when a strong party of foragers — a considerable part of the whole army — had gone out from the

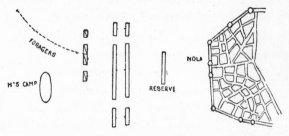

Second Battle of Nola.

Carthaginian camp, Marcellus seized this opportunity of depletion to the enemy's ranks to draw up in battle array outside the town and offered battle. Nothing loath, though not

in force, Hannibal accepted the gage. The distance between
the town and Hannibal's camp was about a mile. In this
space the forces met. Marcellus had armed the citizens of
Nola, and held them in reserve, — a novel thing with a Roman general, for the triarii and extraordinarii were as a rule
the only reserve to the legion; the Carthaginian foragers, at-
tracted by the tumult, returned in season to act as reserve to
Hannibal. The Romans opened the battle by their usual attack, made with great vigor, under Marcellus' inspiring conduct. Equally stanch was Hannibal's defense. The battle
hung in the balance many hours; the fighting was stubborn
and bloody, but apparently without any manœuvring. Finally
Roman discipline asserted itself. That the Roman soldier was
much better than any but the few veterans of Hannibal is
well shown by the victories he won so soon as he got good
generals. The flat ground was not such as to enable Hannibal to take any advantage of stratagem. He was driven
back to his camp — according to Livy — with a loss of five
thousand men killed, six hundred prisoners, six elephants,
and nineteen standards. Marcellus withdrew into Nola,
claiming a loss of but one thousand men. The looseness of
Livy's entire narrative makes one the more regret the loss of
Polybius' books which treated of this subject. Great credit
is due Marcellus for this day's operations. Next day, under
a tacit truce, each party buried its dead.

Thus Livy. But his account, properly summed up, looks
more like a drawn battle than the doubtless overstated Carthaginian casualties warrant. If Hannibal retired to his
camp, so did Marcellus to Nola. If Marcellus had won so
marked a victory, how did Hannibal save his army in a perfectly flat plain? Why should there have been a " tacit
truce " to bury the dead, when Marcellus had control of the
field of battle? That Hannibal did not win a victory seems

certain, for the proconsul held Nola. That Marcellus won one is, to say the least, doubtful. All the statements of Livy, weighed together, point clearly to a drawn battle. None the less credit is due to the Roman soldier ; none the less had Marcellus shown that so far he was the best Roman general of this war. But his retirement to Nola, where he remained and did not interfere with Hannibal's further movements, militates absolutely against Livy's would-be claim of a great Roman victory. Hannibal returned to Mt. Tifata.

Three days after, a body of twelve hundred and seventy-two of his new troops — Spanish and Numidian horse — deserted to the Romans, in whose service they remained throughout the war. This was indeed a hard blow. Happily they were not his veteran troopers. This is the only instance of any but isolated desertion from his ranks.

Fearing that this second failure at Nola might have a bad effect upon his army, Hannibal abandoned his camp on Mt. Tifata and marched for Apulia, where he took up winter-quarters in the vicinity of Arpi. He had been probably accumulating provisions with this object in view, since the call upon him by the Hirpini and Samnites.

Hanno was sent back to Bruttium with the troops he had brought.

It is entirely natural that during the period of Hannibal's success the Romans should have been reluctant to attack him on the march. It was too uncertain a problem. Now that they had found that even he was not invulnerable, it is a curious tribute to Hannibal's ability that, despite their numbers, they never sought to disturb his movements. They limited themselves strictly to following him up and seeking to prevent, so far as in them lay, his securing too large a territory to plunder. They never dared assume the offensive against him in the open field. And now when Gracchus fol-

lowed Hannibal to Luceria with his army, he contented himself with watching him. Fabius remained at Suessula, which
he was able to revictual fully, and strengthening the intrenchments and leaving a large body there, advanced
towards Capua and began to ravage its territory. The
Capuans could oppose him only by partisan warfare, having
no regular troops, but their irregular horse stood them in
good stead. They fortified a camp outside the town and
placed in it six thousand of their foot. Fabius allowed the
Capuans to sow their late crop of grain, in fact retiring to
allow them to do so, and when it ripened reaped and con-
veyed it to Suessula, returning to which place, he went into
winter-quarters. Marcellus, leaving only the necessary garrison at Nola, was instructed by Fabius to send the rest of his
troops to Rome, where it was easier to winter them. Fabius
fortified and garrisoned Puteoli, near Neapolis, which was the
centre of a great wheat traffic.

During this winter there was a constant exchange of combats between Romans and Carthaginians in Apulia. When
Hannibal was not personally present, the Romans generally
had the advantage. These wonderful soldiers were gradually
learning the ways of their foes and regaining confidence in
themselves.

In Bruttium, Petelia resisted eight months all the efforts of
Himilco. When it fell, it carried with it Consentia, Locri,
and, after a fierce resistance, Crotona. Rhegium remained
faithful to Rome. The Bruttians were strongly wedded to
the cause of Hannibal, but individual cities still held out.

The Scipios in Spain, despite lack of money, clothing and
corn, had followed up their successes during the year B. C.
215, had been well sustained by the Roman senate, had advanced from the Ebro to the Guadalquivir and had beaten
the Carthaginians in two pitched battles, with a loss of thirty

thousand killed, six thousand prisoners, ten elephants and one hundred and one standards.

In Sardinia, the Roman arms were crowned with success. Mago, Hannibal's brother, had just got ready to put to sea from Carthage with fifty ships to join the Carthaginians in Bruttium. He had twelve thousand foot, fifteen hundred horse, twenty elephants, and one thousand talents of silver. But at the last moment Sardinia begged assistance from the Carthaginian senate. Mago was therefore sent to Spain, and some Spanish forces under Hasdrubal to Sardinia, which it was thought would be an intermediate point between Spain and Italy, valuable to the cause in every sense. This was true, but the Carthaginian senate was none the less frittering away its resources. The Carthaginians had no success in Sardinia. Manlius Torquatus, with twenty-three thousand men, was too much of a match for them. In two battles he utterly overthrew them, with five thousand men killed and captured, and again subjugated the island. The Carthaginians retired to Iberia. Their men and means were wasted.

Otacilius had won a naval victory over a Carthaginian squadron, but had not succeeded in heading off Bomilcar, who managed to land his troops and money at Locri, and report to Hanno. This petty reinforcement, while of value as far as it went, was of a piece with the shortsightedness of the Punic government.

As a last ounce, the Macedonian ambassadors, returning home from making their treaty with Hannibal, had been taken prisoners by a Roman ship and sent to Rome. The information thus seized enabled the senate to provide for the possible danger from this source. A fleet was sent to Brundisium under the prætor Valerius, who from that port was to raise among the Greeks, if possible, a coalition against Macedonia.

Thus unsupported by his home resources and unable to lure the Romans into battle in the field, Hannibal was gradually but surely losing ground. The fortunes of the war seemed to be going over to the Romans. This was naturally the result of their improved management, and was the due reward of the manfulness of their conduct during the disasters of the first years. The improvement in the fortunes of Rome was, however, less marked in its campaigns against Hannibal than in Spain and Sardinia and at sea.

More strongly in favor of Roman success than anything which the Romans themselves could do, was the despicable policy of the Carthaginian senate. Hannibal had begun his Italian campaign by establishing a base on the Po, where he could receive, and had a right to expect, support from Spain on his right and from Macedon on his left. The chances and demands of the war had led him to a series of brilliant marches and strategic manœuvres, which had carried him to the south of Italy. Here he had established a new base, and he had still more right to expect that his Macedonian allies would now sustain his right, as they could more readily do, and the home government his left. What he had accomplished had been in absolute accord with his original plans. He had been disappointed only in the lack of Italian support and in affairs in Spain.

If we can imagine concord sufficient in the Carthaginian senate to send Hannibal reinforcements to southern Italy, where they might readily land at Locri or Crotona, — for Syracuse was now open to the Carthaginians, and the Roman fleet at Brundisium was held in check by the Macedonians; if we can imagine a descent in force on the Italian coast by Philip; these might, if anything could, have turned the scales of disaster against Rome. These things could have been better done immediately after Cannæ than at any later period.

Hannibal was then at the height of his repute. Only his weakness in men encouraged his opponents to measure swords with him. With such reinforcements as he had counted on, as he was entitled, from his brilliant successes, to expect and demand, Hannibal's campaign could scarcely have been a failure. But while Hannibal was a consummate statesman, he was no politician. He had been brought up in camps. He had no popular leader at home to represent him. The Hanno, or peace party, was uppermost in Carthage, and Hannibal was left to his own resources, and to such fortune as his own unaided genius might compel.

The general scheme of Rome was a defensive one. She must hold the Pyrenees, which her excellent generals in Spain enabled her to do. This forestalled any new descent on the Padane region. She must head off the Macedonian army and prevent its reaching Italy. This danger was ably provided against by Valerius. She must keep up communications with Sicily, for which purpose Messana was the key-point. She must, by constant activity and courage, prevent Hannibal from gaining any more headway. In all these things, aided by the fatuity of the Carthaginian senate, she was measurably successful. The position of Hasdrubal after the defeat on the Ebro was critical. Carthage looked at Spain, not as a means, but as an end, forgetful that unless Rome was defeated at home, Spain would always be held on an uncertain tenure, and diverted the promised help from the Italian to the Iberian peninsula. The Macedonian alliance proved useless; and Rome held Brundisium by land and sea. The Cannæ legions, banished to Sicily, held head against the Syracusans and Carthaginians in the north and east of the island. The considerable forces raised by Carthage in the happy effervescence of Cannæ were frittered away. Hannibal was left alone.

If there was in Rome at the end of this year any one of sufficient foresight and coolness to properly gauge the situation, he could well call the crisis past. Rome was saved. A little more perseverance and the end would come. But Hannibal yet sorely tried their patience.

Signum.

XXXI.

MAKING A NEW BASE. 214 B. C.

THIS year Rome had two hundred thousand men afield. Of this force, four armies, of over twenty thousand men each, were to oppose Hannibal. The Roman plan was the same as last year, but the capture of Capua was projected. Hannibal was obliged to resort to a pure defensive, a rôle which he carried through with wonderful aptness, in marked contrast to his former bold offensive. He was narrowed to the South Italian provinces, but here he held full sway, excepting only Roman fortresses. Capua saw that the consuls were threatening her. She called on Hannibal for help, who left Arpi and marching around the armies in his front, made for Campania. The consuls remained quiet. Hannibal tried to seize on Cumæ, Puteoli or Neapolis as a seaport, but failed. He might have captured either by a siege ; but siege-operations were not his forte. He tried once more to get hold of Nola, but once more Marcellus checked him. Hanno, seeking to join his chief, was stopped at Beneventum and defeated by Gracchus with total loss of his army. Hannibal left Campania, having helped the Capuans to harvest their crops. He had hope of capturing Tarentum, from which city he had received advances, but he reached it three days after its garrison had been reinforced by the Romans from Brundisium. So soon as he left Campania the consuls laid siege to and captured Casilinum, as a first step to attacking Capua, and later ravaged Samnium, and punished all Hannibal's adherents in the cities they could capture. The Romans had made a marked gain this year.

FABIUS for the fourth time, and Marcellus for the third time, were elected the consuls of B. C. 214, the fifth year of the war, and as prætors Fulvius, Otacilius, Fabius, son of the consul, and Lentulus. Rome made still greater exertions than in the preceding year, and placed no less than twenty legions, (that is, twenty Roman and twenty allied), or over two hundred thousand men in all, in the field. They began to see that patience under reverses, and a careful study into the causes of their failures, could accomplish better results than mere brute force. But they kept an abundant force afoot.

In Sicily, the Carthaginians were wasting material which might be of unbounded use to Hannibal. The senate could not see that a peace dictated at the gates of Rome was the only comprehensive or lasting one. The Romans had in the island two legions under Lentulus, and the same force under Q. Mucius in Sardinia, and under Manius Pomponius in cis-alpine Gaul, which, added to the army of Spain, made eighty thousand men in all. When spring opened, the troops left winter-quarters. Fabius had two legions of new levies which had rendezvoused at Cales. Marcellus took command at Suessula with two. Gracchus at Luceria, opposite Hannibal, had two volunteer-slave legions, and backed on Beneventum. The prætor Fabius, in Apulia, had two. Two were in garrison in Rome. Varro, in Picenum, had one, which lay, as it were, in reserve to the two in Gaul. Valerius at Brundisium had one. Otacilius commanded the fleet, and one hundred new ships were built, — making one hundred and fifty in all. The fleet was manned by a direct tax on the wealthy of so many sailors each for so many thousand asses of property.

Of the above twenty legions, fourteen were old; six new ones were raised. This enormous force, of which about one third were new men and one half were Roman citizens, was, directly and indirectly, what Hannibal had to contend with. Nor did it comprise the garrisons in the Roman oppida. The theory of the war continued the same, — to surround the Carthaginian with several armies, to harass and tire him out with small-war, but never, except when the chances were all in their favor, to fight a general battle. Four Roman armies were arrayed in the field immediately against Hannibal: Fabius at Cales, Marcellus at Suessula, Gracchus at Luceria, young Fabius in Apulia. This drew a line which held him to southern Italy, but within this line, excepting only the Roman oppida, he had full sway. While two or more of these armies should watch his movements, the other forces would

Armies opposite Hannibal, B. C. 214.

attack his lieutenants or allied cities. Was ever invader so overmatched?

Hannibal was at Arpi, where he had wintered. Hanno lay in Bruttium, whose ports, except Rhegium, which was protected by Messana, were in Carthaginian hands. No army faced him.

In Campania, the Roman objective was the capture of Capua, the most important of Hannibal's allied cities, as it was the second city of the peninsula. The intention of the consuls was obvious.

The Capuans, alarmed at these extraordinary preparations in Campania, clearly aimed at them, sent word to Hannibal that he must at once come to their aid. Hannibal was in grave difficulty. He was called on to play a waiting game. Nothing but an army from Macedon, or Hasdrubal with troops from Spain, or heavy reinforcements from Carthage, ·could now enable him to do more than hold his own. Meanwhile, he must seek to keep his allies from getting disheart-

ened at the defensive rôle which was forced on him. He en-
acted his part with consummate ability. No one fathomed in
Hannibal any distrust in the future. " We hardly recognize,
in the obstinate defensive system which he now began, the
same general who had carried on the offensive with almost
unequaled impetuosity and boldness; it is marvelous in a psy-
chological as well as a military point of view, that the same
man should have accomplished the two tasks prescribed to
him — tasks so diametrically opposed in their character —
with equal completeness," says Mommsen. He had no less
than ninety thousand men directly opposed to him, whose special duty it was to hamper his movements. The Carthaginian
senate deemed it more essential to hold Spain and play with
Sardinia than to reinforce Hannibal, who was thus left to his
own resources of courage and patience to work out the problem he had undertaken. He had long been compelled to
narrow his field of operations to the provinces lying south
of the Vulturnus-Garganus line. While he was thus near
enough Carthage to be able to communicate with her, as well
as keep a constant pressure on Rome, he had lost his hold
on his original allies of the Po.

Capua's appeal was irresistible. In response to her cry
for help, Hannibal left Arpi at once, and moving boldly
around Gracchus' flank at Luceria, he gained the road to
Beneventum, and by forced marches, no doubt via Telesia
and Caiatia, reoccupied his old position on Mt. Tifata. That
none of the Roman armies deemed it prudent to interfere
with this march seems odd enough. It certainly shows that
Gracchus was wary of approaching him; and it shows either
that the two consuls were equally prudent, or that Hannibal
marched so rapidly as to keep ahead of the Roman messengers who were undoubtedly dispatched by Gracchus to his
chiefs. The latter is improbable. No army can march so
fast.

Arrived on the spot, Hannibal saw that there was no immediate preparation to besiege Capua. But once there, he bethought him to try a diversion to unsettle the intention of

Southern Italy.

the consuls, and if possible seize on a seaport on the Campanian coast. Such a port all his efforts so far had failed to get. Leaving his Spanish and Numidian forces in the camp on Mt. Tifata, he marched straight across the country to the Cumæ region, and established a secondary camp at Lake Avernus, near this city. His purpose was to capture Puteoli, near by. But Puteoli was too strongly garrisoned for a *coup de main*, — it had stout walls and six thousand men, — so that he was fain to content himself with devastating the adjacent territory as far as Misenum promontory, and moved towards Neapolis. Fabius, the consul, hearing that Hannibal was in Campania, joined his army near Cales, to observe Casilinum and Capua, and ordered Gracchus from Luceria to Beneventum, to be replaced by the army of the prætor Fabius.

Neapolis and Vicinity.

About this time Hannibal received a deputation from some of the young nobles of Tarentum, offering to open the gates of this town if he would come to that region. The offer was tempting to the last degree, as Tarentum would furnish him with a harbor of great value, either looking towards Carthage or Macedonia, and he determined to take advantage of the proposal so soon as he could absent himself from Campania.

It was of the highest importance to Hannibal to make for himself a solid base in Campania, where not only was his most important ally, Capua, but which lay singularly well for his purposes, with both the Via Appia and Via Latina leading direct to Rome. But Capua and Mt. Tifata alone could not enable him to operate against Rome, when, as he still anticipated, he should receive reinforcements from home or Macedonia, and should secure more of the Italian allies. For he had no near-by port of disembarkation. He must have either Neapolis or Cumæ, or both if possible, for this purpose. He moved to and fro over the vicinity, seeking an opportunity of gaining the one or other.

Just why Hannibal was so much opposed to sieges, it is hard to say; but to judge by the event, he distrusted his own powers in such efforts. Though part of his army was on Mt. Tifata, he could at this time have sat down before Cumæ, Puteoli or Naples with a fair show of success, and without running any graver risk than his general situation compelled, even if the Romans had attempted to raise the siege. There is something we are not told which is needed to explain this odd aversion to siege-work. That the towns were well walled and garrisoned by Roman soldiers is not a sufficient explanation. Still we must not forget the overwhelming forces surrounding him.

Hannibal's near approach to Nola, when he had reached the vicinity of Neapolis, induced his old friends, the commons, to invite him to renew an attempt on the city, assuring him of the present certainty of assistance from within. But Marcellus, who was Hannibal's black-bogy whenever Nola was the question, opportunely learned of this message from the Roman adherents in the city. He was at Cales in consultation with his colleague. The legions which had fallen to his lot had been wintering in the Claudian camp above Suessula. He hurried from Cales by the roads back of Mt. Tifata, and collecting a picked force of sixty-three hundred men, anticipated Hannibal in reaching Nola and checkmated the scheme. Hannibal had been slow, for he had little cause to place confidence in the Nolan people.

In order to further his project of making a good base of

operations in Campania, Hannibal ordered Hanno, who had recruited his army up to seventeen thousand infantry and twelve hundred Numidian horse, to leave Bruttium and join him in the former province. Nola being on the direct road and held by Marcellus, Hannibal advised his lieutenant to march by way of Beneventum. As matters eventuated, it would have been better for Hanno to march due north to Nuceria, towards which point Hannibal could have moved by his right to join him.

As we have seen, when Hannibal left Apulia, Fabius had ordered Gracchus from Luceria on Beneventum, while Fabius junior should take his place in his absence. This would have been, if intended, a very neat strategic manœuvre by Fabius, — and it has been so ascribed to him by more than one critic, — for as Nola barred one of the roads to Hanno, so the possession of Beneventum closed the other. But Fabius had no idea of Hanno's projected advance. He had occupied Beneventum as a strategic centre, and probably with the hope of cooping Hannibal up in Campania, as on the last occasion he had failed to do. He may have incidentally had in mind the closing of the roads to reinforcements. But there is no evidence of other foresight.

Hanno and Gracchus appear to have reached Beneventum about the same time, but the proconsul got possession of the city by the aid of its Roman garrison, and barred the way. Hanno was unable to join his chief without a battle. The Roman generals were ready enough to fight Hannibal's lieutenants ; but not so the great captain in person, who repeatedly marched past Beneventum in the teeth of Roman armies, without meeting an attack.

Hanno camped on the left bank of the Calor, some three miles from the town. Gracchus moved up and camped within a mile of him. He had four legions, two of which were

composed entirely of those debtors and slaves to whom freedom had been promised if they won their first fight. Up
to this moment all had been waiting for the time to come

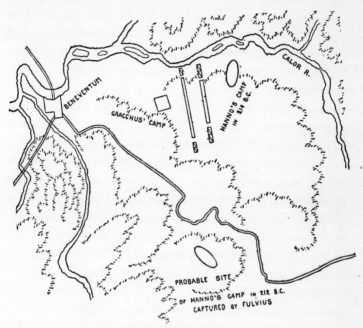

Hanno at Beneventum.

when the redeeming of the promise might be claimed; with
the consent of the senate and Marcellus the consul, Gracchus now definitely promised them immediate freedom if
they did their duty as they should in the approaching battle,
and "each brought him the head of an enemy." The legions, in great joy, assured him that their freedom would
surely be won.

Next day, Gracchus drew up his army in order of battle.
Hanno did the like. His seventeen thousand foot were
mostly recruited in Bruttium and Lucania. The bulk of his

twelve hundred horse was African. Both armies went into action confident of victory. The first shock was remarkably severe, and for several hours the event was doubtful. The slaves were so eager in cutting the heads off the killed and so hampered by many holding on to a head thus got, that they were jeopardizing the battle. Gracchus was obliged to send them word to fight instead of gathering the ghastly trophies, as they had already fairly earned their freedom. At the same time he ordered in his cavalry, until now held in reserve, on Hanno's flanks; but the Numidians fought with so much energy and skill that the fate of the battle seemed to hang on accident. Gracchus again sent round word through the legions that the freedom would not be granted, unless the enemy was speedily beaten. Thus encouraged, the legions made one supreme and desperate effort and drove the Carthaginians back to their camp, entering with them. A number of Roman prisoners in the Carthaginian camp having procured weapons and fallen upon the rear of Hanno's army, the Roman triumph became complete. Barely two thousand men and Hanno himself survived. The Roman loss was some two thousand men; thirty-eight standards were taken.

The well-earned freedom was given to the entire legions, as had been promised. But some four thousand of the men who had not proven themselves as brave as the majority, and had not penetrated the Carthaginian camp, though freed, were punished by being sentenced to eat their evening meal standing during the rest of their term of service. The morning meal, it will be remembered, was always eaten standing; the evening, and heartier one, sitting or reclining.

Gracchus was received at Beneventum, after the victory, with open arms, and his entire army feasted by the citizens. He then marched into Lucania, to prevent Hanno from raising another army there, and after some passages of arms, gradually forced him back to Bruttium.

Livy speaks of Fabius as being the moving spirit of this campaign, though he had but equal authority with his colleague. If he was, he deserves due credit for his intelligent action in bringing Gracchus to Beneventum. To Gracchus must be awarded equal credit for his bold attack on Hanno, for his good management of the battle, and for following him up as he did, to secure the full fruit of his victory.

This unhappy defeat robbed Hannibal of the assistance of his reinforcements, and put an end to any hope of present success in Campania. No such untoward event had as yet befallen him. He was unwilling to leave this province without one more essay on Nola, which, if he could take it, would offset almost any other loss. While Gracchus was campaigning in Lucania against Hanno, Hannibal, having eaten out the Neapolis territory, had broken camp and moved near Nola, camping on its west. Marcellus reinforced himself by bringing Pomponius, the pro-prætor, with the bulk of his forces from the Claudian camp above Suessula, and planned to give battle to Hannibal. He sent his legate, Claudius Nero, with a chosen body of horse, by a long circuit from the east gate, to attempt to fall on Hannibal's rear during the battle which he himself would provoke by attacking in front. On the next morning, he drew up his legions and attacked the Carthaginian army. For some hours the combat raged fiercely, but as Nero was not heard from, Marcellus deemed it wise to withdraw. He had lost four hundred men, and had inflicted a loss of two thousand men on Hannibal. Nero turned up later, alleging that he had lost his way and had not been able to find the enemy. Such are the facts stated by Livy.

It is well to examine these facts. Livy, construed by Livy, often yields light. He says that "the Romans had unquestionably the advantage, but as the cavalry did not come up in time, the plan of the battle which had been agreed upon was disconcerted, and Marcellus, not daring to follow the retiring enemy, gave the signal for retreat when his soldiers were conquering."

From this language one would scarcely assume a marked victory on Marcellus' part; nor can one credit the casualties given. Marcellus had great energy; why should he retreat "when his soldiers were conquering"? The probability is that it was an even thing. Everything points that way.

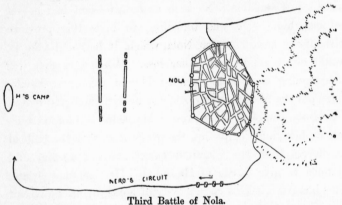

Third Battle of Nola.

Livy goes on to say that Marcellus reproached Nero with having prevented him from inflicting on the Carthaginians a second Cannæ. But Nero was a splendid marcher. His part in the Metaurus campaign is the finest strategic feat of the Romans during the entire war, as well as one of the exceptional marches of history. It is probable that the route cut out for him was too long for the time given, or at least that the fault did not lie entirely with him.

After all said, the third battle of Nola must be set down as drawn. Yet it was a feather in Marcellus' cap, for Hannibal had failed of his purpose. Both the Roman generals and legions were now of far better stuff.

Next day, Marcellus again offered battle. But Hannibal, apparently despairing of ever winning a fight at Nola, declined it, turned face from the town which had thrice repulsed him and marched out of Campania. He had been unable to make a new base in this province, and purposed to turn his attention to the more promising field of Tarentum. He had stayed with the Capuans long enough to forestall the Roman siege for this year and to enable them to get in their harvest. This was all the service he could render them under the present awkward conditions.

The consuls made no attempt to interfere with his leaving Campania. They no doubt breathed the more freely, the further he was from Rome. If Hannibal had been seriously defeated at Nola, this conduct lacked every element of enterprise.

Though his genius never shone so brightly as now and from this time forward, Hannibal's star was paling so far as concerned material success. He arrived at Tarentum three days late. Marcus Livius, an officer sent by Valerius from Brundisium, had anticipated him in entering the city, and had so effectually rallied the Roman sympathizers that no rising could be made in Hannibal's favor when he reached the place. Hannibal acted with sensible moderation in sparing the region, where he still had many friends; and, gathering his store of wheat from Metapontum and Heraclea when the season was over, he left for the north to take up winter-quarters at Salapia. His horse he sent to better foraging grounds among the Salentinians and in the mountains.

It will be observed that Hannibal never lost his hold on the country near Luceria, the key of Apulia. While he was obliged by his failure in Campania to resort to a base in extreme southern Italy, he purposed to hold the avenue by which any possible reinforcements might reach him overland from Spain. This avenue he kept open until the fatal day of the Metaurus wrecked the possibility of help from this direction.

So soon as Hannibal left Campania, Fabius undertook the long desired siege of Casilinum, which he had been prudent enough not to begin in earnest with the Carthaginian army

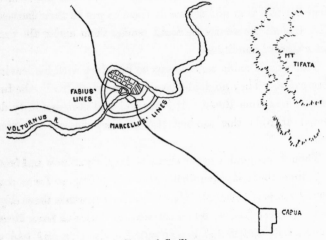

Siege of Casilinum.

near at hand, though he had made a slight attempt on the town while Hannibal was near Neapolis. To make his work tell to the best advantage, he invited Marcellus to move up from Nola to help him on the south bank, where he could at the same time observe Capua in order to prevent its interference with the siege-operations. Nola was strengthened by Marcellus with two thousand men and could take care of herself in the absence of Hannibal.

Casilinum was garrisoned by seven hundred of Hannibal's veterans and two thousand Capuans under Status Metius. Marcellus moved to Casilinum, where he undertook work from the left bank, while Fabius pushed the siege from the right.

Owing to the situation of the town astride the river, their camps were not connected. Marcellus' position was held in sufficient strength to keep the Capuans within walls. The besieged defended themselves with so much intelligence and obstinacy that Fabius was inclined to withdraw; but Marcellus persuaded him to persevere. Finally, hard pressed to the last degree, the garrison capitulated to Fabius, with the understanding that the men should be allowed to retire to Capua. But Marcellus, alleging that he knew nothing of the terms made with Fabius, — at all events without the latter's knowledge or consent, — and being on the side from which the garrison must emerge to go to Capua, took possession of the gates and fell upon the unsuspecting column, killing or taking prisoners all but fifty of the entire number. The prisoners were sent to Rome, except these fifty, who reached Capua in sad plight.

While this unhandsome act by Marcellus was by no means an unusual one, it is one of those which go far to give to the Roman cry of Punic Faith a ridiculous aspect. During this, as well as all their wars, the Romans were so far from immaculate that they can bring no accusation against the Carthaginians, and least of all against Hannibal, whose character emerges unsullied from all their attacks.

The immediate results of Gracchus' victory over Hanno had thus been the forced retirement of Hannibal from Campania and the capture of Casilinum, two brilliant successes which now gave the consuls free scope to lay siege to Capua whenever the occasion should be favorable.

Marcellus again returned to Nola and Suessula. Fabius moved into Samnium, to join hands with Fabius junior in Apulia, and with Gracchus in Lucania, and, in coöperation with them, regain some of the revolted cities. Hanno having retired to Bruttium, the three Roman armies had everything their own way, and took occasion to ravage all the region allied to Hannibal. The Samnites of Caudium especially suffered. Some twenty-five thousand people are said to have perished in this retribution. A number of Roman deserters were captured and sent to Rome for execution. The armies took by storm Compulteria, Telesia and Compsa, Melæ, Fulfulæ and Orbitanium in Samnium; by siege Blanda in Lucania and Æcæ in Apulia, and dealt out severity in abundant measure to all Hannibal's adherents. They then retired to winter-quarters, — Fabius at Suessula, Marcellus at Nola, Gracchus in Lucania, and Fabius, Jr., in Apulia, not far from Hannibal at Salapia. The only ray of light was a severe slap given by Hanno to a lieutenant of Gracchus, "not much less disastrous than he himself had received at Beneventum," says Livy, about the time of the capture of Casilinum.

During this year Hieronymus, king of Syracuse, who had abandoned the Roman alliance, was assassinated by a cabal, and a new treaty with Rome was made by the conspirators. It was, however, of short duration, for the Carthaginian influence again gained ground, and Syracuse declared war on Rome. Many cities of Sicily followed her example. Marcellus was sent with his two legions to calm the storm. Hannibal had never desired the war to extend to Sicily. He was soldier enough to understand the value of concentration, the danger of frittering away one's forces in outside operations. But just because he opposed a Sicilian campaign the Punic senate was glad to foster it, as it had fostered the unnecessary war in the Iberian peninsula. At the same time Philip of Macedon had assembled an army and a fleet with which to invade Italy. But Valerius left Brundisium, sailed to Apollonia, where the Macedonian fleet lay, defeated the army and burned the fleet. Thus ended the Macedonian alliance with Hannibal.

This year and the coming ones were fruitful in instances of Roman patriotism. Private wealth was cheerfully poured into the coffers of the state and the heaviest taxes were honestly paid. Many citizens served in the armies without pay.

The results of the year were entirely in favor of the Romans. The tide had set in their favor. Every element was on their side. The legionaries were not only equal, they were superior to the troops opposed to them, among whom were but few of the Carthaginian veterans. Numbers grew with the Romans as they decreased with Hannibal. Their generals had been trained in a good school, and were doing justice to their master's instruction. To oppose all this there was but one element on the other side, — the burning genius of Hannibal.

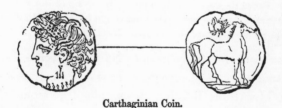

Carthaginian Coin.

XXXII.

TARENTUM WON. 213 B. C.

In 213 B. C. the Romans again raised over two hundred and twenty thousand men. The year had few marked occurrences. Hannibal remained near Tarentum, watching his chance. Marcellus was sent to besiege Syracuse, where Archimedes kept him at bay for eight months with his remarkable mechanical devices. The succeeding year the legions were raised to twenty-three. The Romans found difficulty in recruiting men; Hannibal much more. The Carthaginians had the good fortune to capture Tarentum by treachery; but the Roman garrison kept the citadel, in which they were besieged by land and sea. The Tarentine fleet was in the inner harbor. Hannibal moved it to the outer bay, where alone it could be of use, by carrying the ships through the town on wagons and sledges. The consuls undertook the siege of Capua. This city called on Hannibal for aid, as they had been unable to harvest their crops. Hannibal sent Hanno to Beneventum to accumulate victual and deliver it to the trains which he notified the Capuans to send there. Hanno's part was well done, but owing to Capuan dilatoriness his army was caught by the consul Fulvius, during his absence foraging, and cut to pieces. Hanno escaped.

The consuls for the year B. C. 213 were Tiberius Sempronius Gracchus and the younger Fabius. As prætors were chosen M. Atilius Regulus, Sempronius Tuditanus, Cnæus Fulvius, and Æmilius Lepidus. The Roman armies lay as follows: Gracchus, in Lucania, had two legions with which to continue the war in that province. Fabius remained in Apulia with two legions, his father, late dictator, accompanying him as legate. Æmilius, prætor, was at Luceria with two legions. Fulvius, prætor, succeeded the late consul Fabius at Suessula, where were two legions. Varro remained in Picenum with one. In Sicily were Marcellus and Cornelius Lentulus, — the latter in the western part of the island, known as the Roman province, — each with two legions.

The prætor Sempronius was in cisalpine Gaul with two legions, and the pro-prætor Mucius in Sardinia with two. The Scipios in Spain had two legions. In garrison in Rome

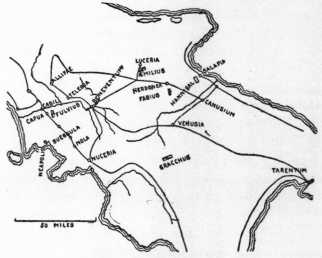

Armies opposite Hannibal, 213 B. C.

were two; while Valerius carried to Greece one legion. Of this enormous array of twenty-two legions, thirteen were in Italy, of which eight were intended especially to confront Hannibal, namely, Æmilius' two at Luceria, Fabius' two at Herdonia, Fulvius' two near Capua, and Gracchus' two between Hanno and Hannibal. It is well to recite this list of legions to show what Hannibal had to contend with. This enormous force of two hundred and twenty thousand men seemed certain to overwhelm his cause. The eighty thousand men who specially surrounded him should be enough, it appears, to put a speedy end to the war.

It is hard to describe the operations of this year. The records are very inexplicit, and like the later years of the Seven Years' War, there was apparently little done by either side. And yet it was a year of intense anxiety to Hannibal, who was hoping against hope; he recognized that the stars in their courses were fighting against him.

The earliest operation of importance in this campaign was the capture of Arpi by Fabius, who attacked the place at night in a thunder-storm, when least expected. The garrison consisted of five thousand of Hannibal's men and three thousand citizen-troops; but a thousand Spaniards went over to the Romans at the critical moment. The Carthaginians made so respectable a show of resistance that they were able to capitulate with right to move to Salapia. The town of Arpi thenceforth remained under Roman control.

Signs of yielding to the pressure, even in Capua, began also to be noticed. A number of the noblemen of this city sent word to Fulvius, the prætor, that they would surrender themselves to the Romans on condition that their possessions might be restored to them in case Capua was taken. Hannibal's structure in Italy seemed ready to go to pieces.

Hannibal's position at Salapia became perilous. His winter-supplies were exhausted, and there was nothing in the vicinity to forage on. Two Roman armies in his immediate front, — one at Luceria, one at Herdonia, — and still another in Lucania, seemed to shut him in beyond possibility of moving. He was not strong enough to undertake an offensive. He was holding himself in Italy in the hope that further reinforcements might reach him. So long as this hope lasted, he would not abandon the peninsula. But Salapia became untenable. He determined to move to Tarentum. His one reliance was in his small remaining force of cavalry, the arm that never failed him; and under cover of a curtain of Numidians, he set out to march along the coast. The Romans deemed it unwise to interfere with his march, and not far from Tarentum he spent the summer, hoping that he might be able to capture it, or that his friends within would induce it to open its gates. Meanwhile, he made a small-war upon some of the towns of the Salentinians. Capua he was compelled to leave to its own resources, but happily it was not molested. Gracchus indulged in a partisan war in Lucania, of no importance. Bruttium began to show awkward signs of a new leaning towards Rome, and some of her cities surrendered themselves to the authorities. Others would probably have followed this example, had not an officer of the allied legions heedlessly begun devastating a part of the province. This general was thereupon attacked by Hanno and badly defeated. Such impolitic cruelty on the part of the allies gave a decided set-back to the sentiment which had begun to run in favor of Rome.

In Spain, too, little was done. The peninsula was then, as later, peculiarly fitted for partisan warfare. The population cared not whether Rome or Carthage won. They were restless, unreliable, and unstable. Such tribes as were within the districts conquered by either party accepted its rule without difficulty. The main utility of this work of the Scipios was to keep the Pyrenees barred, and thus prevent reinforcements from marching to Italy. At Tarraco they made a new Rome, as the Carthaginians had made a new Carthage. They had carried the war almost to southern Spain. Syphax, king of part of Numidia, was induced by the Scipios to join the Roman alliance, and placed his troops under the eagles. This seriously weakened the Spanish cause of Carthage, for Syphax kept Libya in a ferment, and Hasdrubal Barca was called to Africa with the flower of the Spanish troops. Hasdrubal induced Masinissa, prince of the Massylians, to join Carthage. This prince defeated Syphax in a bloody battle, and Hasdrubal was able to return to Spain with reinforcements and an army under Masinissa.

The one occurrence of this year which rises above mediocrity is the siege of Syracuse by Marcellus. In the preceding year, as already noted, owing to the death of the old king, Hiero, and the turbulence of the short reign of his young and weak grandson, Hieronymus, Syracuse had joined the Carthaginian cause, under two of Hannibal's emissaries, Epicydes and Hippocrates, and Marcellus had been sent there to besiege it.

The siege is made principally of interest by the ingenious mechanical devices of Archimedes to resist the approaches of the Romans. The siege of the city by the Athenians in B. C. 415–413 has, in other respects, more interest.

Marcellus began by capturing Leontini, inland eighteen miles to the northwest, and then set to work to shut the city in by sea and land.

Alexander and his engineers had given the first real impetus to the art of fortification and sieges which was to any extent lasting. The Greeks in every part of the world took up the subject, and applied to it all the art and science then known. The siege of Rhodes by Demetrius Poliorcetes, in B. C. 305, exemplified the progress made, and proved the value of the purely scientific man in furthering the commercial interests of every nation, by devising better ships and by constructing better harbors, as well as in fostering their political security by a better system of fortification. This latter gave rise to more scientific means of attacking fortified places.

The centre of learning at that day was Alexandria in Egypt. Pure learning, as well as the allied mechanical arts, throve singularly there. All branches of literary and scientific work emanated chiefly from this great city. Distinguished mathematicians and mechanical engineers of all kinds here had their headquarters. Syracuse, being an important seaport, desired to benefit by all this, and Hiero, the late king, had sent Archimedes, a native Syracusan, to Alexandria, to learn all about the new inventions which had begun to evoke so much interest.

Syracuse.

Archimedes not only learned all that was taught by the Alexandrian savants, but improved upon what he had learned, and put it all into practice in the siege of Syracuse. Without doubt, much is true in all the relations concerning his wonderful mechanical devices and engines. But there is also — probably because the old historians did not fully understand the various mechanisms — some exaggeration in the description of them. It is said by Plutarch that his artillery was capable of wonderful aim and distance, throwing enormous stones with never failing accuracy, and projecting showers of darts into the Roman camps in such a manner as to render siege-operations all but impossible by the land or sea forces. From huge derricks he dropped heavy stones upon the ships which approached the walls, or else chains bearing grappling devices, with which he seized them, and either overturned them or dragged them upon the rocks. It is asserted that by means of burning-glasses he set the Roman fleet afire. This is perhaps not credible, but no doubt exists that Archimedes did, by his fertility in devising means of resisting the approaches of Marcellus, and by his wonderful enginery, render futile all the efforts of the Romans to lay regular siege to the town for eight long months, and converted the siege into a mere blockade. Nor was it on account of the want of skill on the part of Marcellus. This excellent soldier erected all the known machinery of siege and proceeded with his usual energy. He built a huge sambuca, a tower on eight large vessels lashed together, so high that it overtopped the walls. But before this unwieldy structure could be approached to the wall, Archimedes destroyed it by his ballista-fire, and in like manner destroyed the pent-houses and tortoises by which the Romans endeavored to approach the walls to undermine them. When Marcellus, in the idea that Archimedes' engines were so huge that they could only operate at a distance, moved up near to the walls, Archimedes, who had perforated the walls for this very purpose, showered upon the Roman troops such clouds of rocks, darts, and beams, that a hasty retreat had to be beaten. So demoralized did the Romans become that the sight of any new thing on the city walls gave rise to all but a panic.

Finally it was decided that Appius Claudius should remain

with the fleet and part of the troops at Syracuse, while Marcellus should move with the rest into the interior to punish
the towns which had revolted from Rome.

Next year, B. C. 212, owing to the absence of the consuls,
there was first appointed a dictator, C. Claudius Centho, who
chose Q. Fulvius Flaccus his magister equitum. Thereafter
were elected as consuls Q. Fulvius Flaccus for the third time,
and Appius Claudius, the officer who was engaged in the siege
of Syracuse. The prætors chosen were Cnæus Fulvius Flaccus, C. Claudius Nero, M. Junius Silanus and Pub. Cornelius
Sulla. Centho then retired as dictator.

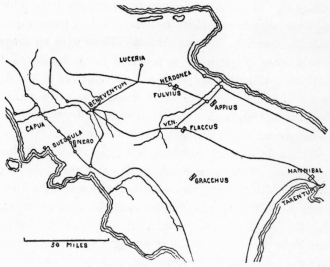

Armies opposite Hannibal, 212 B. C.

Hannibal was opposed by the two consuls, each with two
legions; Nero took post at Suessula with two legions, and to
prætor Fulvius, with two, fell Apulia. Junius Silanus was
sent to Etruria, which threatened trouble. Sulla held Rome.
The usual interchanges of legions took place by lot. Grac-

chus, proconsul, was in Lucania; the pro-prætor of the same name was at Ariminum; Marcellus, proconsul, continued the siege of Syracuse. The two Scipios were still in Spain. Otacilius kept the fleet, Valerius Greece and Mucius Sardinia.

All these forces, twenty-three legions, would be at their full strength over two hundred and thirty thousand men. It is asserted by some that the legions were not filled to the legal strength, and that these twenty-three legions amounted only to about one hundred and forty thousand foot and twenty-five thousand horse, — in all one hundred and sixty-five thousand men. It is true that the population had been exhausted. Hannibal had overrun many provinces which had been wont to contribute recruits, and had pressed many available men into his own service. There were no longer so many men of given age to be raised in the territory held by Rome. Hannibal had weakened the resources of the city by a good half. Moreover, every Roman was not a patriot. Contractors, then as in other eras, were ready to thrive on dishonesty and the sufferings of their countrymen.

Yet the balance of authority is to the effect that these legions were of the legal standard; in other words, that over two hundred and thirty thousand men were under the colors. A new method which placed in the ranks all men of any age capable of bearing arms was adopted to recruit the legions. And those lacking in years or strength could do garrison duty and leave field-work to the able-bodied. When all this was finished the Romans had put five armies, or ten legions, — one hundred thousand men, — into the field against Hannibal. This captain could number in all about forty thousand effective for the field. He had under arms about double this number, but most of his troops were Italians and largely employed in garrisoning the towns in their respective provinces. He could scarcely put in line the force stated, and these fell far below the quality of his old troops, which formed scarcely a leaven, indeed, to the lump, — far below that of the Roman legions. None the less throughout the year Hannibal marched to and fro through southern Italy, in and out among the surrounding armies, and none but kept a respectful distance. No Roman general ventured to meet him in the open field. This testimony to the ability of the Carthaginian is beyond any words. Weak in numbers and resources, with an army composed of poor material, he was yet the dread of the noblest Roman of them all, — and there were able men in command.

This course of the Romans was sensible. It would have been folly for the senate to assume that their generals were able to beat Hannibal on equal terms, and again order an immediate advance on the enemy. They had learned wisdom by the failure of this aggressiveness in the first three years of the war, and they were profiting by it. They were wise, even though their legions had the advantage of experience and their generals grew more expert under Hannibal's tuition. The Roman cause was gaining while Hannibal's was declining. It was becoming hard for the Romans to raise men, but it was doubly so for Hannibal. The senate saw that the policy of starvation was the one to pursue.

This year's campaign was opened by a felicitous event for the Carthaginians. The Tarentines had become much enraged by the execution of their hostages in Rome, on account of an attempt to escape, fostered by Punic emissaries, and a strong party sprang up in Hannibal's favor. The Carthaginian camp was about fifty miles from Tarentum. Communication was opened with Hannibal and a treaty made, under which the city was to be surrendered. Measures were taken to put the Roman garrison in the citadel off its guard.

Hannibal moved up nearer the city at the appointed time, marching in such a way that his approach would seem to be nothing more than a raid of light troops, such as were constantly occurring. He had ten thousand chosen troops under his command, and had covered his advance with Numidians who should seize or kill all peasants or others who could

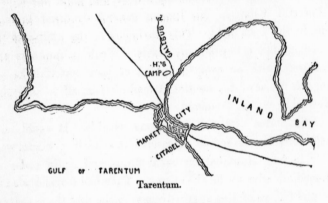

Tarentum.

convey the news of his coming. The Roman garrison-commander sent out a small body of horse to meet the Numidians, who were taken for mere foragers, and received word from prisoners captured that Hannibal was still in his camp.

At night Hannibal moved up to the gate called Temenis (now Porta di Napoli), which faced northwest towards the mainland; this was opened by his friends, who killed the Roman sentinels on duty, while another small party did the like at another gate. Leaving two thousand horse outside, Hannibal marched into the market-place, and dividing two thousand Gauls of his force into three parts, sent each of these under conduct of a friendly Tarentine into a different part of the city, with orders to cut down all Roman soldiers, but to treat the citizens with honor. Aroused by the noise, the Roman garrison assembled, and ascertaining that the city had been captured, hastily withdrew in squads to the citadel,

each one getting there as best it might. Hannibal, not knowing the lay of the land, did not reach it in time to head them
off. But the Romans did not get to the citadel without considerable loss in the darkness.

This capture is a good sample of the manner in which Hannibal became possessed of many towns. It speaks poorly for
the performance of guard-duty by Roman garrisons, despite
the remarkably stringent regulations drawn up for them. The
fall of Tarentum was followed by that of Heraclea, Thurii
and Metapontum, whose garrisons were successively withdrawn by the Romans to save the citadel of Tarentum.

After taking Tarentum, Hannibal armed its citizens and
put it in condition to hold for his cause. But he saw that
unless he had a fleet, he would probably be unable to drive the
Roman garrison from the citadel, which was situated on a
point of land, the sea sides of which were protected by inac-
cessible rocks, and the city side defended by a wall and a
wide and deep ditch. And as the citadel commanded the
harbor, so as to exclude Hannibal from its use, the greater
part of the value of Tarentum had not been gained. For the
citadel stood at a point from which the Romans with their
ships could even aid in besieging the town, and at all events
could harass him in its possession so as to oblige him to hold
it with a large force. The channel from the sea to the inland
bay was cut by a bridge in the hands of the Romans. The
garrison of the citadel was speedily reinforced up to five thousand men with plenty of material of war, but nothing more
was for the moment done.

The citadel was too strong to be taken by assault. Hannibal contented himself with drawing lines of circumvallation
against it and suitably manning them. During the construction of these, he cleverly led on the Romans to make an ener-
getic sortie. His men had orders, in case this happened, to

simulate defeat and retire, some to the rear, in order to lure
on the enemy to a greater distance, some to the side-streets,
where they could fall upon the Romans when they should retreat. This was done. The garrison detachment pursued the
apparently broken Carthaginians, and these, turning upon

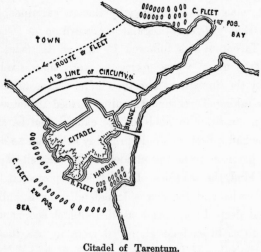

Citadel of Tarentum.

them at a given signal, took them in flank and rear, killed
a large number, and drove the rest into the ditch. But the
citadel had meanwhile been firmly held and Hannibal profited
little by his stratagem.

The lines finished, Hannibal withdrew to a camp outside
the town, near the river Galesus. But, restless under the
menace of the presence of the Romans in the citadel, he soon
returned and attempted siege-operations. These proved un-
successful, as the garrison had been made too strong by a
reinforcement from Metapontum. While he was getting his
siege-machinery into place, the Romans made a determined
sortie upon the works, and managed to burn his towers, vineæ
and artillery. It would seem that the citadel could not have

been impregnable, for while it was hard to approach from the
sea on account of the rocky coast, it was not on an elevated
site, but rather on a level, having but its wall and ditch to
protect it from the town. Sieges in olden times were apt to
be prolonged; and Roman soldiers made a garrison hard to
oust.

In order to starve out the garrison, the harbor, now held
by the Romans, must be blockaded as well. Indeed, to victual
the city, it was essential to have control of the sea; for provisions came in too slowly by land, and the Carthaginian
army required rations as well as the inhabitants. The Roman fleet held the narrow channel from the open sea to the
inland bay, where lay the Tarentine fleet. Hannibal devised
a means of dragging their vessels on wagons and sledges
across the town from the inner harbor into the roadway, and
oversaw the operations himself. In a short time the Tarentine fleet cast anchor before the citadel, much to the surprise
of the garrison. Having given Tarentum control of the sea,
and thus blockaded the Roman garrison, Hannibal withdrew
to his old camp, fifty miles distant.

The consuls undertook the siege of Capua, an operation
which had long been in contemplation. Including Nero's,
they had six legions, nominally sixty thousand men, and this
left four legions, or nearly forty thousand men, in Apulia and
Lucania. Campania was quite at the mercy of the Romans.
The consuls first united their forces at Bovianum in Samnium
as a diversion to withdraw Hannibal's attention from their
real objective, hoping to invest Capua undisturbed. This
succeeded admirably. The Capuans had been closely watched
for many months and unable to sow their crops. Famine was
staring them in the face. They appealed to Hannibal for aid,
and their messengers safely made their way to his headquarters.

Being unwilling to leave matters in Tarentum for the moment, Hannibal ordered Hanno from Bruttium to Beneventum, to make an effort to revictual this devoted city. Gracchus in Lucania was in Hanno's front and Nero at Suessula would, during his march, be on his flank, but so lax was the matter of scouting and reconnoissances, or of procuring information by spies, that Hanno eluded both, safely reached Beneventum and fortified a camp near the place, before his enemies knew of his intention of leaving Bruttium. He had probably marched via Nuceria, from which place country roads led northward over the mountains to Beneventum. Notifying the Capuans to send in haste all their carts, beasts of burden and other means of transport, he amassed in his camp all the grain of the surrounding country. The heedless Capuans were all too slow. "They executed this business with their usual indolence and carelessness." They sent only a small train of four hundred wagons. Hanno, vexed enough at this lax response to his dangerous undertaking, told them that he would not be responsible for the results, and sent them back for more. Before the Capuans got to Beneventum with a second train, this time of two thousand wagons, the Roman consuls in camp at Bovianum, though Hanno had advanced his cavalry as a curtain to his operations, learned from the people of Beneventum what was going on. Fulvius at once made for that city to interrupt the proceeding, and entered it.

Arrived at Beneventum, Fulvius found that Hanno was out with a large force on a foraging expedition, believing himself to be sufficiently protected by his outposts of horse. The rest of the army was in camp, which was admirably chosen in a strong and steep location, and well fortified. But the immense train of wagons and the collection of Campanian drivers and local rustics made it impossible to preserve good discipline.

Fulvius moved at once upon this camp by night, and at sunrise made a sharp assault upon it, despite its difficulties. The attack and defense were both admirable. The first onsets of the Romans were driven back with slaughter. But the Roman troops no longer feared the Carthaginian phalangites. They had recovered their ancient feeling of invincibility when Hannibal was not there. After repeated efforts they reached the ditch of the camp. Here again a bitter struggle ensued, the Carthaginians from above having so nearly the upper hand that Fulvius was about to sound the recall, when Vibius Acculalus, the leader of an allied cohort, and Titus Pedanius, a centurion of the principes, threw their standards over the wall into the camp. This was done without concert between them, and roused the zeal of the legionaries to the highest pitch. They made so desperate a charge at the wall that a number of cohorts surmounted it. Seizing this advantage, Fulvius, instead of the recall, sounded a new charge all along the line, and the entire body of Romans poured as one man into the camp. The Carthaginians were slaughtered wholesale, — six thousand being killed; while seven thousand others, including the Capuans and their wagons, were captured. The camp was destroyed, and Fulvius retired to Beneventum, where shortly he was joined by his colleague, Appius Claudius. Hanno learned of this disaster at Cominium, and escaped to Bruttium with the foraging party he was commanding. Gracchus was as much lacking to allow Hanno to return without molestation as he was to have allowed him to pass up to Beneventum without challenge. On either march he should at least have followed and annoyed him.

This operation was well begun by Hanno, who eluded the Roman armies on his either hand, and made his way to Beneventum with consummate cleverness, and but for the inexplicable sluggishness of the Capuans, might have been entirely successful. The event does credit to the Roman consuls. The determined attack of Fulvius on Hanno's camp, in view of the importance of Beneventum, as well as the conduct of his army, deserves due praise. All this in nowise detracts from Hannibal's intelligent plan in sending Hanno to the succor of Capua. Its failure lay solely in Capuan dilatoriness. The combinations of Hannibal deserved a better fate.

The general manœuvring of the Romans had gained in effectiveness. It cannot be said to have been characterized by any special ability; but in its care and intent, it was in marked contrast to the manœuvring of earlier years. All the Roman generals showed a dread of Hannibal which has no parallel in history except in the case of Frederick; and, as with Gracchus in the march just narrated, they were often lacking in the performance of the evident duty of commanders. But the gain was marked.

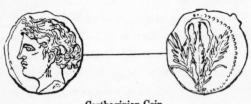

Carthaginian Coin.

XXXIII.

A WONDERFUL MARCH. 212 B. C.

THE consuls now turned to the siege of Capua, which again appealed to Hannibal for help. Four armies, numbering over eighty thousand men, barred the way from Tarentum to Capua; it seemed impossible for Hannibal to make his way to his hard-pressed ally. But he started, and by wonderful marching, of which we have unfortunately no details, and by the dread all Roman generals had of his approach, he reached Mt. Tifata, and next day entered Capua. A battle was shortly fought, in which the Romans appear to have been getting worsted, when some cavalry from Beneventum appeared on Hannibal's flank and obliged him to withdraw. The consuls, in order to draw him from Capua, retired from the siege, one of them towards Lucania. Hannibal felt compelled to follow, lest his holding on the south coast should be lost. Having thus lured him away, both consuls returned and resumed the siege. This work had been ably done. On Hannibal's way back to Tarentum, a Roman army barred his path. This he destroyed, and turning aside to Herdonia, likewise destroyed the army of the prætor Fulvius. Not seeing how he could benefit Capua without further reinforcements, Hannibal returned to Metapontum. He had got possession of nearly all the south coast of Italy, but the Tarentine citadel held out. In Sicily, Marcellus took Syracuse; but the Scipios in Spain were defeated and killed. Despite his destruction of two Roman armies, Hannibal had made a less gain during this than during the former year.

THE siege of Capua now monopolized the attention of the consuls. There was grave fear that Hannibal might again appear to succor the town which had been so devoted to his cause. Large supplies were accumulated on the Vulturnus, in Vulturnum, at its mouth, and at Casilinum, to be used in the proposed siege. Had Hannibal been in Campania, the consuls could not have accomplished this without interruption. But Nero, at the Claudian camp above Suessula, the two consuls surrounding the city with their double army, and the prætor Fulvius, presumably in the Venusian country, watching the Appian Way, closed every avenue and made a network of armies, through which even Hannibal, it would seem, could not penetrate. While they held Beneventum, and there was always a good force here, they were able to prevent Hannibal from thrusting himself in between their

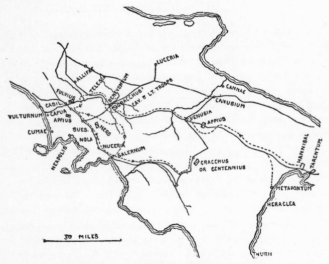

Armies between Hannibal and Capua, 212 B. C.

armies in Lucania and Campania, and thus making their efforts futile by turning on one or other.

The Capuans, foreseeing what was sure to come, again appealed to Hannibal for succor. Though the season was already spent and he had lost heavily in his former efforts in their favor, Hannibal felt that he must again attempt whatever was possible. He sent them as a preliminary two thousand of his matchless Numidian cavalry, which he could himself illy spare, to keep the enemy away from their fields. These admirable light troops succeeded in passing through the Roman cordon of armies and in reaching the city. Mago (not the Barca) appears to have been the commander of this body of horse. He must have been an able partisan.

Hannibal could not well afford to leave the south coast. Some of the adjacent towns of Lucania were falling into his hands. Heraclea and Metapontum had been taken by himself, and Thurii by Hanno. This work was all important to him, as it promised him the entire coast from the Adriatic to the straits of Messana, Rhegium and the citadel of Tarentum alone excepted. The Roman fleet had just broken through the Tarentine navy and revictualed the latter, and Hannibal all the more needed the other harbors from which to communicate with Carthage, and in which to receive succor, if it should be sent. But though loath to interrupt his labors here, he none the less lent an ear to the appeal of Capua, and set out to march towards that city through Apulia. Though well aware of the difficulties besetting his path, he felt that Punic craft outweighed Roman watchfulness.

The battle of Beneventum having disposed of Hanno, for some time at least, Gracchus was enabled to bear a hand in the siege of Capua. He was ordered to leave his heavy infantry, under suitable command, where it could safely watch Lucania, and move to Beneventum with his light infantry and cavalry. The consuls wished to utilize their cavalry for the outlying armies, for they could not but appreciate how inefficiently their outpost duty was performed. The addition of Gracchus' force would concentrate between Hannibal and Capua some seven thousand cavalry, a larger body than usual with the Romans. And the value of Beneventum as a strategic centre was fully appreciated by the consuls.

Unhappily for the Romans, Gracchus was killed in an ambuscade, which, Livy says, was treacherously laid for him by one of Hanno's lieutenants. He was an excellent soldier,

brave, generous, intelligent. After Marcellus, he first obtained successes over Hannibal. His legionaries, largely
slaves manumitted after the battle of Beneventum, feigning
to consider themselves bound personally to him, and therefore released from service by his death, dispersed. Lucania

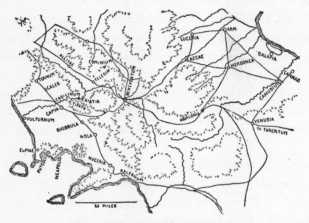

Scene of Hannibal's March to Capua.

was for the moment disgarnished of troops, and the road to
Capua made more easy to Hannibal, when M. Centenius, a
sort of soldier of fortune, of great personal strength and
courage, but of no capacity whatever, was given command,
and raised sixteen thousand men for the defense of the province.

It seems to be commonly accepted by the historians from
whom Livy quotes that the body of Gracchus, on being sent
to Hannibal, received distinguished burial rites. Livy leans
to belief in this fact, and frankly admits the honors paid by
Hannibal to his other fallen foes.

The consuls approached Capua. They entered the plains
and sent out small parties to harvest the half-ripe wheat.
The Capuans sallied out and waylaid these parties, in con-

nection with the Numidian cavalry, under command of Mago, and inflicted a loss of fifteen hundred men on them. This was but a temporary check to the consuls. They camped in front of Capua, intent on making some headway with the siege so long deferred. The Capuans saw the Roman lines of circumvallation growing about them, and felt that their hour had come, when to their extreme joy, and the no less surprise of the Romans, Hannibal suddenly appeared in his old position on the slope of Mt. Tifata, from which place he descended and entered the town.

It is extraordinary that the Roman generals should have so carelessly manœuvred as to allow Hannibal thus again to retake his old position. It should have long ago been seized by the Romans and fortified for their own uses against Capua. Not only would this have kept Hannibal from occupying the place, but it would have furnished a key-point from which a descent on his flank or rear could be made in case he occupied the plain before Capua.

That Hannibal marched from the south coast by way of Beneventum, and no doubt Venusia, we are informed by Livy. By what road he reached Campania from Beneventum is uncertain,— not unlikely by Telesia and the Caiatian country. Or he may have passed by the Caudine Forks, northeast of Suessula. Once past Beneventum, he could march that way without interference save from Nero. The former route is the more probable.

It is incredible almost that Hannibal should have evaded the prætor Fulvius, who was in the Venusian region, such troops as held Beneventum, and who, at least, must have had abundant opportunity to send word ahead of his presence there, and the armies of the consuls near Capua and of Nero at the Claudian camp, and reach Tifata. That he should have been able to march from Tifata into Capua, with the consuls' four legions preparing to besiege the city, and already engaged on their lines of circumvallation, almost passes belief. Still such is the statement of Livy and the other historians.

It is such feats of marching, such inexplicable and unexplained exploits of daring and skill, which place Hannibal so far above other generals. It cannot be supposed that for a forced march like this Hannibal would head a large army; and that he should dare force his way into the very midst of enemies outnumbering him many-fold, through roads which he must expect to find beset in his front and closed behind him, and with every reasonable expectation of battle, shows the Carthaginian to be, in his power of manœuvring, marching and deceiving his enemies, without a peer. It shows, as nothing else can, what the dread of the very name of Hannibal meant. That the common people, or the common soldier, or the centurion, should partake it, is no wonder. But this dread equally possessed the consul, the prætor, the legate, the tribune. We know that the camp and battle discipline of the Romans was good; we know that their system of outposts, reconnoissances and scouting was in quite inverse ratio to it. But nothing except the rarest ability, and the power of making the enemy dread his very approach, can explain such a march as this last one of the Punic leader.

After two days, during which the Capuans were intoxicated with his presence, and felt that they were now safe from their persecutors, Hannibal emerged from the city and offered battle to the consuls. It was accepted. The first shock was handsomely given and taken, but the numerous cavalry of Hannibal, including Mago's and the Capuan, was beginning to make an unfavorable impression on the Roman formation, when a body of horse made its distant appearance on the flank of both armies. It was the cavalry of Gracchus'

army which was being brought from Beneventum towards
Capua by the quæstor Cornelius. It " excited alarm in both
parties equally, lest those who were approaching should be
fresh enemies, and, as if by concert, both sounded a retreat,"
says Livy. But Hannibal of course knew that they could not
be his troops; they must be enemies; and a large body of
Roman cavalry on his flank could not but jeopardize the day.
He was wise in retiring. The Romans, on the other hand,
had every reason to believe that they were friends; and it is

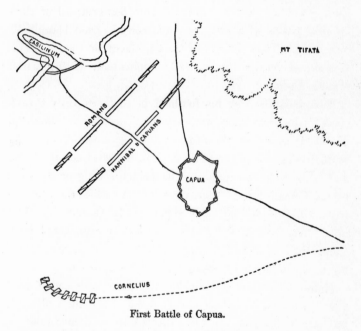

First Battle of Capua.

probable that they had been so roughly handled, as to be on
the point of losing the day, when the appearance of this *deus
ex machina* obliged Hannibal to withdraw. Livy for once
acknowledges a heavier Roman than Carthaginian loss.

It is not desired to convey the impression that Livy is in-
tentionally unfair. How could he write about Hannibal with-

out prejudice? But in order to arrive at the truth, we must often dissect his statements and compare his facts to discover their fair meaning.

It was evident that Hannibal must in some way be induced to leave Capua, or the best efforts of the two Roman armies would be thwarted. To bring this about, the consuls separated and did a really able piece of work. They knew that Hannibal would ask for nothing better than to have them stay about Capua and enable him to lure them into some stratagem, — a thing they had even a more hearty dread of than an open battle with him. So the consuls tried Hannibal's own game. They decamped from in front of Capua. Fulvius moved towards Cumæ, while Appius took up the march towards Lucania.

Hannibal, who saw his foothold in southern Italy threatened, for his force there was very small, decided to follow Appius. He could not allow the results of so much effort on the southern coast to be prejudiced. He marched out of Capua and in the wake of Appius. The sudden raising of the siege by the Romans was of short duration; for while the Capuans were still rejoicing at their supposed deliverance by Hannibal from their foes, Fulvius so suddenly reappeared from Cumæ that he all but forced an entrance into the town; failing in which, however, he again sat down before it.

Hannibal pursued Appius, but the latter, who had a good start, by a series of excellent forced marches eluded him, not unlikely by filing to the left at Salernum, and marching by way of Abelinum to Abella, and down to the plain near Suessula, from whence he returned to Capua and rejoined his colleague. However careless the consuls had been in allowing Hannibal to enter Capua, they had ably retrieved their error. Their stratagem was thought out and carried through with decided cleverness. Capua had benefited naught.

Hannibal saw no good to be attained by a new attempt to aid the city, and concluded to return to Tarentum, where he was greatly needed, when he found that M. Centenius Penula with his new levies barred his passage, intent on battle. Just where this was is not known, but probably in the northwest part of Lucania.

This Centenius had been in several campaigns in subordinate positions, and behaved with courage and intelligence. He was past the age of duty, but had asked and obtained from the senate leave to raise volunteers, promising to deal heavy blows at Hannibal in his own fashion, and to trap him with his own devices; a boast which was credulously heeded by the conscript fathers. The senate foolishly gave him eight thousand men, and in Lucania he doubled this number by recruitment, and now stood athwart Hannibal's path.

No sooner did Hannibal appear than Centenius offered him battle. Hannibal was not loath to accept it. The men led by Centenius made an exceptionally good fight, and for two hours Hannibal was unable to make any impression upon them. But Centenius, overanxious to win a victory, or at best determined not to survive a defeat, put himself at the head of his soldiers. Here he fell, more bravely than discreetly. His men soon lost their confidence, and surrounded by Hannibal's horse, were all cut down except about a thousand of their number who escaped and dispersed.

This victory was in a measure compensation for the failure of Hannibal's pursuit of Appius, but better was to come. Another easy triumph was at hand in the presence of the prætor Fulvius, who had but eighteen thousand men at Herdonia, which he was besieging.

From northwest Lucania, a road led to Venusia, — perhaps more than one. Heading in this direction, Hannibal shortly reached the vicinity of Herdonia, — probably via Aquilonia.

Here he heard that Fulvius was laden with booty and had, from easy successes, become careless in his discipline. Knowing the impatient character of Fulvius, and hearing also that the troops were overeager for a fight and probably in a poor condition for battle, Hannibal chose his camp where a good battle-field lay before him, and preparing during the night an ambuscade of three thousand light foot in some farm yards and woodlands near by, he sent Mago and some two thousand Numidians to occupy all the roads in the rear of the enemy. Fulvius, who had promised his impatient men to fight the next day, accepted the gage of battle so soon as Hannibal had drawn up in front of his camp, and moved to the attack.

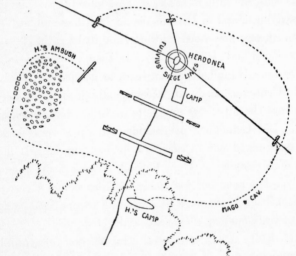

Battle of Herdonia.

Hannibal was superior in numbers as well as skill. Fulvius, in order to make his front equal Hannibal's, decreased his depth against the protests of the tribunes and, mixing the cohorts of the Roman and allied legions in one line, drew up with his horse on either flank, and covered by his light troops.

Hannibal formed as usual in phalangial order, sixteen deep, cavalry on the wings, skirmishers in front. The Roman line scarcely stood the first shock. Fulvius, less daring in deed than in threat, fled from the field at the earliest sign of disaster. His legions, taken in front and flank and rear by Hannibal's phalangites and Numidian horse, were absolutely destroyed. Scarce two thousand men were able to make their escape from the sword of the Carthaginians.

Thus, in a few weeks, the Romans had lost three armies as well as any standing they had gained in southern Italy. Hannibal, despite his success, felt constrained to return again to Tarentum, and here he remained during the rest of the year. He made a fresh effort to capture the citadel, but with renewed failure. He then attempted Brundisium, but this likewise proved too strong for him, as he had no adherents within its walls.

That Hannibal should have moved down to southern Apulia at a time when he had dispersed three Roman armies and when the siege of Capua had reached a culminating point has by many critics been looked upon as a mistake. We can only guess at his motives. His army was probably difficult to manage. Of material absolutely lacking homogeneity, he may often have been unable to allow himself to do what he so easily did in the first three years of his Italian campaigns. That he would have difficulty in maintaining himself at Mt. Tifata was clear. Three armies of over fifty thousand men surrounded Capua, and had so fortified their position that he would have been unable to effectuate anything towards raising the siege, while he would fatigue and worry his troops, and scarcely be able to victual them. He knew that Capua could stand a long siege, and he had reason to expect reinforcements from Carthage. It was these which he was preparing to receive by his efforts to control the southern coast. If they came soon, he would be in position to go to the relief of Capua with a better chance than if he returned there now. Had Hasdrubal come to southern Italy at this time instead of later by way of cisalpine Gaul, Hannibal might still have won a great measure of success. It seems that he was wiser to reserve his efforts in favor of Capua until he could act efficient¹y, than to fritter away his forces on work to which he knew by his late experience he could not succeed in doing justice.

The Roman senate was much disappointed at these reverses, which had been entirely unlooked for. But the promise of a Capuan success came in to compensate for this, and the siege was vigorously pushed. The consuls began to surround the town with a siege wall. They had abundant supplies in their great magazines of wheat at Casilinum and those made at Puteoli and at the fort at the mouth of the Vulturnus, to which corn came from Sardinia, Sicily and Etruria. The men of Gracchus' army who had dispersed were gradually captured and once again assembled under the colors and added to the others; the bulk of the army of Claudius Nero was called from the Claudian camp above Suessula, and the siege was pushed by the three armies from three sides. Two lines of walls as usual, with ditch and rampart, and towers at intervals, were made to resist the Capuans from within and Hannibal from without. These works took all winter, and the Capuans, despite many efforts and one rather severe engagement, in which they appear to have lost by dividing their forces, were unable to break through. Only on one or two occasions and before the line was complete could they even get a messenger to Hannibal to implore his instant help. These messengers found Hannibal at Brundisium, which he was seeking to capture, the citadel of Tarentum having so far resisted all his efforts. He promised, as early the next year as he could move, to go to their aid and to raise the siege, adding with proud consciousness of power (though it must have been with the secret feeling that his was the waning cause) that he had once raised the siege of Capua, and that the consuls would not sustain his approach again.

Some time before, a deputation of Capuans, who were somewhat faint-hearted, had made advances for amnesty to one of the consuls. The Roman senate now gave notice through these officers that to all Capuans who would surrender before the ides of March a free pardon would be granted; but this offer was indignantly rejected by the more courageous citizens, who browbeat the weaklings into silence.

The Roman strategy of the past three years had consisted in constantly opposing two or more armies to Hannibal, and never, unless under the most exceptional conditions, giving him a chance to fight them in the open field. These armies sought to tire him out by fatiguing marches, constant skirmishes and famine. This general military policy they followed from this time on. The consuls always had from eighty thousand men upwards to oppose to Hannibal, whose army was gradually deteriorating in quality and rarely more than half reached those of the Romans in effective strength. It was by his remarkable power of adapting his means to the end to be accomplished that Hannibal maintained himself; until he was recalled to Africa he moved all over Italy, and uniformly marked his progress by defeat of his foes or their retreat from the open.

The constancy of the consuls to their one object of besieging Capua deserves credit. On several occasions they met with disaster which interrupted their prosecution of this work, but they always returned to it with undiminished energy. When their dispositions to protect themselves against Hannibal's approach by occupying Beneventum and Suessula had been nullified by the death of Gracchus and Hannibal's bold march, they might very naturally have raised the siege. They, however, did nothing of the kind, but returned to their work as soon as they had lured Hannibal away, and this they continued with equal heart after the folly of Centenius and the cowardice of Fulvius had lost them a second and a third army. We shall see them hold to their quarry under yet more trying circumstances.

Hannibal's year had been less successful than the last. To be sure he had destroyed three of the Roman armies. But Rome could bear this loss. His gain at Tarentum, after his entire year's work, had been next to nothing, owing to the persistent holding of the citadel by the Roman garrison. He had been lured away from Capua by Appius, and it was no equivalent that the Romans had lost two armies as well as their footing in Apulia and Lucania. On the whole, the Romans again had the best of it in Italy.

We left Marcellus blockading the land side and the port of Syracuse, and raiding in the interior. After Appius Claudius had been elected consul, Marcellus single-handed continued the siege, which for many months resisted all efforts. The Carthaginians sent an army to Sicily, and the Syracusans sent one out of the city to join it. Marcellus' position threatened to become difficult. But during a certain festival which had lured some of the garrison from their posts, the Romans escaladed the walls and got into the city proper. From their position they managed to isolate the Euryalus, or fort on the western extremity of the walls. The allied armies now approached, and, in connection with a sortie of the garrison, tried to raise the siege. But Marcellus held his own; nor was the Punic fleet more fortunate. A pestilence attacked the allies, who were camped on low ground along the Anapus, while Marcellus in the suburbs was well placed. Finally the

Roman general, by tampering with the garrison, got into the "island," and shortly after the gates were opened to him. Marcellus allowed the city to be given over to his army to plunder, and in the confusion Archimedes, its celebrated defender, lost his life. Soon the whole island of Sicily was brought under Roman sway, and so remained. In addition to the success in all-important Sicily, the Roman admiral Otacilius captured one hundred and thirty vessels of wheat in the port of Utica.

The Roman gain in Sicily was offset by an unfortunate campaign in Spain. The Carthaginians had three armies on foot, under Hasdrubal Barca, Hasdrubal, son of Gisgo, and Mago. The Scipios had, after their marked successes of the past few years, been unwise enough this year to divide their forces. Cnæus Scipio, who confronted Hasdrubal Barca, lost the bulk of his army by defection (for his opponent was clever enough to pay his Spanish troops to desert), and was forced into retreat. Publius Scipio faced Hasdrubal Gisgo and Mago, to whom Masinissa, of Numidia, was allied. In a great battle, shortly occurring, the Roman army was all but destroyed and Publius Scipio lost his life. After this the allies turned on Cnæus Scipio and handled his army equally severely. The fate of Cnæus is not known. The wreck of the Roman armies retired north of the Ebro. The Roman cause seemed desperate, but the Carthaginians were again defeated and forced beyond the Ebro by the signal ability of a young Roman noble, L. Marcius, who succeeded to the command, and by several stout blows did much to reëstablish the Roman foothold in the peninsula.

XXXIV.

CAPUA. 211 B. C.

THE Roman plan for B. C. 211 was to capture Capua while acting defensively against Hannibal. The Capuan cavalry had held head against the Romans, until the latter mounted the best velites behind their cavalrymen, — an old device in the East. This recovered their ascendency by making the Roman horse steadier, and confined the Capuans within walls. Again these allies appealed to Hannibal, and again, leaving his south-coast business, the Carthaginian marched to their aid. Reaching Tifata, he sent them word to make a sortie on a given day and hour, and he would attack at the same time. This plan was carried out, but unsuccessfully. The superior force and intrenched lines of the Romans could not be broken. The Capuans were driven back into the city, and Hannibal sounded the recall. Seeing that direct means could not raise the siege of Capua, Hannibal tried an indirect one. He marched straight on Rome. At an earlier stage of the war, fear for the capital would at once have induced the Roman generals to follow; but they had been well taught; they did not budge. Hannibal knew he could not take Rome. He had barely twenty-five thousand men, and Rome had forty thousand. Fulvius, with a picked force of sixteen thousand men, marched to Rome; but this left fifty thousand men at Capua. Arrived at the capital, Hannibal ravaged the land up to the very gates, and then retired. He had failed in his object. Capua was soon after captured, and the citizens executed or sold into slavery. The Carthaginians were now confined to Apulia, Lucania and Bruttium.

THE consuls of B. C. 211 were Publius Sulpicius Galba and Cnæus Fulvius Centumalus, — not the one defeated at Herdonia. These officers entered on their duty as usual on the ides of March. As prætors there were chosen L. Cornelius Lentulus, to whose lot fell Sardinia, M. Cornelius Cethegus for Apulia, Caius Sulpicius, who, with Marcellus, went to Sicily, and C. Calpurnius Piso for the Roman garrison. While Appius Claudius and Fulvius Flaccus continued to conduct the siege at Capua as proconsuls, Sulpicius and

Fulvius, the new consuls, were supposed to hold head against Hannibal. For this purpose they had the two legions of slaves enfranchised by Gracchus, which after his death had dispersed but been again collected, and two legions which had been doing garrison duty in Rome. Their legions were very likely not up to the limit. There is some obscurity as to just what the consuls were doing during the exciting scenes of this campaign. The proconsuls bore the leading part, not they. Claudius Nero assisted the proconsuls before Capua, with his two legions, making six legions besieging the town. C. Sulpicius was ordered to recruit his two legions for Sicily up to the proper standard from the troops defeated under Fulvius in Apulia. These men, like the survivors of Cannæ, were punished by constant service out of Italy throughout the whole course of the war, and were forbidden to take up winter-quarters within ten miles of any town. Their commander, Fulvius, had been exiled, and gone to Tarquinii. The same forces as last year — two legions — were in Etruria, under the pro-prætor M. Junius; two legions were in cisalpine Gaul under the pro-prætor P. Sempronius; two legions each were in Spain, Sicily and Sardinia, the latter under C. Cornelius. Otacilius, with one hundred ships and two legions, and Valerius with fifty ships and one legion, had assigned to them the coast of Sicily and Greece respectively. In all there were twenty-three legions afoot, making a grand total of two hundred and thirty thousand men.

The two consular armies intended to confront Hannibal were supposed to confine him to southern Italy, but not to act offensively. It was deemed of more importance to keep troops in Etruria and cisalpine Gaul than to come to blows with Hannibal, and now that Syracuse had fallen it was in the highest degree essential to complete the conquest of Sicily. The citadel of Tarentum was well-provisioned and safe for

the nonce. The sixty thousand men before Capua sufficed to
hold the lines inclosing that fated city, which had been made
as strong as Roman art could make them, while Hannibal
was to be treated to a strict defensive. Until Capua was
reduced, no active steps were to be taken against him. No
special siege - proceedings were undertaken. The city was
blockaded rather than besieged. Hunger was invoked instead of force.

The Capuans were looking constantly for the arrival of
Hannibal, and made frequent sorties. In these their cavalry,
the basis of which was the Numidian horse sent them by
Hannibal, always proved superior to the Romans, but the
infantry was so far inferior that the sorties were generally
driven back with loss.

Despite this fact, the Romans found that they must do
something to offset the superior quality of the Capuan cavalry, which caused them no little trouble. The Roman light
infantry contained, among much less good material, the most
active and vigorous youth of the nation. The velites had always been thoroughly exercised in rapid movements, and
many of them could act with cavalry in almost all its manœuvres. A new formation was now made. The velites,
who were armed with seven darts, four feet long and steel
pointed, and with short bucklers, mounted and rode behind
the cavalrymen in the swifter manœuvres, and even in the
charges; and when the shock came, they leaped to the ground
and attacked the dismounted enemy with their darts. This
was a very ancient device, and long in use among the Carthaginians; but it was a novel one among the Romans; and a
line of infantry suddenly appearing from the midst of a line
of cavalry so entirely upset the calculations of the Capuans
that their ascendant was lost, both in the cavalry and light
troops. This new body of men proved so useful that it was

added to the legions at Capua, in maniples. Its use did not spread far nor last long.

The Capuans, reduced to the last extremity, and foreseeing speedy surrender unless Hannibal intervened, managed to get a messenger to him (a Numidian, as on the last occasion), imploring him to come at once to their aid. Hannibal was undecided which he must do first, again attack the citadel of Tarentum, or move to Capua, — the possession of the first being of the greatest importance to him, and the loss of the last a calamity he dared not contemplate. He finally decided to go to the assistance of his faithful ally. Leaving his heavy train and sick behind, he started from Tarentum by quick marches and with his best troops, some thirty thousand strong, and the thirty-three elephants brought by Hanno. His direct road lay along the Via Appia, through Venusia and the Beneventum country. He passed unchallenged the walls of Beneventum, and marching rapidly along the familiar roads, reached the confluence of the Calor and Vulturnus, seized by assault on the oppidum of Caiatia, and filing to the left, camped in a valley in the rear of Mt. Tifata. There seems to be no proof that his presence was unknown to the Romans, as is often alleged. It would be practically impossible for thirty thousand men in an enemy's country to appear within five miles of a blockading force of sixty thousand without discovery. As usual, the Romans preferred not to attack Hannibal, but prepared to fight for their lines around Capua. Just what the consuls were doing while Hannibal marched from the south coast to Capua does not appear. Shortly after they were in Rome.

Sending several couriers to penetrate into Capua (of whom one managed to do so) Hannibal gave his friends within the walls instructions to make a sortie at a given hour on the next day, while he would assault the lines from the outside at

the same time. He proposed to debouch from the northern
slope of Mt. Tifata, and attack the Roman lines on the north
of Capua.

Hannibal appeared at the time stated in front of the Roman intrenchments. The Capuan army made a sortie *en
masse* from the city - gate on the Vulturnus side, aided by the
Carthaginian garrison under Hanno and Bostar, while the

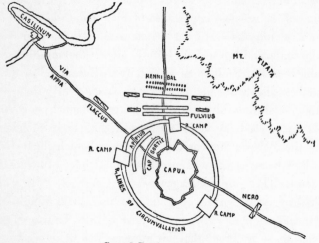

Second Battle of Capua.

citizens on the walls made a horrible din with brass vessels,
"similar to that which is usually made in the dead of night
when the moon is eclipsed," says Livy. At first this joint
attack — which was made suddenly — came near to overcom-
ing even the perfect defenses of the Roman lines, for the Romans were not certain, until they saw Hannibal's approach,
from what quarter to look for the attack. But recovering
themselves, Appius undertook to hold head against the
Capuans, while Fulvius, with the bulk of the army, turned on
Hannibal. The triarii, extraordinarii and velites were left to
man the walls of the camps, as well as the lines of circumval-

lation. Nero was holding the lines towards Suessula and personally occupied the Via Appia with the cavalry of the sixth legion; and the legate C. Fulvius Flaccus, brother of the consul, commanded a body of twenty-four hundred allied horse out towards the river to secure communications with Casilinum.

The task of Fulvius was far from being an easy one. When he saw Hannibal descending the road from Mt. Tifata he seems to have taken the hastati and principes of the three consular armies, nearly forty thousand men, to have sallied from the intrenchments and drawn up in two lines, with his cavalry on the wings. Hannibal had drawn up his whole force in one phalangial line, the elephants behind, and the heavy horse, four thousand strong, manœuvring on the flanks.

Hannibal took the initiative. The shock was delivered with his usual sudden impetus and received with equal stoutness. So bold, however, were Hannibal's men that a simple phalanx of the old Spanish infantry, followed by its quota of elephants, forced its way through the sixth legion in the centre. If Hannibal could have had enough men to form a second line or a reserve, he might have pierced through Fulvius' defense and have penetrated the lines. But the Roman maniples closed up again after the Spanish troops had broken through, and, under the splendid exertions of Quintus Navius, a centurion of gigantic stature, who seized a standard and led on the men, and of Marcus Atilius, the legate, they shut out the brave Spaniards from retreat, while the reserves of the camp, under the legates Licinus and Popilius, stanchly defended the intrenchments against them. The elephants fell into the ditch and were killed; and after a desperate struggle, the Spaniards were surrounded, and died to a man, arms in hand. The Romans, in fighting of this kind, had no superiors. There was no room for manœuvring.

Hannibal, seeing that his task was not to be accomplished, for the rest of his line had not succeeded in making a distinct impression, sounded the recall. He withdrew in perfect order, the horse from the flanks closing in behind the troops to cover their retreat. The Romans did not follow him up. He had undertaken the impossible, out of fidelity to his Capuan allies. Against intrenchments, with fewer men and those of less good material, he had had no chance whatever of success.

In none of his battles, won or lost, was Hannibal so placed that he could not hold his troops in hand. A defeat with him never went beyond lack of success. No one, until the fatal day of Zama, inflicted anything like a crushing blow upon him.

Meanwhile the Capuans, though making an equally brave effort, had been driven in by Appius, who, except for the ballistas and scorpions on the wall, would have entered the city with them. The joint attack had failed, as some authors say, with a loss of eight thousand of Hannibal's army, three thousand Capuans, and thirty-two standards. The Roman loss is not given. Others speak of the attack on Capua as of much less importance.

Hannibal saw that he could not protect Capua by direct means. He resolved to attempt to do so by indirect ones. It was evident that the consuls could not be successfully handled by any force he could bring against them. They had beaten back both the Capuans and himself, and this without seriously depleting their siege lines. He could not remain idle near Capua. Hannibal possessed a keen sense of honor; he felt that he must make still another effort for this gallant ally. He appreciated her fidelity and present strait. As he could not raise the siege by driving the Romans from their work, might he perhaps not lure them away? He gathered at the Caiatian fort all the boats which could be found on the river above the Roman lines, and furnished his men with ten days' rations. He sent out a Numidian messenger who should pass for a deserter. This man managed to penetrate into Capua with Hannibal's notice to his friends not to be alarmed at his disappearance, but to await news of a great success. He lighted his camp-fires at evening, to mislead the Romans into believing him still present, marched his men down to the river after night-fall, crossed before morning to the north bank and burned the boats. Next day, when Appius and Fulvius expected a fresh attack, these officers were astonished to see the Carthaginian camp vacated. Hannibal had marched straight on Rome.

This is the first instance of which we have any record in which a thrust at the enemy's capital has been used as a feint to withdraw him from a compromising position.

It is not probable that Hannibal had any idea that he could capture Rome by a *coup de main.* If after Cannæ he came to the conclusion that it was not a wise step to take, all the more must he have so determined now. But he did expect that his march would induce one or both the Roman proconsuls to leave Capua and follow him, and thus not only raise the siege of Capua, but give him a chance of one more open-field fight with a Roman army. At all events it was an admirable stratagem, and one in which he has had many imitators, but had no predecessor.

Livy states that Hannibal marched along the Latin Way, and also says that Cælius is doubtful whether he did not march through Samnium; and, though there is some disagreement as to what the authorities show, Mommsen leading him "through Samnium and along the Valerian Way past Tibur to the bridge over the Anio," it would seem that his manifest intention of a march on Rome, for the purpose of luring the proconsuls away from Capua, would induce him to take the direct road. Either the Latin or the Appian Way was the nearest route, and the Appian Way was best left to the Romans to follow him up on. There was no necessity of his going so far out of his way as Samnium, and to retire

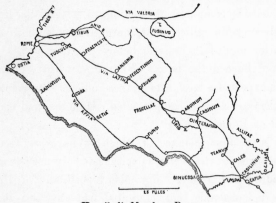

Hannibal's March on Rome.

into that province would not convey to his opponents the very impression he was anxious to produce, namely, that Rome was in immediate and grave danger.

Hannibal did not march fast, — another sign that the capture of Rome was not his objective. He was delayed in places by bridges which the Latins had broken down. But he proceeded at a leisurely gait when he could have forced the marching, ravaging as he went, and looking for signs of the following of the consular legions. But these came not, and, choking down his disappointment as best he might, he followed on his course through Cales, which he reached on the second day after crossing the Vulturnus; Casinum, where he spent two days foraging, — Livy calls it ravaging; then, by Interamna and Aquinum to Fregellæ, where he was delayed at the Liris River by a bridge broken down by the inhabitants; and so along the Latin Way by Frusino, Ferentinum, Anagnia, Præneste, to Tusculum, which he could not enter; until he reached the Anio, on whose left bank he camped, some six miles from Rome. His Numidian horse at once began to devastate the region. The poor countrymen fled from their homes only to be cut down by the wayside.

Fulvius had quickly guessed the design of Hannibal, and had notified the senate, which moreover had been already informed by the inhabitants of Fregellæ, who had broken the bridge on the Liris. The consternation in Rome was great. The scenes after Cannæ threatened to be repeated. Fabius and a few senators kept almost the only cool heads. The majority were for at once raising the siege of Capua and bringing the proconsular armies to the capital. Fabius, who fully understood Hannibal's manœuvre, pointed out the folly of doing just that thing which Hannibal most desired and was aiming to bring about. The garrison of Rome was sufficient. Hannibal had just been repulsed from before the mere siege-intrenchments of Capua; how should he take Rome with its lofty, substantial walls, manned by over twenty-five thousand soldiers, new to be sure, but still Roman soldiers? Finally, a middle course was agreed to. The proconsuls were to be notified of what the garrison of Rome actually was, and left to decide what should be done.

Fulvius did not for a moment lose his head. He sent a courier to inform the senate of what he deemed it wise to do. He knew that Hannibal would probably produce a great commotion at Rome, but he had no fears that the Carthaginian general could capture or would even attempt to capture the city. If after the victory of Cannæ he had not made the attempt, how should he now, after a defeat before Capua? The Roman generals were beginning to feel that they could better cope with Hannibal than of yore. The demoralization of the first three years had disappeared. Fulvius had

decided on what was wise, and he was speedily on the march
to Rome with fifteen thousand chosen infantry and one thousand cavalry, leaving nearly fifty thousand men at Capua under wounded Appius. Knowing that Hannibal had marched
by the Via Latina, Fulvius moved north by the Appian Way,
sending ahead messengers to have rations provided by the
population on the way, at Setia, Cora, Lanuvium.

Fulvius, says Livy, was detained at the Vulturnus by Hannibal's burning the boats, which obliged him to make rafts in
order to cross. This looks as if the bridge at Casilinum had
been broken down. But owing to Hannibal's purposely
slow marches, he arrived in Rome the day Hannibal neared
its walls. Rome thus had, in addition to Fulvius' army, its
own garrison, a part at least of the two consular armies, and
all the troops of Alba, which came to Rome at once. It is
difficult to say what the total force was. The consuls were in
Rome, but we are not told which of their legions were with
them. There were certainly over forty thousand men in the
city. It stood in no danger whatever. Troops were disposed
in the citadel, along the walls, at the Alban Mountain and at
Fort Æsula. This force would have made an assault by Hannibal mere folly, with his much less than thirty thousand men,
even if he had harbored any intention of so doing. He contented himself with advancing along the left bank of the
Anio to within the short distance of three miles of the walls
and making a reconnoissance as far as the temple of Hercules
near the Colline gate. After a slight skirmish, in which his
own Numidians crossed swords with the Numidians who had
deserted him, he retired to the camp which he had established
near by.

The populace in Rome was in such a state of excitement
and terror that the senate passed a law that all former dicta-
tors and consuls should again resume their functions until

the enemy had left the vicinity of Rome. This was necessary to suppress acts of positive madness. Nothing shows the popular scare so well as the fact that the appearance of the Numidian deserters, as they marched through the city to go out to encounter Hannibal, so affrighted many that there arose a cry that the city was taken, and multitudes retired to

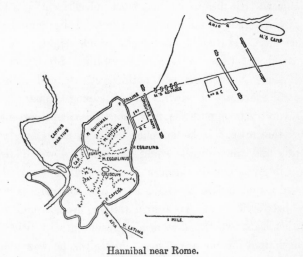

Hannibal near Rome.

their housetops and cast stones down upon their own legions. The other side to this picture is the statement that the very ground on which stood Hannibal's camp was sold in Rome, at the moment of its occupation, for its usual market value. The intelligent Roman was a level-héaded man.

Fulvius had entered Rome by the Capuan gate, had at once marched through the city, and now, with the consuls, occupied a position outside the walls between the Esquiline and Colline gates, reinforced with the bulk of the Roman garrison. The consuls did not propose to be provoked into risking a general engagement, unless they themselves invited it at their own time. Hannibal, who was anxious to fight on anything like even terms, though not ready to shatter his phalanx against the walls of Rome, resented this inaction by pillaging the region, while waiting news from Capua. This soon came in, and much to his chagrin he learned that the blockade was in no sense relieved; but that fifty thousand men still held the lines. He recognized that he had failed in his object. His disappointment must indeed have been keen. He saw at a glance that Capua, that faithful city, must be left to her fate. He could do naught which might avail her. He could not raise the siege by assault. Stratagem had failed him. Even if he had nothing else to call upon his time and exertions, he saw no way of helping Capua. It was useless to try to oppose the fifty thousand troops intrenched before that town. If he marched back by the Latin road, Fulvius and the consuls would have been down upon his rear; if by a circuit through Samnium, they would have reached Capua before he could do so, and his chances would have been still less. To return thither, even, would place him between two Roman armies, each nearly twice his strength, and for no advantage. Moreover he was obliged by the importance of the affairs in the south, on holding his position in which his entire salvation depended, to regain Apulia.

Fulvius and the consuls now moved their camp nearer to Hannibal's, and on the next day drew up in line on their own ground to invite an attack. Livy says the battle was prevented by a heavy storm of rain and hail; and that the same thing occurred on the succeeding day, which the Carthaginians interpreted as a divine command not to attack the city. The cause rather lay in the fact that Hannibal saw no eventual good to be derived from an assault on the Roman position, and deemed it wise to withdraw. He retired along the Valerian Way through the Alban territory and that of

the Peligni, whence striking southerly by Æsernia, Bovianum
and Herdonia, he reached northern Apulia, and continued
his march towards Tarentum.

The consuls harassed his rear, and Fulvius returned to
take command at Capua. At the Anio, near Tibur, whose
bridge had been broken while Hannibal was occupied in
front of the capital, the Romans attacked him, captured a

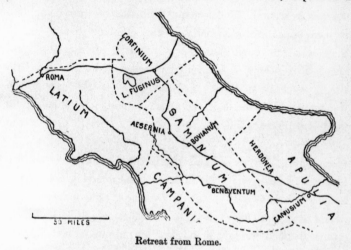

Retreat from Rome.

large part of his booty, and gave him a serious check. But
he shortly paid them off. Turning in his tracks a few days
later, he made on their camp a night attack which was so entirely a surprise that it demoralized and nearly broke up their
army. The consuls beat a hasty retreat in far from good
order, nor stopped till they reached a position well into the
mountains. Livy tells us little about it.

Reaching Apulia, Hannibal continued his march through
Lucania, and from here made a rapid diversion into Bruttium, against Rhegium, hoping to surprise this town, so important to him. But disappointed in so doing, he returned
to Tarentum. Here he learned the surrender of Capua from
hunger.

So soon as the devoted town got news of what had happened, the citizens gave way to despair. Though the Roman senate offered his life to whomsoever would come over before a stated day, no faith was put in the promise, and no one accepted it. Many of Hannibal's adherents took their own lives by poison. Hanno and Bostar remained in control, as every one else lost his head. After some days the senate nominally, though the commanders in reality, were compelled to surrender unconditionally. The Romans put to death those who had been the chief supporters of Hannibal, and expatriated others. The citizens were generally sold into slavery, and all property was confiscated to the uses of the Roman people. Most of the artisans and poorer inhabitants were left undisturbed, and a prætor was sent to govern the city.

The fall of Capua obliged Hannibal to change his tactics. Masters of Campania, the Romans could debouch upon Apulia or Lucania at will. He was no longer able to retain the numberless small cities in these provinces, which he had hitherto garrisoned and made of use, not only as a moral force, but to control the territory adjoining them for foraging. He saw that his campaigns must be narrowed to a small section of southern Italy. The number of his enemies, and want of reinforcements, were tightening the toils around him, — though indeed no opponent had yet dared to come too near his reach.

In the past ten years Hannibal had taught the Romans how to make war. This march on Rome, one of his best pieces of strategy, which abundantly deserved success, if undertaken at the opening of his campaigns, would certainly have accomplished its object of luring away the Roman generals from their quarry. Now it had accomplished nothing. His pupils were graduating in the school of war, and commanded means which their master lacked more than ever. We, who owe so much to Roman civilization, recognize the fact that Hannibal could not succeed, ought not to have succeeded. Our military regrets are easily swallowed up in our historical satisfaction. But one thing we may be proud to owe to Hannibal. He was the earliest teacher of the Romans in the broader lessons of war. From him they learned what strategy can accomplish against force ; and this knowledge, improved by them as the Romans improved everything they touched, has descended, among their other great legacies, to civilized mankind.

The Romans, though in a certain sense successful, and though Fulvius' cool calculations, under the trying ordeal of Hannibal's march on the capital, deserves the highest encomium, could scarcely congratulate themselves upon what had been accomplished this year. Hannibal, with a tithe of their force, had once again marched throughout Italy, and not only defied the capital, but devastated its territory to the very gates. For one hundred and fifty years this had not been done. He had marched in and out and between the Roman armies, had beaten them whenever the odds were not all against him, and had retired unharmed from before forces thrice his own in number. He still had a solid foothold in the south.

Altogether, this year, while favorable to the Roman cause, and while showing great advance in self-reliance and ability on the part of the Roman generals, must be considered as vastly more brilliant, in a military sense, for the great Carthaginian. The darker his cause, the brighter the effulgence of his genius. There are things to which words can do no justice. It is well to read and reread, to trace upon the map, the operations of the years of Hannibal's decline in Italy, as we would sit and gaze at the canvas or marble of a great master. To those who know what war in its intellectual sense can be, such lecture will best show what manner of man this giant was.

Etruria this year showed decided signs of discontent; the Latin colonies were weary of the burden of the war, and grew more restless; in Spain the death of the two Scipios gave Hasdrubal abundant opportunity to join his brother in Italy. Had he done this, — had he landed in Bruttium, as he could well have done, — the fate of the world might have been changed.

To repair the disasters in the peninsula, Claudius Nero was sent to Spain, with some thirteen thousand men. His early manœuvres were excellent. He succeeded in shutting Hasdrubal up in his mountain fastnesses, where he could compel a surrender. But Hasdrubal managed to outwit him by perfidy, as the Romans phrased it, and escaped. Nero, "harsh, irritable and unpopular," was an excellent general, but lacked the political wit to keep the Spaniards in subjection. The Roman senate, far from content with the result accomplished by Nero, dispatched thither Publius Cornelius Scipio — now twenty-four years old — to take command. But it was too late in the year to do aught but go into winter-quarters.

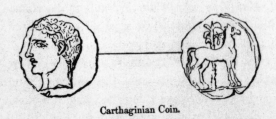

Carthaginian Coin.

XXXV.

ANOTHER ROMAN ARMY DESTROYED. 210 B. C.

THE plan of 210 B. C. was to take from Hannibal as many of the towns he had captured as possible. There were two hundred thousand men under arms. Hannibal was unable to hold as much territory as before, and evacuating a number of his strongholds in order to utilize the garrisons, he destroyed them. The consul Fulvius, with twenty-two thousand men, was corresponding with Herdonia, which was ready to betray its Carthaginian allies. Hannibal was in Bruttium. He gathered a force of thirty thousand men, and rapidly marching on Herdonia, drew up in line of battle, before Fulvius heard of his arrival. In the succeeding conflict Fulvius was killed, and his army cut to pieces. Hannibal destroyed the town, and sent the inhabitants to Bruttium. He then retired to Numistro. Here Marcellus followed him up. A battle ensued, with indecisive results. Both the Romans and Hannibal had begun to marshal their armies in two lines, as they found that one line was not sufficiently solid. In both these late battles such was the formation. Hannibal retired from Numistro, followed by Marcellus, who exhibited marked ability in his manœuvres. Sicily was entirely reduced this year. In Spain, Scipio (later Africanus) captured Cartagena by a bold and able *coup de main*. Hannibal wintered at Tarentum; Marcellus at Venusia.

MARCELLUS and M. Valerius Lævinus, who had done so well in Greece, were consuls of the year 210 B. C. The prætors were Publius Manlius Vulso, L. Manlius Acidinus, C. Lætorius and L. Cincius Alimentus. The plan of the year was to conduct a small outpost-war against Hannibal, and endeavor to rescue from his holding as many towns as possible; to leave the citadel of Tarentum to take care of itself; and to reduce the forces somewhat by consolidation of legions, discharging the highest paid soldiers from motives of economy. Twenty-one legions remained on foot, — the reduction still left over two hundred thousand men under arms.

Valerius had been fighting Philip of Macedon. Before leaving Greece to enter upon his consular duties, he concluded an alliance, offensive and defensive, with Ætolia, which gave Philip enough to do to keep his own territory from invasion for him to seek to invade Italy.

The taxes rendered necessary by the war were weighing very heavily on all the citizens and colonists of Rome. The constant sacrifices increased. General discontent was rampant. Lævinus, on the assembling of the senate, protested against the severity and inequality of these imposts, and urged that the upper classes should give an example of their patriotism. He moved that each senator should present to the coffers of the state all the gold, silver and jewels he possessed, except only what was suitable and proper for the uses of his wife, daughters and table. This proposition was hailed with acclamation. At the closing of the senate on that day, the Forum swarmed with the rich, accompanied by their slaves bearing burdens, each vying with the other in laying his offering at the feet of the fatherland. The example was followed by every class; and the treasury was filled more easily and to better effect than it could have been by any species of taxation. And this with abundant satisfaction to all.

Marcellus, first assigned by lot to Sicily, exchanged with his colleague for the war against Hannibal. A soldier of exceptional capacity, Marcellus was of a harsh, uncompromising disposition, and had made numberless enemies in Sicily. He took command of two legions in Samnium; Cnæus Fulvius, proconsul, headed a force of two legions in Apulia; Q. Fulvius remained at Capua with two; Valerius took charge of Sicily, where he had four legions and the fleet, — for, fully to reduce this island was imperative. The other armies remained much the same.

Hannibal's entire scheme was now changed. He still looked forward to receiving reinforcements from home, or to Hasdrubal's joining him from Spain, though heartsick at the hope deferred, and foreseeing failure in the end from the ill-concentrated effort. But with or without aid, he would not leave Italy until driven from it or recalled by the Carthaginian senate.

He could no longer afford to hold so much territory in Samnium, Lucania and Apulia. He needed the garrisons of the many towns now under his sway for service in the field. His army was dwindling, and he must concentrate his forces in lieu of dispersing them throughout the friendly colonies. The fate of Capua had produced a disastrous effect on these allies, who began to see that the Carthaginian was the losing side, and Hannibal feared that his garrisons might many of them be attacked by the citizens of the towns as present enemies, even if late friends. He therefore evacuated a number of the least important places, and lest they should fall into the Roman hands he razed most of them to the ground. This proceeding, however essential as an act of war, of necessity operated much in his disfavor with the colonies.

In Apulia, Salapia was the first town to fall by defection to the Romans, and its garrison of five hundred Numidians, after a very desperate resistance, was massacred. In Samnium, Marcellus captured Narronea and Meles, and about three thousand Carthaginians in garrison.

The proconsul Cnæus Fulvius Centumalus lay encamped before Herdonia. This was one of the first cities which had joined Hannibal after Cannæ. Hannibal learned that Fulvius was corresponding with the people of Herdonia, and fearing lest relaxed discipline might enable Fulvius to capture the town, he left his baggage in a safe place in Bruttium, where he had been camping, and taking a force stated at thirty thousand men, of which six thousand was horse, he advanced in light order and by rapid marches to Herdonia, where he at once went into camp near Fulvius. Under cover

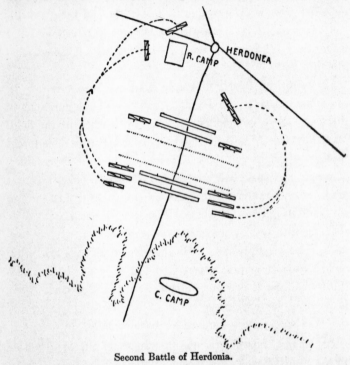

Second Battle of Herdonia.

of the hills, before the latter heard of his arrival, Hannibal drew up in line and offered battle. Fulvius had but twenty thousand infantry and less than two thousand horse; but he was unwilling to decline the combat. He hastily formed his men in two lines of cohorts, one Roman and one allied legion in each line, the velites in the front, the horse on the flanks. Hannibal likewise had two lines, both of foot and heavy horse, the latter having the light-mounted men in their rear.

It will be noticed that the habit of making two lines of cohorts was growing. In battles against the nations so far encountered, the Romans had found the one line of cohorts, that is, one line having the principes, hastati and triarii, sufficient. But against the violent onslaughts of Hannibal, the Roman generals had begun to double their lines. The Carthaginians had found the same device serviceable against the wonderful tenacity of the Roman legionary, and used two lines in many cases, beginning with this period. As about this time there was a transition in Hannibal's organization, so that his phalanx was gradually adopting some of the features of the legion, it is hard to say how heavy a line this made.

The battle opened by an advance of infantry on both sides, the horse remaining *in situ*. Noting that the attention of the Roman general was exclusively devoted to his line of cohorts, Hannibal thrust out his second and third lines of cavalry to fall on the Roman flanks. By a rapid circuit the Numidians on the right attacked the second Roman line in the rear; the horse of the left charged down on the extraordinarii in the camp. While this was going on, Hannibal moved his second line up to strengthen his first, and made another forward movement. The Roman legions fought stanchly and without losing ground or formation, until one of the legions of the second line, — the sixth, — attacked by the Numidians, fell into disorder and communicated this disorder to its leading legion, — the fifth. Perceiving this, Hannibal redoubled his efforts, and the Roman army, thus compromised, speedily showed signs of demoralization. The defeat at once turned to massacre. Fulvius, eleven tribunes, and a vast number of soldiers were killed. The rest, except some three thousand men who escaped to Marcellus in Samnium, were captured. From seven thousand to thirteen thousand men are said to have been slain.

Herdonia, which Hannibal no longer trusted, was destroyed, and its inhabitants sent to Metapontum and Thurii. The traitors who had corresponded with Fulvius, he executed. He then returned to northern Lucania and camped on an eminence west of and near Numistro, proposing either to capture the place or make a bid for Marcellus to attack him. Marcellus, who was essentially a fighter, seemed anxious to wipe out the defeat of his colleague, and moved from Samnium on Numistro and camped. The day after his arrival he drew up in the plain opposite Hannibal, with his left not far from the town. He likewise marshaled his legions in two lines of cohorts, in each line two legions, and as usual the velites out as skirmishers and the cavalry on the flanks.

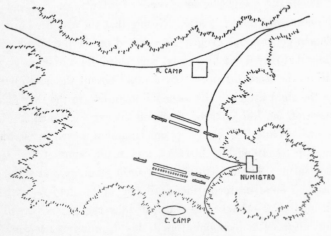

Battle of Numistro.

Hannibal did the like, his right leaning on the hills near the town, his heavy infantry in two lines, the Spaniards in the first, the Africans and Gauls in the second, with the elephants between the lines and the light troops and Balacrean slingers in front.

When the light troops of both sides had opened the fight, the elephants were driven forward, but apparently met with no success. The two first lines maintained the struggle with alternate success from the third hour till towards night. They were then relieved by the second lines, on which darkness fell before either had produced any impression on the other. This battle is so entirely unlike Hannibal's usual tactics, that one is fain to doubt the accuracy of the narration. As a rule, he showed originality of conception and execution. Here, neither was the common parallel order varied from, nor the fighting forced, nor anything like grand-tactics put to use. Frontinus says the victory remained with Hannibal.

Next day Marcellus again offered battle, standing in line from sunrise till late in the day, but Hannibal declined it. He was beginning to distrust the stanchness of his troops, and he had gained a distinct admiration for the steadiness of the Roman legions when well led. Marcellus, says Livy, spent the day under cover of his line of battle, gathering spoils and burning his dead. During the coming night Hannibal stole a march on the consul and moved away, intending to make for Tarentum. Marcellus followed hard upon his heels and reached him at Venusia. Hannibal made halt and about-face. Here for several days, Marcellus kept close to him, and annoyed him by frequent small outpost-attacks, not coming again to open conflict. Hannibal then retired in a zigzag route through Apulia, making many night-marches and taking refuge in numberless stratagems to lure Marcellus into a fight under disadvantageous conditions. But Marcellus could not be so trapped. He would neither march at night nor come to battle, unless he himself dictated the terms; but he followed and watched his opponent for many weeks, harassing him with small-war in true Fabian style, cautiously feeling every step. For this reason he marched only by day and after careful scouting. He exhibited in this pursuit uncommon ability. But the fact always remains marked that, however able his opponent, when Hannibal failed, his army was never seriously damaged; when he won, the enemy was apt to be destroyed. The fact itself so constantly recurred, that frequent reference to it can scarcely be avoided.

Hannibal returned to Tarentum to winter, and Marcellus took up his winter-quarters at Venusia. The citadel of Tarentum was suffering for want of provisions, but still held out. An attempt to victual it was made from Rhegium, but was beaten off by the Tarentine fleet. The tenacity of the Roman garrison was remarkable.

In Sicily, Valerius succeeded in mastering the whole country. He was greatly aided by Mutines, a distinguished Numidian officer whom Hanno, by unjust treatment, had disaffected, and who had surrendered Agrigentum to the Romans and embraced their cause. Some of Mutines' campaigning is among the best samples of the use of cavalry in large bodies to be met with in history. The bulk of the Sicilian troops could now be used for the *coup de grâce* against Hannibal. Syphax, a Numidian king, concluded an alliance with Rome, and ambassadors were sent to Africa to stir up further illfeeling against Carthage.

Publius Cornelius Scipio, son and nephew of the Scipios lately killed, had succeeded Nero in Spain, at the early age of twenty-four. During the first part of this year, he captured New Carthage, dealing a serious blow to the Punic supremacy in that country.

This was a fine example of the seizure of a strong place out of hand. Scipio was not at the head of the Roman soldiers of the Second Punic War, as his victory at Zama over Hannibal and the favoritism of Livy are wont, in the minds of most readers, to place him. But he was an able general, and he was now exceptionally fortunate in his lieutenants, Lælius and Silanus.

This capture of New Carthage was unquestionably a fine bit of work. It was early spring. Scipio was aware that Hasdrubal Barca was expecting to force his way across the Ebro in the effort to reach Italy to join his brother. He had some thirty thousand men, a force none too big to hold head against Hasdrubal. He determined to make a dash on Cartagena, the Carthaginian-Spanish capital, not only for the sake of the place, but to draw the spirit from the enemy by

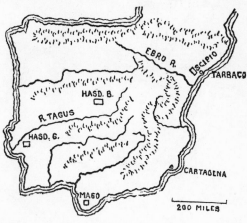

Forces in Iberia, B. C. 210.

doing them a damage. If he left any force behind to defend the Ebro, he would not have enough men for his enterprise. He decided to run the risk. Breaking up from Tarraco early in the spring of 209 B. C., he led his whole force southward, before the Carthaginians were afoot. Hasdrubal Barca lay with his army at the head-waters of the Tagus; his namesake, son of Gisgo, was at its mouth; Mago was at the Pillars of Hercules. No Carthaginian army was within twelve days' march of Cartagena.

Scipio marched fast. Herein lay the success of the plan.
The fleet under Lælius accompanied him. In seven forced
marches he reached the place, and the fleet sailed into the
harbor on the same day. The city had a garrison of one
thousand men.

The city of Cartagena lay on a high and rocky tongue of
land running out into the harbor, with a salt-water lake on
the west, whose mouth discharges, into it close by the town.

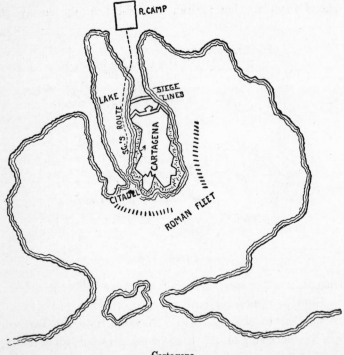

Cartagena.

The garrison woke up suddenly to the fact that they were
surrounded on three sides by the fleet, and on the fourth by
the Roman army. They had not even a chance to send to
their distant friends for succor. But the commander, Mago

behaved gallantly. He had sufficient arms, and he made the citizens man the walls. He attempted a sortie, but it was driven back with loss. Scipio immediately began siege-advances along the narrow neck of land, and worked his men hard to tire out the garrison. This he succeeded in doing by constant relays of fresh troops.

Scipio did not expect to capture the city from this point. He had learned that there was a weak spot in the wall on the lake side, approachable when the sea was at ebb tide and the lake less full; and here he calculated to make an assault. None but isolated fishermen had ever used this path, which was probably unknown to the Cartagenian garrison. Re-doubling his efforts on the land side and ordering the fleet to make a feint to draw the attention of the besieged, at midday when the tide was out and a strong north wind blew the water towards the harbor, he headed a party of five hundred escaladers with ladders, and led them along the beach to the spot, the men wading to the middle in some places. As he had expected, and indeed had been able to observe from an eminence outside the city, the wall here was found undefended. The Romans made their way into the city and easily took it. Mago, who had thrown himself with five hundred men into the citadel, surrendered.

Immense booty, great supplies of military stores, prisoners and hostages of high rank, and the best harbor in Spain, rewarded Scipio's bold enterprise. Having accomplished this *coup de main* within a week after his arrival before the city, Scipio held a review and manœuvre of his army and navy.

"On the first day the legions under arms performed evolutions through a space of four miles; on the second day he ordered them to repair and clean their arms before their tents; on the third day they engaged in imitation of a regular battle with wooden swords, throwing javelins with the points covered with balls; on the fourth day they rested; on the fifth they again performed evolutions under arms. This succession of exercise and rest they kept up as long as they stayed at Carthage. The rowers and mariners, pushing out to sea when the weather was calm, made trial of the manageableness of their ships by mock sea-fights. Such exercises, both by sea and land, without the city, prepared their minds and bodies for war." — Livy.

This describes the exercises constantly indulged in by the Roman army and navy, both in peace and war, and is interesting on this account.

Having put the town in a proper state of defense and suitably garrisoned it, Scipio marched rapidly back to Tarraco, which he reached before Hasdrubal had got ready for the spring campaign. He deserves great credit for his intelligence and courage in this matter.

The fatal grip of Roman numbers was gradually tightening around Hannibal. Alone, with but himself to rely upon, he was obliged not only to resist this mighty people, but to contend with bitter political enemies at home. He was well aware that everything was on the wane for him; that nothing could enable him to make headway in Italy but speedy and large reinforcements. These had been so often promised and so often delayed that Hannibal must have lost faith in their ever coming. We cannot suppose that Hannibal was not keen-eyed enough to see that failure was but a question of time. With full appreciation of what he had done, with full confidence in what he might have done if properly sustained, he must have felt that his ground was slipping from under him, that he could not at the same time fight Rome and Carthage.

XXXVI.

TARENTUM LOST. 209 B. C.

THE senate in 209 B. C. decided to besiege Tarentum. Fabius was one of the consuls, and undertook this duty, while the other consul, Fulvius, was to engage Hannibal's attention in Samnium and Lucania, and Marcellus do the like in Apulia. The force on foot was much the same. The financial condition of Rome was distressing; famine was threatened, and some of the Latin allies refused their quotas of men. But the republic held on. Marcellus began operations by moving on Hannibal. The latter felt like saving his men rather than fighting, as his plan now was to wait for reinforcements from Carthage or his brother, Hasdrubal, from Spain. He moved from place to place, Marcellus cleverly following. Finally it came to battle near Asculum. On the first day Hannibal beat Marcellus badly; on the second, Marcellus won, according to Livy, a victory. But he shut himself up in Venusia for the rest of the campaign, while Hannibal marched throughout the country. This did not look much like a Roman victory. The Romans this year recaptured many of Hannibal's allied cities, and besieged Caulon. While Hannibal sought to raise the siege, Fabius managed to get possession of Tarentum by the treachery of a part of its garrison. The loss of this city was a grievous blow to the Carthaginian.

IN B. C. 209 there were elected, as consuls, Q. Fulvius Flaccus, the hero of Capua, and Fabius Maximus. The former was chosen for the fourth, the latter for the fifth time. The prætors were Veturius Philo, Quintus Crispinus, Hostilius Tubulus, and C. Arunculeius.

The plan of campaign made by the senate was as follows: Fabius, with two legions, was to besiege the city of Tarentum, still held by the Carthaginians and their allies, so as to deprive Hannibal of this storehouse and convenient point of communication with Macedonia and Carthage. This was perhaps now the most important objective of the Roman arms.

Once driven from Tarentum, Hannibal would be near to being driven from Italy for want of a base. The Romans still held the citadel, but its capture by Hannibal had on several occasions been imminent, and the Roman efforts to re-victual it had not always been successful.

To Fabius fell this important duty, mainly because he was a patrician, and received the support of the controlling class. Fulvius had gained reputation by capturing Capua; Marcellus, by taking Syracuse. Both had fought Hannibal in the open field with credit. But despite these facts, and the additional one that Fabius had not proved himself a fighter, — and to fight was still the Roman's chief boast and characteristic, — he enjoyed not only the confidence of the patricians, but all classes saw that he first had grasped the theory of the war which must be waged against Hannibal, unless Rome was to succumb. The Roman theory of government was that men should not be elected too often to the highest office, nor continued too long in any one command. It was felt that there was less danger to the republic in changing frequently — even if the right man was taken from work well done — than in leaving any one man too long in a position which might lead to abuses. Despite this, Fabius was again honored with the consulate. There was a general feeling that there could be no danger to the republic from him.

Two armies were to aid the siege of Tarentum by indirect manœuvres. Fulvius, with two legions which had returned from Sicily, was to lay siege to other towns in southern Samnium and Lucania, which were still held by Hannibal, but were wavering in their fealty to him; while Marcellus near Venusia, with the two legions he had commanded before, was to amuse Hannibal by constant diversions, so as to keep him in northern Apulia, and thus aid these several siege-operations. Crispinus, prætor, had two legions in Campania, with headquarters at Capua. C. Hostilius commanded in Rome; Veturius went to Gaul; Arunculeius to Sardinia; Sulpicius remained in Macedonia.

Valerius Lævinus was again sent to Sicily as proconsul with L. Cincius, and in command of four legions. Here he organized additional troops from the Numidians of Mutines and the Syracusans, for the defense of the island. From Sicily he was to victual Fabius at Tarentum, and assist him with vessels. A force was dispatched by him to operate near Rhegium, and another one to attack Caulon. The fleet assisted in these movements, protected Sicily, and made descents upon Africa to annoy the Carthaginians and spy out their plans. Scipio remained in Spain, his command being indefinitely continued. The total force in the field was twenty-one legions, in addition to the Sicilian levies. The whole plan of the year's operations was skillfully devised.

The financial straits of Rome were serious. The currency was debased, but this afforded no permanent relief. Soldiers were not paid. Contractors furnished supplies on credit, and cheated the republic because they had made themselves necessary. The farms were not cultivated for lack of labor; the price of wheat was thrice the usual figure. A famine would have occurred but for supplies from Egypt and the fact that Sicily was no longer a battle-field, but again bore abundant crops. On the other hand, evidences of patriotism were many. Officers and many soldiers served without pay. The owners of the manumitted slaves waited for their purchase - money. The wealthy, who relatively were the worst sufferers, aided the state with great alacrity.

The Romans now learned that Hasdrubal had made large levies in Spain, intending to join his brother in Italy. This news was made more bitter by the refusal of twelve out of the thirty Latin socii to furnish their yearly contingent of

men or money, alleging that they had been drained to the
bottom and had no more.   There was, moreover, much dissatisfaction among many of the allied cities, about the treatment of the Cannæ soldiers.   If the example thus set should
spread, Rome was beyond question lost.   Why had not Hannibal at this moment reinforcements from home?   Here was
the chance which even Cannæ had not brought about.   The
temper of these twelve confederate cities conclusively show
what Hannibal had been able to do with his bare handful of
men and his scanty means.   Without a great victory for
seven years, his own tireless patience, his marvelous manœuvring, and his skillful policy had brought twelve out of thirty
of the socii to the point of refusing to go on with the war.

The crisis was alarming.   But the consuls were equal to
the emergency.   Their influence on the deputies of the eighteen still faithful allies was such that these responded not
only to the demands of Rome, but held themselves ready to
do all that Rome might ask.   The twelve recalcitrant allies
were simply ignored.   No present punishment was attempted.

Money was still harder to get this year than last.   Supplies, arms and clothing for the large armies in the field were
often pitifully wanting.   But if Rome thus suffered, what
may we imagine Hannibal without any resources whatsoever,
to have undergone?   Instead of a patriotic people at his
back, he had a jealous, abusive opposition, or at best a silent,
stingy lack of support at home.   Instead of allies who —
with small exception — generously gave their all to the cause,
his adherents were gradually falling away.   And yet this
year his genius stood him in stead of weapons, clothing, rations, friends.

The news of Hasdrubal's probable march to Italy was indeed a terrible one for Rome.   It was plain that Hannibal
must be beaten before the arrival of his brother.   The Car-

thaginian captain had marched from winter-quarters in Tarentum to Canusium, with intent to capture the town. Most of his allied cities had been rent from or had deserted him, but he felt that he must hold the high road through Apulia. Only by keeping this open could he hope to join hands with his brother. He had no idea of being penned in, be it by one or by a score of Roman armies. He did not want to fight, but was ready to do so to secure his end. And the question of rationing his army was dependent upon having elbow-room.

Acting under the general plan agreed upon between the consuls, Marcellus decided to move upon Hannibal. The Roman generals, from Hannibal's being so often obliged to decline battle, had begun to assume that he had lost his ability to fight, — that, in other words, they had formerly overrated him. Marcellus held the same opinion. He broke up from Venusia as soon as there was forage and marched against Hannibal, thinking to harass him by smaller operations, and perchance engage him in battle; at all events do what would enable Fabius the more easily to progress with his siege-operations against Tarentum. Hannibal was worse beset than ever. Fulvius had marched into Lucania. Caulon was being besieged by the Sicilian fleet and some land forces. All the towns the Carthaginians had held in Samnium had surrendered. While Marcellus was planning to keep Hannibal in northern Apulia, his footing on the southern coast was threatened to be cut away from him. If ever a captain had a desperate game to play, to this great soldier's lot it had now fallen. It had become a mere question of existence until he received help to continue the war.

Hannibal's genius and energy rose to the occasion. Marcellus approached Canusium. Hannibal, with his wonted determination not to strike until his blow should tell, retired

from the open plains to the uplands on the right bank of the
Aufidus, west of Canusium. The ground here was much cut
up and wooded. Marcellus followed him day by day, camp-

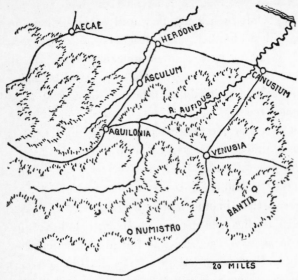

Canusium-Numistro-Herdonia Region.

ing near by and constantly offering battle. Hannibal had
no men to lose, even for the honor of a fruitless victory, and
avoided everything but the daily skirmishing of light troops
and horse. The Romans could replace their men lost in action; not so Hannibal.

It soon appeared that if Hannibal continued upstream too
far he ran the danger of getting entangled in the mountain-
region and of being shut in between Fulvius, who was in
Lucania, and Marcellus. He therefore chose to cross to
the north side and moved to the plains between Asculum
and Herdonia. Marcellus followed him sharply up and
came upon him just at the moment when he was busy fortifying his camp. The Romans, elated with the pursuit of

what they already deemed a beaten enemy, fell upon the
working parties with such suddenness and energy that Hannibal found himself compelled to turn and offer battle in
pure self-defense. The action lasted till night without material gain on either side, and each army retired to its fortified
camp, — the two being on either side of the Asculum valley.

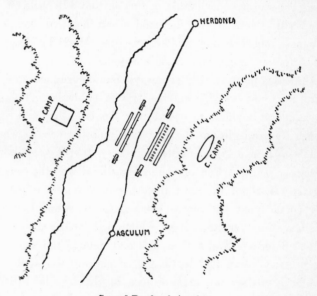

Second Battle of Asculum.

By daylight next morning both armies drew up in order
of battle for a renewal of the conflict. Hannibal was tired
of the pursuit of Marcellus, and though he could not afford
to fight — men were so scarce with him that he must accomplish his ends by manœuvring rather than by attrition — he
saw that nothing less would rid him of his enemy. His line
was twofold, with the elephants between them. Marcellus'
army stood likewise in two lines. In the first was the right
allied legion, then the extraordinarii, then the twentieth Ro-

man legion; in the second, the eighteenth Roman and the
left allied legions.

The battle was fiercely contested from the outset. After
some two hours of desperate fighting, the right allied legion
and the extraordinarii were driven in, and though Marcellus
quickly ordered up the eighteenth to their support, the entire
line gave way in considerable confusion and fell back on its
camp with a loss of two thousand seven hundred men, two
tribunes, four centurions and six ensigns. Marcellus deserves
credit for saving his army from a massacre.

Marcellus punished the runaways, but determined to fight
again next day, to wipe out the stigma of defeat. This he
proceeded at daylight to do, placing the left allied and eighteenth Roman legion in the first line, and the cohorts which
had lost their ensigns between them. In the second line
were the twentieth Roman, the extraordinarii and the remaining six cohorts of the right allied legion. Marcellus personally commanded the centre, his legates Cornelius Lentulus
and Claudius Nero the wings. Hannibal wondered at Marcellus' determination to face a second defeat, and regretted
the necessity of another battle, but as nothing else would suffice, he also drew up in two lines, in the first his Spanish
veterans, — few indeed now left, — and the elephants, as on
yesterday, between the lines.

Again came the shock of battle, sharp, severe. The strain
was long maintained, but without result until Hannibal ordered forward the elephants. These unwieldy animals,
equally dangerous to friend and foe, at first brought the
front Roman line into some disorder, — so much in fact that
had not the tribune Decimus Flavius seized the ensign of
the first maniple of hastati of the eighteenth legion, and rallied the Roman legionaries about the spot where the elephants
were committing havoc, the confusion would have spread

beyond repair. But under this leadership the Roman soldiers regained heart and the wounded elephants were driven
back through the Carthaginian ranks, where they bred more
mischief than they had done in the Roman cohorts. The
Roman generals utilized this moment for a general advance,
and attacked the Carthaginians with such fury that they
were driven back to their camp in some disorder. The gates
of the camp being obstructed by dead elephants, the phalangites, in seeking refuge, were obliged to climb over the walls,
and a great number of them perished in the ditch and at the
stockade. The Carthaginian loss (perhaps for both days)
is stated by Livy at eight thousand men and five elephants,
the Romans at three thousand. No mention is made of the
cavalry of either side. Though it is probable that Hannibal's cavalry had been much reduced in number, it must
have borne some part in the fight.

Such is the account given us by our only original source,
the Roman historians. But mark the result. Hannibal next
day retired unopposed to Bruttium, where the siege of Caulon by the Romans demanded his attention. Tarentum he
felt that he could rely on to hold out. Marcellus, whose
great number of wounded, says Livy, prevented him from
following Hannibal, — though Marcellus was a man of exceptional energy and would scarcely have allowed this to
stand in his way if there was not a more serious reason, —
withdrew into Venusia, which place he did not leave the rest
of the year, though Hannibal confessedly marched through
the length and breadth of the land. Marcellus " was kept
from pursuing by the number of his wounded men, and re-
moved by gentle marches into Campania, and spent the summer at Sinuessa, engaged in restoring them," says Plutarch,
while "Hannibal ranged with his army round about the
country, and wasted Italy free from all fear." Plutarch

mistakes the locality, but agrees in the main fact with the other authorities. This looks less like a defeat of Hannibal on the second day than the result of a brilliant victory. And it is fair to read this victory between the lines of Livy. Certainly, Marcellus' task had been to keep Hannibal in northern Apulia; he had failed to perform it; and under Livy's statement, in view of what he himself further records, Marcellus can scarcely be credited with a day won.

Moreover, at the close of the year in Rome, at the time of canvassing for new consuls, there was a vast deal of criticism of Marcellus' conduct at this time, and he was openly accused before the Roman public in the Flaminian circus by the plebeian tribune Publicius of losing both these battles. " Marcellus was under an ill report, not only because he had failed in his first battle, but further, because while Hannibal was going wherever he pleased throughout Italy, he had led his troops to Venusia in the midst of summer to lodge in houses," says Livy. It will not do to underrate Marcellus. He was a brave and excellent soldier, whose ability stands out in cheering relief above the average of Roman generalship in these years, but too many victories must not be ascribed to him. There is no doubt that Hannibal had been undesirous of fighting, and now retired into Bruttium, partly because he must recruit his battle-torn ranks, partly to relieve Caulon, but he does not appear to have been driven away by a bad defeat. The Romans continued to occupy upper Apulia, Marcellus in Venusia being the centre-point.

Fulvius, having nothing in his front, now made a raid into the Hirpinian, Lucanian and Volcentian domain in lower Samnium. Left without support or hope of it, these peoples, hitherto strong adherents of Hannibal's, surrendered their towns and the Carthaginian garrisons, without attempt at opposition. Fulvius was politic enough to treat the towns

with moderation, and, as a result, a number of others in Lucania followed suit. Even some in northern Bruttium began
negotiations with the Romans.

Fabius opened operations among the Salentini. Here he
first captured Manduria, with a four-thousand garrison of
Carthaginians. He thus cleared from his rear a stronghold
of the enemy which might be awkward for him while he attacked Tarentum. Reaching this latter place, he camped on
the south side of it, hard by the mouth of the harbor. The
Carthaginian fleet had just sailed away to Corcyra to aid in
the Macedo-Ætolian war. Fabius utilized this opportune occurrence to collect ships from all sides and build artillery and
towers both for land and ship use, prepare for a vigorous siege
of the city, and to act in common with the Roman garrison
in the citadel.

Meanwhile Hannibal had marched to Caulon. Here the
besiegers, who consisted largely of freedmen and slaves, raised
the siege, and withdrew to an adjoining eminence. The position was strong, but Hannibal soon managed to surround the
force, shut it in, and after the lapse of a few days compelled
its surrender. While relieving Caulon, Hannibal had fully
counted on Tarentum being able to hold its own, as without
treachery it would have done. No sooner had he put aside
the danger, than he started with forced marches for this city,
intent on disturbing Fabius at his task. But he was just too
late. He had nearly reached Tarentum, when the news of its
surrender came to him. His chief port was thus in the hands
of the enemy.

Fabius had expected a long and tedious operation in front
of Tarentum, though he held the harbor and the citadel. But
luck was on his side. He had managed, by fostering a *liaison*,
to treat with one Philomenus, the commanding officer of a
Bruttian detachment of the city garrison, who agreed to give

up to him a certain portion of the wall where he commanded. To carry out his scheme, Fabius moved with a portion of his fleet from his position on the south round to the east side of the town near the spot agreed upon. On the next day, before daybreak, at a given signal, demonstrations were made all along the line, with trumpets blaring and as much noise as could well be made. Nico and Democrates, in command, scarcely knew to which side to turn, and under cover of the confusion, the Roman legionaries landed from the vessels, mounted that part of the wall which had been selected and which was found deserted, and speedily opened the gates. At daybreak all Fabius' troops forced their way into the town. Nico and Democrates made a stout resistance in the market place, but were overpowered and both slain. The slaughter was immense. The city was given over to plunder, thirty thousand inhabitants were sold as slaves and much treasure was taken.

Hannibal, on reaching the vicinity, camped three miles distant from Tarentum. But as he could now accomplish nothing, in a day or two he withdrew to Metapontum. From this place he tried one more stratagem on Fabius. He caused letters to be sent by the authorities of the town to this general, proposing surrender on given terms on a certain day, while he, with his army, marched out and lay in ambush on the road he hoped Fabius might take. The cautious Roman came close to falling into the trap, but, held back by inauspicious sacrifices, he finally remained in Tarentum. Seeing his scheme thwarted, Hannibal definitely took up his quarters in Metapontum, where he was watched at a distance by the three Roman armies. Despite the serious reverse in the capture of Tarentum, it appears that Hannibal remained practically master of the entire region within the boundaries of the Roman forces. He marched to and fro on his foraging excur-

sions and gathered victual. He burned and destroyed or captured whatever seemed good to him. None of the Roman
generals, nor indeed all of them together, saw fit again this
year to try conclusions with him. Well indeed was he characterized as dirus Hannibal.

In Spain, Scipio had proceeded in a politic as well as ener-
getic manner, and had largely brought over the Spanish tribes
to the Roman idea. Those along the Iberus had almost uniformly joined his cause, and Indibilis and Mandonius, two of
the highest chiefs of Spain, came over to him. There being
no more danger at sea, he beached his vessels near Tarraco,

Iberia.

and broke up his navy to increase his land forces, so as to be
able to guard northern and invade southern Iberia at the
same time.

Early in the spring, he crossed the Iberus and moved south
to Cartagena, from whence he undertook a campaign against
Hasdrubal. The latter was still in southern Spain, but was
intending to advance north, hoping to cross the Pyrenees.
It came to battle at Bæcula, near the river Bætis. Hasdru-

bal fought defensively, in a strong position on an eminence difficult of access. Scipio attacked him stoutly in front, and created a lively diversion on both his flanks. Despite his position, Hasdrubal's army was badly beaten, as the Romans claimed, with a loss of eight thousand killed and twelve thousand captured. With the remnants of his force, army-chest, elephants and best troops, Hasdrubal withdrew behind the Tagus. This retreat was well-managed, if his defeat was as serious as claimed by Livy. As there seemed small prospect of holding Spain, Hasdrubal now concluded to march to Italy.

It was arranged that on his leaving, Hasdrubal, son of Gisgo, should retire into Lusitania, and avoid all conflict with Scipio ; that Masinissa should patrol southern Iberia with three thousand horse, and that Mago should go to the Balearic Islands to recruit and from there endeavor to ship his forces to Italy, should this prove advisable. Hasdrubal himself, after filling up the gaps in his ranks as well as he might with such men as the few remaining Spanish allies could furnish him, finally made his arrangements to move through Gaul. It was several years too late.

The Romans might properly be disappointed with the result of this year's campaign. They had, to be sure, recovered Tarentum, but they had by no means accomplished results commensurate with the force they had in the field. Marcellus, against whom the largest amount of criticism was launched, defended himself by claiming that no Roman general had yet defeated Hannibal in the open field, and he at least had more than once been bold enough to fight him. He did not in his defense assert that he had beaten Hannibal, though Marcellus was not noted for modesty. He claimed that he had fought him on many occasions and had come out of the fray without losing his army. This indeed was, in view of the Roman experience in this war, a sufficient plea.

But it adds weight to the assumption that Hannibal was the victor at Asculum. Perhaps there are no statements more apt to be unreliable than those concerning campaigns or battles, emanating from the parties concerned. We have seen this demonstrated to the fullest extent in our own civil war. And as we are following in this case the Roman historians, we may be sure that we are giving Hannibal in no event too much credit.

Legionary's Pack. (Antonine Column.)

XXXVII.

MARCELLUS' DEATH. 208 B. C.

MARCELLUS and Crispinus, consuls of 208 B. C., faced Hannibal in Lucania and Apulia. The Carthaginian was growing weaker year by year, but he still held to his work, he was still the terror of Roman generals. From Metapontum he advanced to Venusia as a mere attack in self-defense. Here both consuls joined forces. Marcellus was anxious to bring Hannibal to battle; but before he completed his plans he fell into an ambuscade and was killed. He was, with Scipio and Nero and Fabius, the stay of Rome. His career had been an enviable one. Hannibal gave his body honorable sepulture. Having taken Marcellus' seal-ring, Hannibal tried to use it to capture Salapia, but was foiled. Crispinus, wounded in the same ambuscade, shortly died. The Carthaginians remained masters of southern Italy. Scipio in Spain won victories, but he did not prevent Hasdrubal from escaping him and marching towards Italy. In this far he failed of his object. Scipio had shown himself brilliant rather than solid. Rome looked forward to fighting two of the lion's brood instead of one.

MARCELLUS had hosts of friends. His defense to the attacks brought against him was voted to suffice, and in the eleventh year of the war, B. C. 208, he was elected consul for the fifth time, with Titus Quinctius Crispinus as his colleague. The prætors were Licinius Crassus, Licinius Varus, Sextus Julius Cæsar, and Claudius Flaminius.

Nearly all the Spanish tribes having left the Carthaginian alliance, there was no danger to be anticipated in the affairs of the peninsula. But though Hasdrubal had been beaten by Scipio, it was a question whether this had not led to a still more dangerous condition of affairs. For, having finally learned by bitter experience that Spain could not best be held for the Carthaginian cause by fighting in Spain, Hasdrubal was about to seek his fortune in Italy, as Hannibal had done before him, and as he himself should much sooner have done, and to leave the wreck in Spain for future attention. The Romans had little to fear from Hannibal's army. This had been so weakened that it had naught left but the strong will of its commander. The body was hectic, wasted, exhausted by long marches, desperate fighting and constant privation; but as the heart of the man will surmount the weakness of the body, — as you may read in the flashing eye the un-altered devotion to the cause, the unflagging courage and the unchanged ability to do great deeds, so was Hannibal the soul and impulse of this army. And one may read in his every act that heart and head are to the army what they are to the man, — that an army crawls on its belly but in one sense.

So far from Hannibal being an actual threat to the Romans, it was he who was in narrow straits. But the news that Hasdrubal was about to join his brother was naturally alarming beyond its actual danger. In anticipation of this invasion, the Roman colonies in Etruria were on the eve of rebellion, and the senate was obliged anew to take hostages, — from Aretium alone, one hundred and twenty senators' children, — and cisalpine Gaul had already revolted. In Carthage there were great preparations evident for some purpose, but for what purpose was not known. Rome had gained so hearty a dread of Carthaginian generals in the past dozen years that it was difficult for her to calmly survey her position. One had brought her to the verge of ruin. What might two do?

The forces of the Romans were divided as follows: Marcellus and Crispinus, each with his army of two legions, faced Hannibal in Lucania and Apulia. Claudius occupied Tarentum and vicinity with the old army of Fabius, two legions strong. Fulvius was in Capua with a legion. The army

was again reduced by two legions, twenty-one only being in
active service.   Etruria, cisalpine Gaul, Sardinia, Sicily and
Spain were still held as heretofore, and two legions garrisoned Rome.   The fleet was much increased, so as to provide
for a proposed descent upon the African coast and to protect
the southern shores of Italy.

Crispinus had been engaged in besieging Locri, on the
southern coast of Bruttium, and had accumulated a vast
amount of siege-material and supplies.   To counter this menace Hannibal marched to Lacinium, and by his threatening
presence effectuated a raising of the siege without a fight.
Crispinus was fearful of being bottled up in the toe of the
boot.   It had been determined that the consuls should act together, and finding that he could accomplish nothing at Locri,
Crispinus joined Marcellus, who had been some time at Venusia.   The consular camps were some three miles apart east
of this city between Venusia and Bantia.   Hannibal, who had
wintered in Metapontum, on learning of Crispinus' junction
with Marcellus, had deemed it wise to follow up the movement, — a mere attack in self-defense, but with no intention
of forcing battle, and now lay an equal distance south of
them.   His own force we do not know; but he had forty
thousand men in his front; twenty thousand men were in rear
of his right wing at Tarentum, whence they could debouch at
any moment to coöperate with the consular armies.   This was
in any event more than double his effective, not to speak
of the superior quality of the Roman troops.   He was in a
dangerous situation, for in case of disaster his only retreat
was on Metapontum or Heraclea, his last two strongholds on
the coast, and to retire might be a difficult operation, with
active enemies ready to fall upon his rear and flank.   But he
was used to such positions.   Bruttium was his natural base,
and most of the towns he still held.   He must do his best to

keep this one province free from invasion, and a simple defensive would encourage the Romans too much. His advance accomplished thus much, but he limited his touch of the consuls at Bantia to mere feinting.

Hannibal was always in motion. This was partly necessary for subsistence; it was partly his method. He was always an unknown quantity to the Romans; and the fact that they never could guess where he would be next day, or what his aim might be, explains to a certain extent their constant dread of him. This dread too, which is frankly acknowledged by Livy, and lasted till Hannibal left the country, goes far to show that the so-called victories of the Romans were questionable. If they had found that they could beat Hannibal in open fight they would have been far less liable to the panic they exhibited whenever they came within his reach.

While lying here, Hannibal learned from Thurii that a force from Sicily had been ordered by the consuls to take Crispinus' place at Locri, and that a legion from Tarentum had been instructed to join them. He at once sent a body of two thousand cavalry and three thousand infantry from his best troops to intercept this last detachment. These forces placed themselves under cover of the hill of Petelia so as to ambuscade the Roman legion, which, not suspecting the presence of an enemy, was marching from Tarentum in careless order. The stratagem was well-planned and fully successful. Falling upon the Roman flank, the Carthaginians killed two thousand men, captured twelve hundred, and sent the rest terror-stricken back towards Tarentum, having accomplished which brilliant feat, they returned to camp.

Marcellus, whose courage was always of the best, was anxious again to bring Hannibal to battle. He was not foolhardy enough, however, to do this without an effort to get the conditions on his side. Marcellus deserves abundant credit for his courage; but it was coupled with a sensible appreciation of his own limitations. Hannibal was this year still less able to indulge in the costliness of general engagements, and saw that he must avoid crossing swords unless to gain a signal advantage. He was the more driven to stratagem, as he had both consuls to engage.

There was between the two camps a little wooded eminence not held by either army. The Romans were unacquainted with the slope towards the Carthaginian side, and Hannibal had not considered the hill as well fitted for a camp as for an ambuscade. In the woods, well out of sight, he had placed a Numidian post with this object.

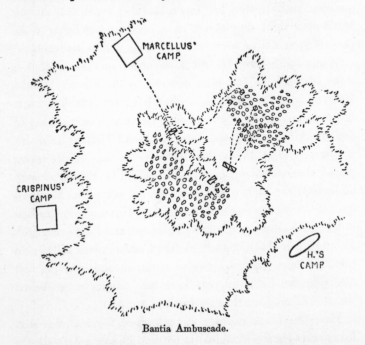

Bantia Ambuscade.

The consuls thought the hill an excellent place for an outpost-camp, or indeed for a camp for the entire army, which, well-intrenched, might be of value in bringing about an active encounter. "There was a general murmur in the Roman camp," says Livy, "that this eminence ought to be occupied and secured by a fort, lest if it should be seized by Hannibal they should have the enemy, as it were, immediately over their heads." It seems that under even the best leaders the legionaries gave expression to their opinions. Leaving orders for the troops to be ready to change camp, in case they should decide upon occupying the hill, the two consuls set out to reconnoitre the ground for this purpose. They were accompanied by the tribunes Marcellus, who was the consul's son, and Manlius, two præfects and but a small body of two hundred horse. The approach to the hill was through a short ravine, opening on the plain where lay the Roman camps. The Numidians posted in the wood had videttes out, but in concealment. These saw the approach of the party, and, recognizing the consuls, gave notice to the commander of the outpost, who hurried a few horsemen around to occupy the ravine behind the consular party, and as they approached the height fell upon them with great suddenness and fury. The Roman cavalry escort were partly Etruscans. Of these some of doubtful loyalty turned and fled. The rest of the escort were Fregellans, about forty men. They surrounded the consuls and fought for their own and their leaders' lives. But there was no chance of safety. Marcellus soon fell with his death wound, and Manlius and one of the præfects were killed. Among the severely wounded were Crispinus and Marcellus the younger. The latter both managed to escape with the handful of uninjured, but Marcellus' body remained in Hannibal's hands, who buried it with all honor. It is well to note the fact, stated by the Roman historians, that Hannibal uniformly paid this tribute to his dead foemen. It makes all the more prominent the horror of the treatment of the body of Hasdrubal, after the Metaurus, and aptly illustrates the weakness of the Romans in their slur against Hannibal for what they call his savage cruelty. The cry of Punic Faith and the accusation that Hannibal was barbarous are about on a par.

After this, for the Romans, lamentable event, Hannibal moved forward and occupied the hill as a camp, perhaps thinking he might see an opportunity of benefiting by the temporary dismay of the Roman legions. Crispinus retired to the protection of the hills and guarded himself carefully against Hannibal's approach.

Marcellus was sixty years old. His military career had been an enviable one. He had conquered the Gauls; he had captured Syracuse, he had several times fought Hannibal and only on one occasion been decisively defeated. This last, despite the disparity of numbers in his favor, is praise enough. He ought not to have conducted a simple reconnoitring party which a subaltern might have headed; or, if he did so, it should have been with more care or a larger force; but this is small criticism. His death was a severe blow to the Roman cause, and a large gain to Hannibal. While the Carthaginian was unable to fight battles during this campaign, he was skillful enough to strike smaller blows whose effect was almost equal to a victory over a consular army. We can scarcely sustain Livy in characterizing the ambuscade at Bantia as " Carthaginian treachery."

The seal ring of Marcellus had fallen into Hannibal's possession. Crispinus was afraid that he would use it for some stratagem, and sent word to all the principal towns to be on their guard against all things smelling of ruse. Hannibal did in fact endeavor by its use to again secure possession of Salapia. He needed to hold northern Apulia so as to retain a means of joining hands with his brother Hasdrubal when he

should arrive. He wrote the city word under Marcellus' seal
to be ready on a given day in case he should want the garrison for any service. At the appointed time he approached
the town, the van headed by some Roman deserters. But
Salapia had received warning and had her chosen warriors at
the gates. On the arrival of the Carthaginians the portcul-
lis was raised as if to receive the troops, and some six hundred were admitted, when suddenly it was dropped; those
who had marched in being at once cut down, while the walls,
previously manned, showered arrows, darts and stones upon
Hannibal's army. The stratagem thus failed. Hannibal was
not with the van. He had a way of mixing caution with
boldness, as no one else.

After the affair at Bantia, with some intermediate and un-
important manœuvres, the army of Marcellus, under his son,
took refuge in Venusia, and Crispinus in Capua, where the
consul died of his wounds. Hannibal, foiled in his hope of
worsting the Roman army, turned back and marched on
Locri, besieged by Cincius, who had brought his force and
material from Sicily. Mago was in command of the town,
and at Hannibal's approach made a sortie in force with great
suddenness and vigor. The resistance was sharp, but short
and vain. Taken in front and rear, the besiegers fled to their
ships, leaving on the field all their camp equipage, victuals
and siege-material.

Thus Hannibal remained master of southern Italy. No
army disputed him its possession. The situation was one of
armed and warlike quiet. Hannibal was able to forage at
will. He held the entire province. Interest now centred in
Africa and the north, to which Hannibal must look for valuable succor as the Roman senate for danger. The Carthaginian winter-quarters were in Metapontum.

It was evident, though Scipio claimed the victory at

Bæcula, that Hasdrubal had not been prevented from accomplishing his object. Scipio had shown energy and skill, but his youth had outrun his discretion. The Spanish programme was clearly to keep reinforcements from coming to Italy. The elder Scipios (this one's father and uncle), and even C. Marcius, with very inferior forces, had accomplished this end. But Scipio was young and ambitious; unwilling to content himself with a defensive attitude, he had launched out into activity greater than demanded by the circumstances, and had allowed Hasdrubal to escape him. Of what consequence was Spain to Rome, if Rome should find Hannibal, with Hasdrubal to back him, too much for her resources and skill in Italy? A judicious offensive was no doubt Scipio's best method : but he lost sight of the fact that his main object was defensive, that is, to protect Rome from another Barcine invasion. This Scipio had not done. He had so manœuvred as to place Rome in greater peril perhaps than at any other time. But fortune was always on Scipio's side. Nero came to the rescue and at the Metaurus rectified Scipio's error. Rome forgot the peril he had caused her, and Scipio still remained the hero of the day. While not denying Scipio the praise he justly earned, it is clear that the larger part of his success came from the favor of the fickle goddess.

During the autumn news came from Massilia that Hasdrubal had crossed the Tagus, had turned the sources of the Ebro and entered Gaul, where he had enlisted numberless recruits. He had made his way to the northern coast of Spain, had marched along its shore and passed the Pyrenees by the western gaps. He had followed the line which Wellington later took after the battle of Victoria. He passed the winter of 208–207 B. C. in Gaul, and was waiting for spring to cross the Alps on the same route Hannibal had pursued. It was a woful pity for the Carthaginians that he had waited or been delayed so long. Had he even been able to join his brother during the campaign just conducted, the chance of success for the Carthaginian arms would have been many fold what it was after another winter. Hasdrubal's arrival after the death of the two consuls would have been a thunder-clap.

Rome thus could expect next year to have two of the lion's brood to fight. If one had been so hard to combat, what could she do with two, when Marcellus was dead, Fabius beginning to be enfeebled by old age, and none of her generals able to engage Hannibal even with a vast preponderance of power? Rome did not yet know Caius Claudius Nero.

Boar. — Gallic Ensign.

XXXVIII.

HASDRUBAL AND NERO. 207 B. C.

NERO and Livius, consuls of 207 B. C., had Hasdrubal to face in the north, Hannibal in the south. The latter undertook the northern problem, with three armies of twenty thousand men each. Nero had an equal number. Hasdrubal left Spain too late to cross the Alps the same year. He crossed early in the spring, but did not push to a junction with his brother, engaging in the useless siege of Placentia instead. The Romans knew his movements well; not so Hannibal, to whom news could only come through two sets of armies and a hostile country. Hannibal twice advanced to northern Apulia, hoping for news, but both times was pushed back from lack of men, losing heavily in affairs forced on him against his will. At Grumentum Nero and Hannibal crossed swords, to Hannibal's loss, if we can credit Livy. Certainly his army was now of very poor material, and Nero, save only Marcellus, the stoutest opponent the Romans had yet sent against him. Despite defeat, Hannibal again advanced to Canusium, where he awaited news from his brother. Nero closely watched him. Hasdrubal's messengers fell into the hands of the Romans, who found out his plans and were able to take means for meeting them, while Hannibal was ignorant of the projects of both.

THE thirteenth year of the war, the twelfth campaign in Italy, B. C. 207, was opened by appointing to the consulate the most competent of the Roman generals, Caius Claudius Nero. For several years he had held important commands, and had done them justice. To him was joined M. Livius Salinator, an old man, who twelve years before had been consul, and had then given proof of capacity. He had been accused of peculation, but on trial been acquitted. The accusation had embittered him; he desired to keep out of public life, and at first refused to serve. He had for some reason a particular prejudice against Nero. But the entreaties of the senate prevailed. Livius accepted the consulate, and was publicly reconciled to his colleague. The prætors were Lucius Porcius Licinius, Caius Mamilius, Aulus Hostilius Cato and Caius Hostilius Cato. In view of the approach of Hasdrubal, two additional legions were put into the field. Scipio sent reinforcements from Spain, and Mamilius from Sicily, more than fifteeen thousand men, all told.

To Livius was given the task of holding head against Hasdrubal in the north. His own two legions were supplemented by two others under Porcius, already in cisalpine Gaul. A third army of two legions, under Varro, was in Etruria. Thus Hasdrubal was to be welcomed by three armies of twenty thousand men each.

In the south, Hannibal had likewise to face three armies:

Armies between Hannibal and Hasdrubal.

that of Nero, which had been Marcellus', that of the proconsul Fulvius, lately Crispinus', in Bruttium, and the two legions in the territory of Tarentum and the Salentinians, under the pro-prætor Q. Claudius. These three armies, like those of the northern country, were later consolidated into two, by the consul taking the Tarentine legions to double up his army, which being done, the army of Bruttium moved to the Tarentine territory. One legion, under C. Hostilius, stayed in Capua; two defended Rome. Aulus Hostilius was in Sardinia, and C. Mamilius in Sicily. There were in Italy but fifteen legions this year; but under the eagles there were nine armies, in all twenty-three legions. These were supplemented by three fleets, in Spain, Sicily and Greece.

Hasdrubal was without question a good soldier, but he appears to have been of a careless habit. He is considered by some to have shown himself Hannibal's equal; but the pattern of Hannibal has been paralleled but a few times in the world's history. Hasdrubal's campaigns in Spain were not characterized by much success accomplished. His campaign against the Scipios was brilliant, but the rest of his operations bore uniformly no fruit, and this generally from want of good management rather than want of ability. His movement from Spain was delayed beyond reason. Had he joined Hannibal after beating the Scipios in 212 B. C., while Hannibal was still near the zenith of his success, and held Capua and Tarentum, had destroyed one consular army at Herdonia, and had dispersed another, the Barcas would have come nearer the fulfillment of their purpose. It was well for Rome that Hasdrubal did not do so. The intervening four years were the ruin of the Carthaginian cause in Italy.

It would have been wiser for Hasdrubal to seek to join Hannibal in southern Italy. To force a junction with him over the wreck of all the enormous intervening armies, if he entered northern Italy, was a task to overtax even his brother. It was a far greater risk than to face the Roman fleet in transporting a lesser army across the sea. He no doubt counted on Gallic aid ; but when he reached the Po, he made no efficient use of his Gallic allies, and they were in no sense of the same value to him, with Hannibal already in Italy, as they had been to Hannibal when he had to fight Rome single-handed. When Hasdrubal set out to march overland, though he had Hannibal's experience to guide him, he left Spain so late that he had to winter west of the Alps, and thus gave his enemies abundant time to make preparations to meet him. That they did not do so even more efficiently was due to the Gallic insurrections and to Roman laxness, not to Hasdrubal's activity.

Hannibal was the first who ever led a regular army, with its baggage, not to speak of elephants, across the Alps. Hasdrubal's crossing can in no sense be compared to his. The only mountain passage recorded in history which does compare to it is Alexander's crossing the Parapamisus. Hannibal's passage was made against serious opposition, and with none but unreliable information about the ground he had to cover. Yet, from his entrance to his exit from the Alps was a bare two weeks. Hasdrubal encountered only friendly greetings and assistance from the transalpine Gauls, receiving guides, food, and even troops. The past dozen years had made the intercourse by this route over the Alps much more frequent, and the roads were correspondingly better. The tribes had learned that the Carthaginians were not enemies they themselves had to fear, but that they were aiming at the equally dreaded and hated power of Rome, which all the Gauls now were eager to see humbled.

Hasdrubal took a much longer time than Hannibal in his entire passage ; but he finally descended to the valley of the Padus. Once there, his first efforts should have been to push as straight and as fast to a junction with Hannibal as properly reconnoitred but forced marching could carry him. But

Hasdrubal had not the keen military insight of a great soldier. His first effort was a mistake. Under the impression that he would by its capture inflict grievous damage on the Romans, he sat down before Placentia, and unable to take it by a first assault he began to besiege it. His project was a dismal failure, and its consequences fatal. Here, too, he deemed it wise to wait for reinforcements which were on the way from Liguria and Gaul, — another foolish step, — and not until then did he march on Ariminum. He did not grasp the fact that for every thousand men he could gain, the enemy would find time to concentrate five against him; nor, indeed, that Hannibal would count on him to push through at once, and would act accordingly. Hasdrubal's tardiness might not have worked against him years before. But the Romans had received a dozen years' good schooling, and they better knew how to take advantage of mistakes.

The consternation at Rome, on the news of Hasdrubal's arrival being spread, was only equaled by the dismay which followed Hannibal's early victories. It was not now one son of Hamilcar over whom success must be won, but two, and Hasdrubal's ability was overrated. Should both the brothers win in the coming battles, what would become of Rome?

The Romans were quickly and fully advised of Hasdrubal's arrival and movements. But not so Hannibal. News could come to him only through the enemy's double lines, those facing himself and those facing his brother. Spies were of small use. Porcius, who was in Hasdrubal's front, had retired on his approach, retarding him as much as possible, while Livius marched towards his lieutenant, who had already fallen back to the line of the Metaurus, and from this point still farther back to the little river Sena. Here the consular army sat down in its camp to await the new-comer.

As in a number of cases, so here the location of the battle-

field is uncertain. On the whole, it is safest to follow the
account of Livy, who states that Livius' camp was near Sena.
It is rather hard to explain why the consul should pitch his
camp at this place. The direct road from Ariminum to Rome
— one branch of the Via Flaminia — turned from the coast
at Fanum Fortunæ, north of the Metaurus, and ran southwest towards the capital; and as, at Sena Gallica, or on the
line of the Sena, the consul could not hold this road, it would
seem as if he would take up the only position which commanded both branches of the Via Flaminia, the one which
ran inland and the one which followed down the coast. The

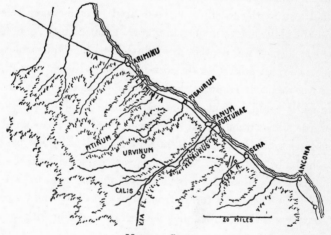

Metaurus Country.

consul's task was to protect the road to Rome as well as the
coast road, by which Hasdrubal could join his brother. At
Fanum Fortunæ, at the mouth of the Metaurus, he protected
both; at Sena, but one. Fanum was the key-point; Sena
had no importance whatever.

The movements of Hannibal are not clearly set down by
the ancient historian. It appears that he left his winter-

quarters at Metapontum before the new consuls were afoot, moved through Lucania to Apulia, where he went as far up as Larinum, near the Tifernus. This was unquestionably in the hope that Hasdrubal would very early seek to push south to join him; or in the expectation that if he did not find Hasdrubal's army he would procure news of it on which he could himself act to advantage. He did hear news, but to his great disappointment it was that Hasdrubal was besieging Placentia, instead of marching immediately south to a junction with him. And as he foresaw the danger he was running of being hemmed in away from his base by the numerous Roman armies then changing stations to correspond with the lots drawn by the consuls; as he desired to understand Hasdrubal's plans before undertaking any serious march; and as the south coast was a necessary future base for both armies, which he must protect at all hazards, he moved back to southern Lucania. If Hannibal had any understanding with Hasdrubal, it could be but a very partial one; and to advance towards him without definite knowledge of his whereabouts was to risk the loss of the campaign as well as of his base. He had but one army. The Romans understood and acted on this fact. Hannibal's evident programme was to keep quiet and preserve his forces from injury until he could communicate with Hasdrubal, and then, in coöperation with him, deliver one hearty blow.

It was on his march back, just as he was leaving the territory of Larinum, that, according to Livy, C. Hostilius, who, before the consul Nero had joined the army, was marching northward from Tarentum to meet his chief, ran across Hannibal on the march, and cut out from his column four thousand men and nine ensigns. This is another of the actions which are so imperfectly described that nothing can be stated but the bald fact, and this subject to doubt. If it is as stated, it goes to show that the quality of Hannibal's present forces was very low. Unless he had a great deal of ragged material under his colors, his column was not apt to march in straggling order, as Livy says he was doing when attacked by Hostilius. We know indeed that his veterans had practically disappeared, and that most of his men had been forced into the service; but the few words devoted by Livy to the subject are not convincing.

All this may look like unwillingness to credit Livy, who, in many respects, is the most valuable of the Roman historians. But during the past thirty years, we Americans have seen so many utterly unreliable statements with regard to our civil war put before the public in good faith by well-equipped witnesses of the event, that it appears wise to distrust the statements of one of Hannibal's worst enemies, unless we find them well vouched for by the attendant circumstances. Many of Livy's facts are contradicted by what he tells us himself in some other place.

Nero now joined his forces to those brought by Hostilius, which made an army of forty thousand foot and twenty-five hundred horse. His headquarters he established at Venusia, and his main object was to prevent Hannibal from marching north to join the new army, which after weary waiting had come to his relief. Hannibal found it necessary to retire to Bruttium. His recent losses were directly traceable to Hasdrubal's delay.

In Bruttium, Hannibal reinforced himself with all the garrisons he could spare, and moved along the great road from Rhegium on Grumentum in Lucania, intending once more to reach out towards Hasdrubal, and hoping on the way to capture Grumentum, which had been one of those towns which through fear had surrendered to the Romans. He camped near the city. He was anxious to avoid the attrition of bat-

tle by every means in his power, until he could strike in connection with Hasdrubal. At the same time, Nero, with much
precaution, moved from Venusia on Grumentum, and occupied a camp about a mile from Hannibal's. He was soldier
enough to know that Hannibal did not want to fight, and to
be anxious to force a battle on him if it could be done on
advantageous terms.

The Carthaginian rampart was only five hundred paces
from the city walls. Between the camps the ground was
level. Hannibal lay with the town in his rear, the Aciris on
his right, Nero facing him, the Aciris on his left. On Hannibal's left were several naked hills, not at all fitted, apparently, for an ambuscade and unsuspected by either party.
Hannibal had probably grown to believe that ambuscades
were of no further use, and that the consul would be on his
guard against them; but if the account of Livy is accurate,
he paid no heed to the operations on his own flanks. On the
open plain were daily skirmishes between the outposts and
light troops. Nero kept close in camp, as if intent only on
barring Hannibal from a march northward to join Hasdrubal.
Hannibal, however anxious to get away, fearing that he could
not well advance or retire without a battle, drew daily up in
order and awaited Nero's attack. He understood the character of his opponent well, but thought that if he could get
Nero to make a direct attack he could beat him.

Nero was unwilling to run the risk, but concluded to try
upon Hannibal one of his own stratagems. He managed to
send, under command of Tiberius Claudius Asellus, a tribune, and P. Claudius, a præfect of the allies, by night and
unperceived, five cohorts and five maniples, to the rear of the
hills on Hannibal's left, with orders to debouch from cover
at a set time.

Next morning both parties made ready for battle, Hanni-

bal giving the earlier orders, and the armies filed out from
camp and deployed into line. Hannibal's hastily raised
levies had not yet been subjected to careful discipline, and
the deployment was irregularly made on the Carthaginian
side, with considerable confusion in the lines. Nero at once

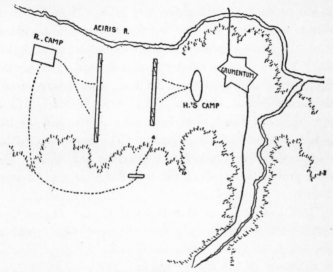

Battle of Grumentum.

took advantage of this confusion to make a sharp and unexpected attack on Hannibal's light troops with his cavalry.
Hannibal's presence, however, began to restore order; the
Roman right wing was coming steadily into action, and the
battle was fully engaged before any regular formation had
been completed on either hand. The Romans were under
better discipline and had the advantage .of the ‘initiative.
The Carthaginians showed no demoralization, and resisted
the spirited Roman assaults with great determination. "Hannibal among the terror and confusion would have drawn up
his troops while fighting, which would not have been an easy

task unless to a veteran general with veteran troops," says Livy, and the Carthaginian lines were pretty well holding their own, as fresh detachments were hurried up to fill the gaps. Hannibal was busily occupied in restoring order and with considerable success, when the Roman detachment, which had been sent round back of the hills, debouched with its war-cry on the Carthaginian left flank. Hannibal's men were at once seized with fear lest they should be cut off from camp, and made a speedy and confused retreat to its protection. Nero pushed his cavalry upon their rear. Had not the camp been near at hand a second Cannæ might have occurred, claims the Roman historian. The retreat was not without eight thousand killed, seven hundred captured, and the loss of nine ensigns and six elephants. The consul limited his casualties to five hundred men, Romans and allies. The event proved the result of this so-called victory to be more like that of a drawn battle.

These lost battles of Hannibal's, if we were to give them entire credit, would as fully show the wretched material he now had in his ranks as they would prove the great advance in steadiness of the Roman troops. The evidence of Livy, who makes constant efforts to rehabilitate the Roman reputation for fighting, is clearly to the effect that it was the poor quality of Hannibal's army to which so frequent defeat was due. This in no wise robs Nero of the full credit of conducting a brilliant stratagem under the eyes of the very father of stratagem. While we cannot accord to Nero a victory on this field, it is nevertheless true that Marcellus and he were the fighting men of Rome as Fabius was the originator of its better policy. Nero in some respects stands at the head of all the Roman generals of the Second Punic War, though the Romans had a habit of calling Marcellus their sword and Fabius their buckler.

Next day Nero again offered battle, but Hannibal was not strong enough to engage. Nero, according to Livy, buried the dead, — a token of victory, — and harassed Hannibal as much as he could with his cavalry, and by daily advancing to the very ramparts of Hannibal's camp, "so near to the gates that he almost appeared to be carrying in his standards."

Hannibal felt compelled to withdraw. This he did in the third watch of the night, by leaving his camp-fires lighted, and the foremost rows of tents standing, with a few Numidian sentries left behind to make an appearance of occupation, which they did, and afterwards joined the column. He marched straight for Apulia. Nero did not find out his absence till late next day, having been singularly cautious about approaching the Punic camp; and after he found it out he lost much time in plundering. Hannibal had evidently not lost his ability to march. But when Nero started, he pursued the Carthaginians vigorously, and coming upon them near Venusia, by a sudden and unlooked-for attack, cut out some two thousand men from the column. Hannibal, who had moved on Apulia, in renewed fruitless search of news from Hasdrubal, was too much weakened by these losses to make it safe to try to hold his own, without still further reinforcements, in the midst of so many Roman armies. He turned back to Metapontum, "marching by night and over mountain roads to avoid a battle," in search of new levies, which he sent out Hanno to pick up. On their arrival he again advanced by the same route to Venusia and thence to Canusium. Nero had constantly dogged his footsteps, even as far as Metapontum, leaving Q. Fulvius in Lucania during his absence. Hannibal's persistency as well as his skill in eluding Nero and his better army, which, consisting of a selection from the two consular armies of the past year, were old and seasoned troops, over forty thousand in number, was marked.

Thus, despite the defeat described by Livy, Hannibal had won his point. He aimed at gaining a position in Apulia, where he could await messengers from Hasdrubal. That he had not been defeated must be assumed from this fact alone. No doubt he suffered severely in the drawn battle at Grumentum, but Nero was unable to prevent him from gaining Apulia and, after he had gathered recruits to replace those he had lost, from holding himself there. All the facts here narrated are taken from Livy, without addition or detraction. But that Livy's facts are not beyond question it is well to point out. If we had a history of Napoleon from only the English standpoint, or a history of our civil war from only southern or northern writers, we should come far short of accuracy. Indeed, a meeting of the veterans of the Third Corps of the Army of the Potomac, under distinguished leaders, in 1886, deliberately voted that the opening days of Chancellorsville were "one of the most noted tactical victories of modern times" for the Union arms!

But were the relation of these constant victories of the Roman armies over Hannibal true, it would in no wise militate against his skill. It can be readily understood that Hannibal, whose Spanish and African veterans had all but disappeared, and whose means of recruiting, arming and equipping his men — let alone disciplining his heterogeneous mass of half-hearted Bruttian allies — were very limited, was often able to offer but a poor resistance in open combat to the enormous odds of excellent troops under the best generals Rome afforded, his own pupils of a dozen years' standing, and all instinct with the one set purpose of crushing the hated invader. But it becomes difficult to understand, if we accept as accurate the number and extent of his defeats and losses, how Hannibal could still maintain his footing as he did. If these victories were won by the Romans, how came

it that Hannibal was never so badly defeated as to have his
retreat cut off, or be totally disabled? The fact remains, on
Roman testimony, that Hannibal was able to move about at
pleasure, and that, when he retired from before great numbers
or because his own weak condition did not allow him to fight,
he none the less, by some flank manœuvre or night march, accomplished substantially what he sought to do. That he was
apt to be beaten in open fight, after the Romans had learned
to be cautious about stratagems, is natural; that he was able,
even when beaten or when he failed of victory, still to compass his ends is the wonderful feature of his work. His
later campaigns are an everlasting pattern of defensive manœuvring, as his early ones are of offensive strategy. On
the Roman side it seems curious that no attempt was made
to operate on Hannibal's communications while he was at the
front. His base was depleted of troops, and the evident objective of one of the Roman armies was Hannibal's rear.
But as none of the consuls and prætors liked the task of
meeting the Carthaginian in the open field, so most of them
even fought shy of his lieutenants in his allied cities.

Nero had been closely following up Hannibal. Why he
did not again attack him at Canusium, — just where indeed
Nero was, — we do not know. But he had evidently made his
way to a position north of Hannibal, to head him off from
marching farther towards Hasdrubal.

Hannibal had forty thousand men in his front, twenty
thousand behind him at Tarentum, ten thousand on his left
at Capua and twenty thousand in Rome. His own force we
do not know. It was probably not over thirty thousand men,
of whom two thirds were Bruttians of recent levies. He was
not strong enough to force his way on either side of the
Apennines through this barrier to join his brother. Every
main route was held by the enemy in force. He had prob-

ably hoped, by advancing into Apulia, to oblige the Roman generals to concentrate their troops, and thus enable Hasdrubal's messengers to penetrate to him. He had no doubt of their being on the road. He had twice been driven back to Bruttium to recruit his forces, which battles fought against his will had depleted. He had again advanced. His marches at this time seem erratic; but they are explained by the weakness of his army, the necessity he was under of saving it all he could, and his desire to communicate with Hasdrubal. He was ready to march forward to join hands with him, or even to fight his way through, so soon as he knew what direction Hasdrubal would take, who, from the Padus, might pass either by way of Etruria or Umbria. Now less than ever, while looking forward to what he had awaited for many years, could Hannibal afford general engagements for any other than the one purpose of forcing a junction with Hasdrubal.

It was in the hope of receiving some message from Hasdrubal that Hannibal now remained at Canusium. It was a dangerous position to occupy, surrounded by Roman armies and with such an able general as Nero on his heels wherever he turned. Nothing in the Roman annals excites our admiration more than Nero's excellent manœuvring, within its limitations, against the great Carthaginian. But Canusium was as good a position as Hannibal could well occupy until he knew how to coöperate with the newly arrived army of invasion. Until he heard from it, he could undertake nothing.

As might have been expected, Hasdrubal had failed in his siege of Placentia, and then had finally turned towards Ariminum to join his brother. He had sent messengers from Placentia, telling Hannibal of his throwing up the siege and proposing to meet and join in Umbria. Hasdrubal was to follow the Flaminian road along the coast and then at Fanum, at the mouth of the Metaurus, turn across the Apennines to

Narnia, hoping to meet Hannibal on the way. The messengers, four Gallic and two Numidian horsemen, had, curiously enough, traversed all Italy in safety, at the time Hannibal was retiring towards Metapontum, but had got off their track, turning towards Tarentum and not Metapontum, and had been made prisoners near Tarentum. They were bearers of Hasdrubal's entire plan of operations written in Carthaginian vernacular. This was not a clever device. Hasdrubal might better have dispatched one man or two every day for some time with false plans to deceive the enemy, and with the real plan confided to the messenger's memory. Hasdrubal risked the outcome of the entire campaign by risking the loss of the knowledge of it. The messengers were captured by some Roman foragers and taken to Caius Claudius, pro-prætor at Tarentum, who, after some delay and the exhibition of instruments of torture, ascertained who the men were. He at once sent them with an escort of cavalry and Hasdrubal's unopened letter to the consul Nero.

When Nero had got this plan, he had already half beaten the enemy. Had Hannibal received Hasdrubal's message, it is certain beyond a peradventure that he would at once have attacked Nero, and thus have forestalled all which this wide-awake and enterprising general did; or else would have stolen a march around his flank and made his way north.

This mishap of the messengers is but one more fact which forces on our attention Hannibal's crass bad luck. If Alexander was born under a lucky star, so, assuredly, was Hannibal born under a luckless one. It seems as if Fortune delighted to betray him and to thwart his best-laid plans. While fortune is largely of a man's own making, it cannot be admitted that there is not in war, as there is in all human events, such an element as simple luck.

XXXIX.

THE METAURUS CAMPAIGN. SUMMER, 207 B. C.

Possessed of Hasdrubal's plans, Nero had a splendid opportunity, and he used it in a manner to show the stuff that was in him. He notified the senate of his purpose, but waited for nothing. Secretly taking seven thousand men, the pick of his army, and leaving the legions under a legate in front of Hannibal, who, owing to Nero's careful method, knew nothing of his departure, the consul started north to join his colleague. With the aid of wagons for the infantry, he marched two hundred and fifty miles in seven days, and reached Sena, where lay Livius. This march of Nero's, his conduct at the Metaurus and his return to Hannibal's front, are a fine example of the use of interior lines. They form the most brilliant page of Roman achievement in the Second Punic War. Hannibal had no idea that the Roman consul had left his army, which to all appearances was still intact. Hasdrubal had advanced to the Sena but had not manœuvred ably. He had lost a chance to evade Livius and march towards Hannibal, and when he found that Nero had arrived, he seemed to lose moral force. He retired from the enemy's front, and back to the river Metaurus. The consuls followed him up, and forced battle on him. Hasdrubal drew up his men ably, and fought stoutly. But his army was demoralized, and a flank attack by Nero decided the day. Hasdrubal was killed and his army destroyed, in a second Cannæ. Nero then hastened back to his army. In two weeks he had marched five hundred miles and won the great Roman victory of this war.

Nero, then, became possessed of the messengers who bore the plans of Hasdrubal. These were translated by an African deserter. Here was one of those opportunities which show a man in his true colors. There was an extraordinary danger. It must be met by an extraordinary means. Nero at once advised the senate — as he was bound to do — of what he had learned, and of the plan he had devised to check the Carthaginian brothers in their proposed junction in Umbria. This the senate promptly confirmed. They believed in Nero and acted up to their belief. The Capuan legion was called to Rome; new troops were enlisted in the city garrison and the two city legions were sent up to Narnia.

Nero did not wait. He proceeded with his plans. Mounted messengers were dispatched along the road through Picenum to Larinum, Marrucia, Frentana and Prætutia, ordering the farmers to collect all the victuals, wagons, beasts of burden and fresh horses at convenient places, to help forward the march of an army. Nero made preparations for leaving the bulk of his army in front of Hannibal, while he himself should march at high speed, with a small but chosen band of his best troops, on whose devotion he could rely, to join Livius. Acting with Livius he hoped to destroy Hasdrubal, and then be able to turn upon Hannibal before the latter could accomplish anything against his lieutenant. What he left in Hannibal's front sufficed, if properly handled, to hold him there, or else to follow him north if he should break through, so as to reinforce the Roman army wherever Hannibal should attempt to strike it.

To prevent Hannibal from knowing what he was about to do, he gave out, even in his own camp, that he was preparing an expedition to Lucania to attack some of Hannibal's cities. He made the most careful arrangements to prevent a knowledge of his real direction from reaching Hannibal. It is to be regretted that the details of what he did are not known. Not one of his soldiers had any conception what the objective was, till they had marched a good many miles north. He had with him but six thousand foot and one thousand horse, but these were of irreproachable quality. Sufficiently far on his way, he explained his plan to his men, showed them how much depended on their strength and courage, and called on them for the one exertion of their lives. He explained the situation fully to them; convinced them that what was apparently rash was really the safest, surest road to victory; that Livius' army was the largest and best of all the Roman forces, and that with their aid the enemy must be defeated. His men were wrought up to the highest state of enthusiasm and confidence.

Scarcely a soul in Rome but was frightened at the bold scheme of Nero's. He had left his army in charge of a lieutenant whose capacity in large commands was not yet proven. He had withdrawn from Hannibal's front the very flower of his troops. He was marching to meet the man who had overcome him by deceit in Spain. What if Hannibal should attack his army, thus left behind under a legate, and contrive another Cannæ? What if he should escape the legate, follow Nero and destroy his small force on the way? What if Hasdrubal should again defeat him by ruse, as he had once defeated the Scipios in Spain? To the Romans, Hasdrubal was as dreadful a foe, for the moment, as Hannibal. Again was the excitement and dread of defeat at its highest pitch in Rome.

The progress north of Nero's small army was a triumphal march. The tired infantry was carried in wagons. The entire population was devoted to speeding them on their way, and lined the roadside in crowds to welcome them, encourage them, and pray the gods for their success. They marched night and day; they eat their rations without stopping. Nothing was allowed to arrest the constant motion of the column.

This manœuvre of Nero will always remain, not only a wonderful instance of marching, but a sample of the finest strategy, — the first of its kind. It is one of the best examples of the proper use to be made of interior lines in either ancient or modern times. There was of course danger that Hannibal would follow him. But this was remote, for Hannibal must take fifteen days to do what Nero was able to accomplish in seven, aided as he was by every soul in the population. The main danger lay in Hannibal's discovering his absence and attacking his army, which he had left under the legate Quintus Catius, while he himself was away. But war is a game of risk. Nero could not eliminate this element. It is he who limits the risk best who wins. This Nero did by keeping his own counsel and acting with extreme speed.

Nero made the extraordinary distance of two hundred and seventy Roman miles — say two hundred and fifty English — in seven days. And a considerable number of old soldiers and youths under age, met on the way, catching the infection, voluntarily joined the ranks of the consular army for the campaign. He arrived with a larger and better force than that with which he had started.

Nero, while on the march, sent forward messages to Livius to ask how he would prefer to have him join his army, — by night or by day, — and whether as a separate body or a reinforcement, suggesting that it was best to conceal his own arrival from Hasdrubal. Livius opened his camp to the new-comers, some of the men crowding into tents in double numbers, each tribune receiving a tribune and each centurion a centurion, so as not to increase its size. Having no baggage and being few in number, this was not difficult : and as Nero hid himself in the valleys until he could make his junction at night and in the protection of some hills, Hasdrubal knew as little of the arrival of Nero as Hannibal knew of his leaving. No more camp-fires were lighted than before, and the utmost secrecy was kept.

A council of war was immediately held, the prætor Porcius being present. The majority were for giving the newly-arrived troops a day's rest, but Nero strenuously opposed such a suggestion, lest a day lost should bring Hannibal upon them or upon Nero's own army, which lay in Hannibal's front; and it was agreed by all to force a battle on the morrow. According to Livy, the council was held on the morning after Nero's arrival, and the troops drawn up for battle immediately after. If this is so, Hasdrubal must that day have managed to decline the engagement.

The two consuls were, according to Livy, in their intrenched camp near Sena, and Hasdrubal was camped less than half a mile distant.

Why Hasdrubal, when he found that the road to Rome was left open, by the consuls taking position at Sena instead of Fanum, did not steal a march on them and advance towards Narnia, as he had notified Hannibal that he would do, sending other daily messengers to Hannibal to give him notice of his movements, cannot be said. He may, before Nero's arrival, have ascertained that he had but one consul before him, and have believed that it would be wiser to seek to beat him, than run the risk of moving farther on into the bowels of the land, and by such advance enable the consuls to join forces and thus incur the risk of having two to fight. At all events, he chose battle as a first step.

At point of day after the council, the Roman legions deployed in battle order in front of their camp. Hasdrubal was prepared to accept the gage, and backed up against his intrenchments. Before attacking he rode forward with a small escort to reconnoitre. There was an apparent increase of the Roman forces. He noticed that many of the shields looked rusty, instead of bright, as a Roman legionary's shield always was on the day of battle. Many of the horses he saw looked thin, as if they had recently made a long march. These and other indications raised his suspicions. He drew back, and sent out some scouts to examine the matter further, and make some prisoners if possible. He told them to ob serve the men going to the river for water, if any were more sunburned than usual; and sent another party to ride around the camp and see whether it had been increased, or the signals were sounded more than once.

The scouts reported that they heard only one in Porcius', but two signals blown in Livius' camp. Nero had been anxious to conceal his arrival until he could force battle on the enemy. When he came face to face with him, and Hasdrubal could no longer avoid the combat, Nero proclaimed the fact that he had two consuls to meet instead of one. He believed this would impair Hasdrubal's morale, as indeed it did.

The report of the scouts, and his own observation, convinced Hasdrubal that he had both consuls before him as well as the prætor Porcius. He feared that some great disaster had befallen Hannibal; that the second consul had eluded him by a stratagem he could not credit. Or had his own messengers to Hannibal been captured? Without knowledge of this plan how should Nero be there? Troubled by these thoughts, Hasdrubal held his own all day, evacuated his camp after nightfall, and retired towards the Metaurus, purposing to cross so soon as he could do so.

What Hasdrubal's eventual purpose may have been in retiring, we cannot guess. If he did not care to engage both consuls, now was his time to show himself able to manœuvre. If, instead of retiring on the Metaurus, Hasdrubal had left a strong rear-guard in camp, and had moved by his right towards the Flaminian Way, he would have found his road open, and, assured that the consuls were both at Sena, could have escaped them, and made some distance towards his brother before they followed. But it looks as if Hasdrubal was acting from demoralization. The task which Hannibal had performed unruffled for a dozen years, and under vastly more difficult conditions, seems to have overtaxed Hasdrubal at the outset. Hannibal had been alone; Hasdrubal was marching towards a friendly army. Hannibal and he were, to be sure, operating on exterior lines and were seriously hampered by the forces interposed between them, which prevented their manœuvring with common purpose. But this does not explain Hasdrubal's sudden retreat. The loss of moral force following such withdrawal was alone enough to forfeit the battle which must ensue. It is unlike the man; Hasdrubal was more apt to err on the side of boldness than discretion. He was no longer himself. Having advanced to the vicinity of the enemy, he should by all means have fought him. His object was to join Hannibal rather than to beat a Roman army; but this was a matter to have considered beforehand; he could not afford to retreat when in presence of the enemy, particularly with his heterogeneous and unreliable forces, with which prestige was everything. An advance along the Flaminian Way towards Rome would have encouraged his army; a retreat to the Metaurus must inevitably draw their temper. Hasdrubal's conduct looks like that of a man who is not abreast of his work. One finds instances like this in every great war; in our own civil war notably that of Hooker at Chancellorsville.

It is related that Hasdrubal was deceived by his guides; he may not have been careful in watching them. They escaped. one by hiding, and one by swimming the river, and Hasdrubal lost his way. In the darkness, the troops straggled, broke ranks and mixed up organizations, so as to place the army in the worst possible condition for meeting the enemy. Having reached the Metaurus, Hasdrubal, to preserve order, instructed the ensigns to march along the banks, so that each taxis and syntagma might keep its proper place. But in the dark these ensigns could not be seen, and the rolling ground, wooded for the most part, without guides, was a

very labyrinth, while the increasing steepness of the river-
banks along which Hasdrubal was seeking a ford for the
army, broke up all semblance of formation. It seems curious
that he could not find his way back over the route he had
advanced on. The march of an army leaves a wide track.
Finally, after the march had been continued all night and
most of the succeeding day, and many of the men — especially
the Gauls — were almost dropping from fatigue and inanition, they were reached by the Roman van-guard of cavalry
under Nero, shortly followed by the light troops under Porcius. These attacked his rear of column smartly, and brought
Hasdrubal to bay.

The Romans were eager for battle. Hasdrubal was badly
dispersed. He was not much more than ten miles west from
Fanum in a direct line. No ford was at hand. He saw that
he could not cross the river with the Romans at his heels; he
must stop and fight for it. His troops were discouraged and
the effect of this retreat on the Gauls had been fairly disastrous: they had no rations; they had lost their rest; they
were in sorry condition for battle. Livius soon arrived on
the ground with the heavy foot, ready to engage, and there
was no more chance of avoiding the conflict.

It is hard to decipher from Livy — Polybius' account is
very short — whether the battle was fought the same evening
or the next morning. It is probable that both parties camped
and drew up their forces for battle the succeeding day.

Hasdrubal deserves credit for marshaling his forces so
well under such trying circumstances. He spent the night
collecting his men, and drew up his phalanx in good order to
resist the Roman attack. His line lay along a slight rise in
the ground. His left flank was covered, probably by a small
brook or low piece of ground, at least an obstacle difficult
to pass. The African and Spanish foot was on the right,

with which Hasdrubal personally proposed to make his
strongest effort; the Ligurians in the centre; the Gauls, always unreliable on his left, covered by the obstacle.   His ten

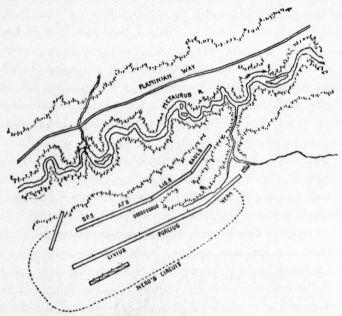

Battle of the Metaurus.

elephants were in front of his centre. Cavalry is not mentioned. If Hasdrubal had any amount of this arm, it was
probably in the rear. His "line was rather long than deep,"
says Livy, "rather deep than long," says Polybius.

We do not know the size of Hasdrubal's army. It has
been thought by some authorities to have been far superior to
the Roman army. As Livius and Porcius had been unwilling
to attack it before Nero's arrival, it may have been numerically equal to the forty thousand men now in the Roman line.
But in quality it was far less good.

In the Roman line Nero with his seven thousand chosen

men stood facing the Gauls; Porcius was opposite the Ligurians. Livius had the Spanish and African infantry to contend with. The Romans were in the usual formation by cohorts. The Roman horse, there being no Carthaginian horse
for it to cope with, was in rear of the triarii.

Hasdrubal saw that he must win this battle, or forfeit
every hope for which he had crossed the Alps. His Gallic
allies were protected by the obstacle in their front; his Li-
gurian allies were stanch; he hoped to win an advantage with
the Spanish and African foot on his right, as the Romans
would probably attack this wing, the left being under cover.
This prompted him to open the battle by a hearty attack on
Livius. Soon the fighting became general all along such
parts of the line as could be reached. Livius and Porcius,
though their legions fought with true Roman grit, could make
no impression on Hasdrubal's Spanish and African phalanx.
The elephants were as usual equally dangerous to both sides.
At first they were sent against the Roman line and created
grave confusion in the Roman ranks, but being driven back
made similar havoc among their own friends, and "ranged
to and fro between the two lines . . . like ships floating about
without rudders." Nero did his level best on the Roman
right, but without results. He could not cross the ground in
face of the Gauls, who, despite their weariness and hunger,
which drove many to desert, held the lines in good style.
Finally, having convinced himself by repeated efforts that the
same obstacle which prevented his own success would in the
same way prevent theirs, should the Gallic troops attempt
a serious attack, Nero left the front line of maniples to hold
head against this wing, and moved those of the principes and
triarii by the rear of the Roman army over to their left.
This manœuvre showed the same *coup d'œil* and was similar
to that which won Marlborough such renown in the battle of
Ramillies.

It was a complete surprise to both Carthaginians and Romans, when Nero, debouching from behind the rolling ground, appeared in line on the Carthaginian right flank and sharply attacked the Spaniards in the rear. The front attack of Livius was at once doubled in vigor and effectiveness. This timely manœuvre decided the victory. The Spaniards and Ligurians, surrounded and crushed, fell to the last man facing the foe. The Gauls were cut down with scarce a show of resistance. Many in fact were found asleep in the fields and woods. They lacked that courage which can stand a long drain upon the physical powers.

Hasdrubal had in the combat acted with courage and good sense. He "called back the flying and restored the battle in many places where it had been given up." Finally, after heroic efforts to redeem the day, "sharing equally in every danger," seeing the battle irretrievably lost, he rode into the midst of a Roman cohort sword in hand and died "as was worthy the son of Hamilcar and the brother of Hannibal."

No such defeat had taken place since Cannæ. Livy sets the slain at fifty-six thousand men, with fifty-four hundred taken. Except some six thousand prisoners, and such as escaped the Roman sword, the whole Carthaginian army perished. The Roman loss was eight thousand killed. Polybius gives a much less number, — ten thousand Carthaginians killed in battle, and two thousand Romans; but he says that, excepting a few distinguished prisoners, the whole army of Hasdrubal was put to the sword. Whatever is the truth, Cannæ had been avenged, and Nero had bitterly repaid Hasdrubal for the deception practiced on him in Spain. The Punic phalanxes were destroyed, and Hannibal's last chance of conquering Italy disappeared with them.

"So completely were even the victors satiated with blood and slaughter that the next day when Livius, the consul, received intelligence that the cisalpine Gauls and Ligurians, who had either not been present at the battle or had made their escape from the carnage, were marching off in one body without a certain leader, without standards, without any discipline or subordination; that if one squadron of horse were sent against them they might be all destroyed, he replied, ' Let some survive to bear the news of the enemy's losses and of our valor.' " — Livy.

This whole campaign reflects the greatest credit on Nero, and is far from creditable to Hasdrubal. Every step in the undertaking was carefully studied by the Roman, and he never failed to get time — in such operations the one needful element — on his side. In this instance, it was all the more essential to the safety of the army he had left behind. Speed is one of the greatest values in war. Nero had marched to better effect than any Roman before him. The march from and back to Hannibal's front is a lesson to all military students. Not one among the Roman generals had profited as had Nero from the lessons of his great antagonist. The manner in which he utilized the moral effect of his junction with his brother consul, away beyond the numerical reinforcements he brought him, was masterly; we have seen its effect on Hasdrubal.

Hasdrubal's fault was essentially lack of speed and decision. The delay in moving out of Spain, the siege of Placentia, were fatal errors. As to join Hannibal was his one object, so soon as he met Porcius and Livius, if he did not propose to give them battle, he should have withdrawn with the precautions Hannibal was wont to use, and have sought touch with his brother by the Flaminian Way. It was his delays, coupled to his unwise method of communicating with his brother, which defeated him.

Just what Hannibal was doing during the full two weeks

of the enactment of this to him fatal drama, history does not reveal. That portion of Polybius which should deal with this question is lost. Livy is silent on the subject. His remaining thus quiet makes Nero decidedly the hero of the act. The character of Hannibal shows so much both of energy and precaution, and he was as a rule so extremely careful as well as skillful in procuring information of the enemy's whereabouts, that we are at a loss to explain how he could in this instance have been so blinded, even by the excellent precautions of Nero, as to have remained quietly in camp while Hasdrubal was being destroyed. There are facts connected with the matter which we do not know. While his rôle was necessarily to preserve his army intact and wait for news of Hasdrubal, the fact that Nero was able to deceive him as he did gives this consul a credit beyond all his fellow-generals of the Second Punic War. Still we must remember that the consular army itself remained in Hannibal's front. Nero had only taken a small part of it with him. Hannibal was in the enemy's country, where information was not easy to get, and his Numidians, his eyes, had all but disappeared.

Nero hastened back to Apulia, bearing the head of Hasdrubal. He returned by the same route and means, and this time made the march in six days. He had thus put behind him considerably over five hundred miles, and had fought perhaps the most important battle of this eighteen years' war, in the short space of two weeks. Scipio's victory at Zama ended the war, but Nero's skill at the Metaurus alone made Zama possible. Reaching the vicinity of Hannibal's camp, Nero stuck the gruesome symbol of his victory on a pike in front of the Carthaginian outposts, or else threw it in among them, "repaying in this way his great antagonist, who scorned to war with the dead, for the honorable burial which he had given to Paulus, Gracchus, and Marcellus."

It was found by the outposts and carried to Hannibal. The Carthaginian prisoners were also exhibited at a distance, and and two were sent into the camp to tell the story.

Hannibal thus learned of the death of his brother and the destruction of his own plans at the same moment. He gave utterance to one of the few expressions of his of which we have any record, that in this sad spectacle he recognized the impending doom of Carthage. He withdrew to Bruttium, and with him took all his auxiliaries of Metapontum and other towns in Lucania. Good as the occasion was for Nero to pursue Hannibal, he made no attempt to do so. Probably Hannibal could have foiled him, but the advantage of following up a victory was rarely understood in ancient times.

The danger had been as great as after Cannæ; the defeat of Hasdrubal made it certain that Rome was saved. The capital was in a delirium of joy. The effect of the victory of the Metaurus was enormous on both citizens and allies. For the first time in twelve years Rome breathed freely, and saw the triumph of a victorious general. For to Livius, as commander in the province and of the bulk of the forces at the Metaurus, was granted the greater triumph; to Nero the lesser, though they were associated in the same procession. History, however, recognizes better than the Romans to whose skill, courage and clear conception the victory was really due. And it is said that this too was understood by the senate and people, as well as by Livius' army, which had been recalled and took part in the triumph; for "it was observed that the men wrote more verses in their jocular style upon C. Claudius Nero than upon their own general," says Livy. Nero, though an unpopular aristocrat, was the hero of the day.

Remotely, it was Scipio's successes in Spain which won this victory, as it was Scipio's carelessness which had allowed Hasdrubal to march to Italy. The one offsets the other.

Had Hasdrubal kept his Spanish resources and his fleet on the coast, he might have joined Hannibal in southern Italy, instead of crossing the Alps, and we can readily conceive how differently the Italian campaigns might have eventuated. But Scipio had robbed him of the power to do this. If not in the small galaxy of stars of the first magnitude, Scipio may fairly claim rank among stars of the second. Men are — indeed must be — judged by success. Scipio was beholden to Fortune far more than to his own ability; but he honestly won his way, and is entitled to the laurels won by ending the war both in Spain and Africa. For to him — under good fortune, and aided by the unwise administration and intestine broils in Carthage — Rome owed her eventual salvation.

This year in Spain, Hanno, with a third army of reinforcements from Carthage, had supplanted Hasdrubal, son of Gisgo, who had been filling the vacant place of Hasdrubal Barca. Mago had returned from the Balearic Islands. Both these generals moved into Andalusia, but were defeated by Silanus, Scipio's legate, and Hanno was captured. The relics of their armies retired to the province of Hasdrubal, son of Gisgo. This officer, placing garrisons in such Andalusian cities as he still controlled, shut himself up in Gades. Masinissa, with his light horse, scoured southern Spain. The work of this cavalry-general affords one of the most interesting examples of the proper use of cavalry on a large scale in the history of war. He and Mutines were born commanders of horse. Gades was too strong to attempt, but having captured Oringes (near modern Seville), and garrisoned it, Scipio retired into winter-quarters at Tarraco. Spain was all but cleared of Carthaginian forces.

The fleets, meanwhile, had had fairly good fortune on the coast of Africa and against Philip.

XL.

SCIPIO. 206–205 B. C.

THERE were still nineteen legions in service the next year. Rome was well armed, but her conduct was lax. The farmers could begin to return to their devastated homes. Hannibal was confined to Bruttium; but the Romans could not drive him from Italy. The fear which even the best Roman generals exhibited of Hannibal speaks volumes; and this fear is acknowledged by even Livy. In Spain, Scipio fought a battle at Bæcula, in which the tactical manœuvre was handsomely devised and executed. Hasdrubal, son of Gisgo, was defeated and his army dispersed; and Scipio reduced the entire peninsula. Scipio was a brilliant rather than a great general. He had many qualities which command popular suffrage; his personality was in his favor. But had he been placed where Marcellus or Nero was placed, he would have failed. In 205 B. C. he was made consul, and to his lot fell Sicily, from which island every one believed he would soon carry the war into Africa. Scipio was apt to take the bit in his teeth, and there was a strong element against him in the senate, because he was thought to be unwilling to serve the republic with perfect subordination. Still, much power was left to him. Mago, Hannibal's brother, landed at Genoa, and began to collect an army of allies, in addition to over twenty thousand men he brought. But the Roman armies in his front neutralized his efforts. The war in Bruttium had become a mere raiding war, and the sole event of the year was the loss of Locri by Hannibal. In 204 B. C. Scipio as proconsul was permitted to continue his long-delayed preparations for a descent on Africa. Epidemics ravaged the armies in Bruttium. Little was done on this account.

Q. CÆCILIUS and L. Veturius Philo came into the consulate in the thirteenth year of the war, B. C. 206. They had particularly distinguished themselves as legates at the Metaurus. The prætors were C. Servilius for Sicily, Cæcilius Metellus in the city, Tiberius Claudius Asellus in Sardinia, and Q. Mamilius Turinus on foreign duty. The situation of affairs had undergone an entire change. The disaster at the

Metaurus had put Hannibal upon the strict defensive in Bruttium and Lucania, and the senate saw its way to decreasing the number of legions to nineteen, of which only four — the two consular armies — were placed in Hannibal's front. Capua and Tarentum were held each by a legion; and Rome and Etruria, Sicily and Sardinia, were defended as before, the usual shifting of stations taking place. The naval force underwent no particular change.

It was quite natural, though unwise, that, upon the severe moral strain and depletion of resources which Rome had undergone, there should follow a laxity of purpose in the prosecution of the war. Every intelligent citizen of Rome could see that the war had definitely turned in her favor, and that it was but a question of time when Hannibal would be driven from Italy. But, though nearly two hundred thousand men were under arms, there was little energy put into ridding the republic of its harassed but still redoubtable enemy.

Up to this moment, for some years past, all the country people had, by instructions from the senate, taken refuge in the towns. They were now ordered back to their farms and to tillage. This order was carried out so far as possible in the provinces not too near the seat of war, as well as in the vicinity of Rome. But there was little left to be done by those farmers who were poor. Their lands had been devastated, had got choked up with weeds and scrub growth, and they had almost no means of restoring them to productiveness.

When lots were drawn, Cæcilius took Nero's army, Veturius that of Q. Claudius, the pro-prætor. The consuls chose for opening the campaign to make a raid on the district of Consentia, in upper Bruttium, which they began to ravage; but they were cleverly entrapped in a defile by some partisan bodies of Bruttians and Numidian archers, and escaped with difficulty. They then retired to Lucania, which they readily brought into subjection.

Hannibal could not move out of Bruttium. His forces were quite unequal to fighting or even campaigning with any promise of success. He was hoping against hope for some further recognition from home, some aid in men and material. He could undertake nothing, but clung to his work with a despairing grasp. Weak as he was, however, neither of the consuls chose to come within reach of his arm. His patience and constancy under these trials, and the dread his name still inspired, show him up in a far greater measure than any of his triumphs. Even Livy, who is full of depreciation of Hannibal's abilities, says : " The Romans did not provoke him while he remained quiet, such power did they consider that single general possessed, though everything else around him was falling into ruin ; " and is compelled to follow up this statement with a panegyric.

For thirteen years Hannibal had held more or less territory within the bounds of the Roman confederacy, far from home and his natural base. His old army had quite disappeared, and a motley array of hybrid material had taken its place. For three or four years he had had nothing which he could oppose to the Roman legions without danger of, — without actual defeat. His troops had often neither pay, clothing nor rations ; their arms were far from good ; they may have foreseen eventual disaster as did Hannibal. And yet the tie between leader and soldier never ceased to hold ; the men he had were all devotion to his cause. Driven into a corner, where he must subsist his army on a limited area, which he could only do by forcing under his standard every man possibly fit for service ; among a people whose greed for gold and plunder was their chief characteristic, he was yet able not only to keep his phalanxes together, but to subject them to excellent discipline,— not such of course as that which was the legitimate pride of the Romans, but under the conditions remarkable. The Carthaginians had only dreamed of keeping Spain; their one great captain, with all his possibilities, they had blindly neglected. He was left absolutely to his own resources. And yet,— it is so wonderful that one cannot but repeat it again and again, — though there were around him several armies of Roman veteran legions, for nearly all Romans were veterans now, such was the majesty which hedged his name, that neither one of the opposing commanders, nor all together, dared to come to the final conflict with him. Even after the Metaurus, when the Romans knew what the effect of this defeat must be on the morale of Hannibal's army, if not on himself, this dread of the very name of Hannibal, even by the best of the Roman commanders, was unparalleled. They must have each and all recognized that it needed but one joint effort to crush out his weakened and depleted semblance of an army, and yet none of them was apparently willing to undertake the task. Whatever the Roman historians may tell us about these years, is not here really a great and stubborn fact which testifies to more than a thousand written pages?

When we look at the condition of Carthage, its political imbroglios and the bitterness of its factions, it ceases to be a matter of curiosity that so little was done to aid Hannibal. Spain had been a mine to Carthage, not merely self-supporting, but yielding vast revenues. The peace-party had not the foresight to comprehend that every nation which had to do with Rome must eventually be neutralized if not swallowed up by her, and it was natural that they should prefer to hold Spain to winning in Italy. They believed that they could do the first, they doubted the other. They were lavish of their means to Spain for this reason; and the victories of Hanni-

bal seemed to them, described by the oily tongue of Hanno,
no greater than those of Hasdrubal. That a durable peace
could not be conquered in Iberia did not appear to be understood.

Hannibal, on the contrary, could see, as his father had seen
before him, that there was no *modus vivendi* with Rome until
she had been taught such a lesson that she would act a defensive rôle and not again venture to attack Carthage. Like
Napoleon, Hannibal saw that a peace, to be a peace, must be
conquered at the doors of the enemy's capital. This was his
policy. It was the proper one; but it failed because he
could not control the resources of Carthage.

Yet it is passing strange that the jealousies of the Carthaginian ring should have been such that it could not see that
wherever Hannibal was not, there was failure; that Hannibal
was the man for their opportunity; that not Spain but Italy
was the battle-field on which they could win. Spain had
been constantly, steadily reinforced, while within her own
borders there had been everything to draw from; the Roman
forces against Carthage there had never had overwhelming
odds; yet Spain was falling away from her grasp.

Scipio this year fought a decisive battle in Spain, the tactics of which were original and crowned with success. Hasdrubal, son of Gisgo, and Mago had lain in front of Gades.
They had collected at various places in Bætica, an army
stated as high as seventy thousand foot, forty-five hundred
horse, and thirty-two elephants, of which force, however, less
than half were Africans and Numidians, the balance being
made up of hastily-raised Spanish militia. With part of
this numerically respectable, but intrinsically weak, body —
what might not the half of it have accomplished under Hannibal's discipline in Italy? — the two Carthaginian generals
moved up the left bank of the Bætis and crossed to Ilipa

(or Silpia), a place above modern Seville, on the right bank
of the river, where, by adding reinforcements, they reached
the number stated, and proceeded to Bæcula. The Carthaginian camp was on the slope of a hill facing a valley, with
a similar slope running up from the other side, and with
the right flank of the camp towards a small affluent of the
Bætis.

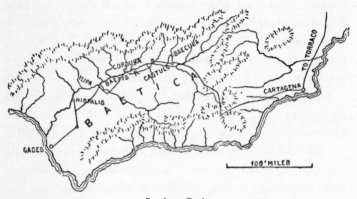

Southern Spain.

Scipio had four Roman legions and an equal number of
Spanish levies. Remembering the fate of his father and
uncle through the treachery of their Spanish allies, he had
been wise not to overbalance his force. He had been in
winter-quarters in Tarraco, from which place he advanced to
Cartagena, whence west to Castulo on the Bætis, intending
to give battle to the enemy. After leaving garrisons along
the route, he had left some forty-five thousand foot and three
thousand horse — of which number twenty-four thousand
were the Roman and allied legions. His movement against
Hasdrubal and Mago was on such a line as would cut them
off from the nearest road to Gades, which lay along the south
bank. If he beat them, he could the more certainly compromise the whole army. This was another instance of attack-

ing the enemy's strategic flank. He went into a camp on the opposite slope from the Carthaginians, with his left towards the stream mentioned.

Mago and Masinissa sharply attacked the Romans with their cavalry while they were going into camp, but Scipio had anticipated a possible attack, and had kept a body of Roman horse in hiding, while, as usual, protecting the building of the camp with his light troops and some cohorts. The foot held the Carthaginians in front, and the Roman cavalry took them in flank, and drove them off with loss. Both armies lay facing each other across the valley. For several days nothing but outpost-skirmishing occurred, in which the new levies on either hand were sizing up each other, and each army was marshaled before its camp. But neither offered battle. It must be remembered that no army attacked uphill if it could be avoided, because the enemy's spears, darts, arrows and stones had so much more effect from a height. An army in line in front of its camp was rarely attacked.

The usual habit with the Carthaginians was to place the African foot in the centre and the Spaniards on the flanks. During these days of waiting, Scipio placed his Romans in the centre and his Spanish allies on the flanks. It grew to be understood in both camps that such was to be the formation for the approaching battle. Acting on this knowledge, Scipio formed his line. He proposed not to pit Spaniard against Spaniard, but to oppose the Spanish infantry in the Carthaginian army with his Roman legions, and to use his own Spaniards against the African centre. Like Wellington in a later age, he preferred not to put too great dependence on his Spaniards in battle. Scipio would naturally force the fighting with his Roman legionaries, and this would bring the brunt of the attack upon the flanks.

The day on which Scipio designed to offer battle, he had

his men eat their morning meal at a very early hour and filed out of camp with so much commotion as to induce Hasdrubal to leave his quarters before his men had broken fast. The battle was opened by the light troops and horse of both sides, and the formation of the line went on behind them. The Carthaginians had as usual placed the African foot in the

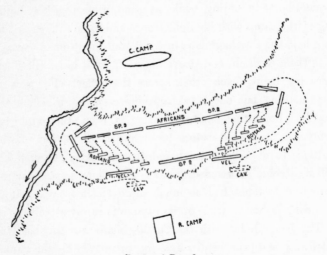

Battle of Bæcula.

centre, the Spaniards in the wings, the elephants in front. When the Carthaginian cavalry was withdrawn, it was placed, the heavy in rear of the flanks, the Numidians outside the heavy. The Carthaginian army, without its morning meal, was not in good condition. The Romans were well prepared. Scipio had retorted on Hasdrubal the ruse of Hannibal at the Trebia. He could profit by others' experience.

Scipio had prepared his troops for an exact and difficult tactical manœuvre. His Roman and allied legions were on the flanks and were pretty sure to beat the Spaniards in the Carthaginian army; but the Spaniards who were in his centre, opposed to the excellent African infantry in Hasdrubal's, were apt to fail at a critical moment. For this possibility he sought to provide.

Some five hundred yards from the enemy, Scipio brought his heavy foot into line, still covered by his skirmishers. The Spanish legions, as well as the Roman and allied, all stood in the usual checkerwise order by maniples. On the withdrawal of the skirmish line, the men fell back through the intervals and formed, the velites in rear of the flanks of the legions, the cavalry again in their rear. This done, the cohorts moved forward. It was too late for the Carthaginians to change their dispositions if they so desired. Scipio had purposely prolonged the contest of the light troops so as to keep the enemy busy without allowing him to change formation, and tire him out from lack of food.

The Carthaginian line extended some distance beyond the Romans' either flank. When within two hundred paces, Scipio gave the order to the centre to continue its movement straight forward, but at a slow and regular step; to the wings to oblique at a rapid gait, the right wing to the right, the left wing to the left by cohorts so as to strike the Carthaginian line at its extremities, while the light foot and horse, by a turning movement at a *pas de charge*, surrounded the right and left flanks of the enemy respectively. Scipio commanded the right cohort, to give the direction; Marcius and Silanus the left. Within striking distance, the oblique movement ceased, the legionaries moved to the front and struck the enemy a staggering blow, while the light foot and horse fell upon their flanks. As intended by Scipio, the centre had not yet got up to engaging distance, and was held back so as to continue to threaten the Carthaginian centre and prevent the African infantry from coming into action, but without risking its blow.

Scipio thus had a concave line of battle, or rather a double oblique line with centre refused. Whether the wings ad-

vanced in echelon or not cannot be said; no doubt they advanced in some similar oblique order. The entire manœuvre
appears to have been executed with the utmost skill and pre-
cision, just as planned. The Carthaginian horse, nonplussed
at the novelty of the dispositions, was late in charging, and
thus lost its first momentum. The elephants, wounded by many
spears, rushed back towards the Carthaginian line, inflicting
upon it the damage intended for Scipio. In a short but sharp
and decisive struggle, the Carthaginian cavalry and the
Spanish phalanx proved entirely inadequate to resist the onset of the Roman wings, and were dispersed and largely cut
down. The African centre, however, which Scipio's Spaniards
had kept in place, could not be demoralized. It withdrew
in good order, and enabled the wreck of the wings to rally
upon it.

The whole battle is a pattern of excellent tactics, as skillfully designed as brilliantly executed. The strategic soundness of Scipio's dispositions is shown in the fact that the Carthaginians were, as he intended they should be, thrown back
off the line of retreat on Gades, which was across the river
and ran down the left bank; the army was compelled to retreat down the right bank. Nearly all the Spanish allies of
the Carthaginians forsook them. Scipio followed up Hasdrubal's retreat. On reaching the mouth of the Bætis, Hasdrubal was about to go into a fortified camp, but Scipio again
attacked him, and but six thousand men saved themselves in
the camp out of the fifty thousand who fought at Bæcula.
Most of these six thousand deserted in a few days to the Romans. Hasdrubal fled by sea and reached Gades. Leaving
a force of eleven thousand men under Silanus to watch the
camp, which not long after surrendered, Scipio retired to
Tarraco.

During the balance of the year Scipio captured Gades, and

subdued the rest of the peninsula. Spain became a Roman province; but it was subject to constant insurrections, and there was always danger that it would rise in favor of Carthage.

Much of his success Scipio owed to his lieutenants. Lælius and Silanus were of an ability to command higher rank than they enjoyed. They did much for which brilliant Scipio managed to reap the credit. Still there is much which is admirable in Scipio's work.

Hasdrubal sailed to Carthage. Mago, Hannibal's brother, with large treasure, sailed for Minorca, where he wintered, with authority from the Carthaginian senate to go to cisalpine Gaul and raise troops to join his brother, Hannibal.

Thus Scipio's marked good fortune and fine abilities had enabled him to end the war in Spain. The cause of Carthage had all but reached its ebb tide. But Scipio had once again allowed a lion's whelp to escape him. What Mago might accomplish remained to be seen.

Marcellus had ended the war in Sicily; Publius Sulpicius that in Greece; Scipio that in Spain. But the war still went on in Italy, though the best generals and troops were at hand in the peninsula.

Scipio was a brilliant rather than a great general. He had early begun his career, as we have seen, by saving his father's life at the Trebia. When, as it is related, he was chosen by the people for the Spanish army because he was the only candidate who presented himself to undertake this difficult mission, he became at a single leap the favorite of the people, and always so remained despite his errors, which were many and serious. Scipio was handsome and manly, enthusiastic and courageous, intelligent and full of self-confidence. He was not the man to constrain fortune, but he was born under a lucky star, which was better. When he failed from the result of his own errors, Fortune always came to the rescue. She did as much for him as for Alexander, while Scipio did but a tithe as much for himself as the son of Philip. Scipio believed in his own star and was adroit in acting up to his belief. He was honorable, envied no man, treated all with consideration. He was highly educated and refined, and a general favorite. But he considered himself above criticism, and often acted in what was really a high-handed manner. He was never called to account for many acts which in others would have been insubordination. He did no more for Italy than Marcellus, less than Nero, but he has descended into history as a greater character than either. Less able in many respects, his work was supplemented by opportunities not awarded them, and what he did bore fruit which all men could see. Scipio never hid his light under a bushel. Had Scipio faced Hannibal when Marcellus or Nero was called on to do so, he would probably have failed. Fortune saved him for Zama, when Hannibal had no longer an army and he himself had inherited the best of its size Rome had put into the field.

It was just that Scipio should be rewarded with the consulate the next year, B. C. 205. P. Licinius Crassus was his colleague. There were still nineteen legions under arms. The prætors were Cn. Servilius for the city, Spurius Lucretius for Ariminum, L. Æmilius for Sicily, and Cnæus Octavius for Sardinia. Q. Cæcilius remained in Bruttium as proconsul. To Crassus the care of the situation in Bruttium was confided.

To Scipio's lot fell Sicily, but it was understood by him, and by all who wisely scanned the situation, that the war should now be carried over to Africa. Though he was not the only good soldier in the service of the republic, he was the one whose personality captured the suffrages of the average citizen, and all Rome looked to Scipio as the man to give the finishing touch to the struggle. There seems to have been much the same glamour about Scipio as there was in 1861 and 1862 about McClellan. But Scipio met the tests he was put to after a better fashion. In the senate, however, and among the most thoughtful, was a division on the question of moving into Africa. A considerable faction distrusted Scipio, not on account of his military conduct, but because he showed a disposition not to ride to orders, but to look at things *de haut en bas*. Fabius Maximus was among those who opposed Scipio's being sent to Africa. Livy asserts that Scipio had openly declared that he would transport an army into Africa through the medium of the people if the senate opposed him; and on being publicly asked in the senate whether he would submit to the conscript fathers and abide by their determination in the matter, replied that he would act as he thought was for the interest of the state, facts which accord well with Scipio's character, but are more consistent in a politician than in the military servant of a republic. The result was that supplies were withheld from Scipio. But as he had permission to accept volunteers, an appeal to the allies soon enabled the new consul to create a fleet, and later the senate gave him fuller support. Nor was Scipio idle. That twenty quinquiremes and ten quadriremes could be built and launched in forty-five days, as was done, shows diligence on his part and experience in shipbuilding among the allies.

Mago had raised twelve thousand foot and two thousand horse. He set sail towards summer from Minorca, landed at Genua and took the place. Soon large numbers of the native tribes joined his standard. Carthage sent him some seven thousand men, seven elephants and money. But M. Livius from Etruria, and Lævinus with the city legions, four in all, by moving, the one to the Ariminum country, and the other to Arretium and its territory, not only arrested Mago's expected supplies of Gallic troops, but cut off his advance into the interior as well.

The war in Bruttium had taken the form of forays. Hannibal's Numidians had set the example in the business, and they were quickly followed by the Bruttians, with whose character a raiding war well comported. The Romans were not slow to follow suit. But the campaign had practically been nullified by violent epidemics in both the Roman camp and Hannibal's. The sole incident of the year was the loss to Hannibal of Locri. He had previously abandoned Thurii. While Scipio was completing his preparations to go to Africa, he was led by certain rich exiles from Locri to make an attempt to seize on this town, and thus still further hem in Hannibal. He managed through these exiles, who were in Rhegium, and some Locrian prisoners taken by the Roman raiding parties and ransomed for the purpose by the exiles, to get into communication with the garrison of one of the citadels of Locri, and, by the aid of a conspiracy excited among some of them, who then helped the Roman forces from within, to seize upon it. The operating force was three thousand troops from Rhegium under two military tribunes, Sergius and Matienus, and the pro-prætor Q. Pleminius. Hamilcar, commander of the Carthaginian garrison of Locri, appears to have been careless, and the Carthaginian soldiers under bad discipline. A panic seized the garrison upon the first attempt of the Romans to scale the walls, which was done by but a small party, and the first citadel was lost. Hamilcar hereupon withdrew into the second citadel. The townsmen held the city between the two citadels, which were not far apart, awaiting events. Pleminius held one and Hamilcar the other.

Hearing of the threatened capture of Locri, Hannibal at once moved thither, and sent orders ahead from the river Butrotus for Hamilcar to make a vigorous sortie when he

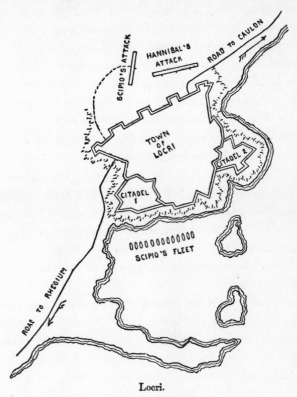

Locri.

himself should attack the town and the citadel held by the Romans. Scipio at Messana heard of Hannibal's movement on Locri, and, setting sail with the next tide, arrived in the port a few hours later on the same day that Hannibal put in an appearance. During the night he landed his men and hid them in the town, whose population leaned towards the Romans. When Hannibal next day advanced to the attack of the town, Hamilcar having begun the battle, and was placing his ladders in position, Scipio led out his troops from one of the town gates and attacked him in flank and rear. Quite unexpected, this attack demoralized Hannibal's raw levies, and, completely upsetting his plans, forced him to retire to camp; when hearing that Scipio was in command, and that the Locrians were favorable to him, he left Locri, and ordered Hamilcar to evacuate the second citadel and follow him. Scipio left a garrison in Locri under Pleminius, and returned to Sicily. Hannibal's Bruttian levies were now of such poor material that he was often unable to get them to face the Roman veteran legions. He had to acknowledge defeat on more than one occasion from this cause.

The Carthaginian rule had been severe, but Roman cruelty and rapacity surpassed everything the Locrians had so far endured, and they had good cause to regret the change. The account of the conduct of the Roman troops and their commanders shows that even Roman discipline could be lax, and Roman laws disregarded, among themselves as well as towards outsiders.

During this year the Macedonian imbroglio was brought to an end by a treaty of peace with Rome. The Carthaginian senate, too late aware that its failure to sustain Hannibal had brought about the danger of a new descent upon Africa, now sent to Philip to urge a fresh invasion of Italy. It was in vain. A small Macedonian corps sent to Carthage was the only response. When Carthage could be saved, the senate would not; now that the senate was willing, Carthage was beyond saving.

Scipio was not elected consul the succeeding year, B. C. 204, but was allowed, as proconsul, to continue his preparations for a descent on Africa. He does not seem to have been very expeditious about the business. In this he resembled McClellan, as well as in his popularity. All thinking men

saw that the best manner of ridding the country of Hannibal, who, like the Old Man of the Sea, had bestridden Italy
for so many years, was to force his recall from the peninsula
by attacking Carthage on her own soil. Scipio could see this
fact, and he appeared anxious to cross the strait; but his
tardiness looks as if he too may have been wary of too close
a contact with the giant, however weakened, unless he could
have things his own way.

The consuls were M. Cornelius Cethegus and P. Sempronius Tuditanus. To the latter was confided the task of
watching Bruttium with freshly levied legions; to Cornelius' lot fell Etruria, with the old army. Two additional
legions were continued in Bruttium, under Licinius. The
total force under arms was again nineteen legions. The prae-
tors were Claudius Nero in Sardinia, Marcius Ralla in the
city, Scribonius Libo in Gaul, Pomponius Matho in Sicily.

The twelve Latin confederates which had in B. C. 209 refused to furnish their contingents were punished now that
Rome had recovered her equipoise. They were Nepete, Su-
trium, Ardea, Cales, Alba, Carseoli, Sora, Suessa, Setia,
Circeii, Narnia, Interamna. They were compelled to furnish
double the number of men which were properly their quota;
and these were not only drafted from the wealthy classes,
but were sent out of Italy on the hardest service. A heavy
tax was imposed upon these socii.

Epidemics still raged in the camps of the Romans and
Carthaginians in Bruttium, which prevented Hannibal, if inclined even, to undertake any special operations. As he had
waited, year after year, for the advent of Hasdrubal, conducting practically but a defensive system of warfare in a country
he had invaded, so now, again hoping that his brother Mago
might have better fortune, he based his hopes on what Mago
should accomplish in Liguria, and patiently held his ground

on the enemy's soil, eager to seize any opportunity which
good fortune might present of joining forces and once more
becoming an active menace to Rome.   His army, weak years
ago, was still more so now.   His inability to relieve Locri
shows the poor quality of the force he headed.   He was
hand-tied.   As servant of the Carthaginian senate, he could
do nothing but await orders where he stood.   As adviser
of the Carthaginian senate, he had found in his days of prosperity that he was not hearkened to, — how should he be
heeded now ?   And yet he knew full well that the war was
drawing to a close ; that the term of his usefulness as a soldier had expired.

Among Scipio's political successes while in Spain had been
the detaching of Masinissa, a king of Numidia, and Syphax,
king of Massæsylia, from the Carthaginian alliance.   Hasdrubal, son of Gisgo, on his return from Spain, had however
managed, by giving him his daughter in marriage, to reclaim
the latter to the Carthaginian cause.   It became essential
that Scipio should hurry his preparations for the African
campaign, lest his men should catch alarm by hearing of the
defection before sailing ; lest, indeed, the defection should
spread.   For the alliance of the native kings was one of the
conditions to which Scipio and his army attached a peculiar
value.

Gallic Swordsman.   (Antonine Column.)

XLI.

ON TO CARTHAGE. 204-203 B. C.

SCIPIO sailed from Lilybæum in the spring of B. C. 204. He had over thirty thousand of the best troops, mostly Cannæ survivors, hardened by many years' service in Sicily. He landed near Utica. Carthage was terror-stricken. She had small means with which to resist a good army. But Hasdrubal and Syphax raised a respectable force, though it was of poor material, for the defense of the capital. Hanno was pushed out with a cavalry division to reconnoitre, but was defeated and cut up. Scipio was but a day's march from Carthage, which was practically undefended. If it be held that Hannibal, after Cannæ, should have marched on Rome, twelve days distant, well defended and with allies by the hundreds of thousands, what shall be said of Scipio for not seizing this opportunity? Yet, by some critics, Scipio is ranked with Hannibal as a soldier. Scipio besieged Utica, while Hasdrubal was raising an army. When this appeared, Scipio was in bad case. He retired to winter in an intrenched camp. Opposite Hannibal in Italy there was little doing. In a battle near Crotona he won the first day, and lost the next; but he still held on. This quiet continued through the winter. Hannibal hoped that Mago might win some success. In Africa, Scipio, in the early spring, beat Syphax and Hasdrubal, and destroyed their armies. These generals got together another only to have that also destroyed. Mago, in northern Italy, was defeated by the Romans, and died of his wounds. Hannibal was ordered back to Carthage. No hope left, the great captain embarked his army and landed at Hadrumetum, where he wintered. Rome was finally freed of the worst enemy she had ever encountered.

HAVING completed his arrangements, by the permission of the senate to take with him whatever troops from Sicily he chose, Scipio set sail from the port of Lilybæum, and, after some danger on the passage, landed not far from Utica, at the "Fair Promontory," in the spring of B. C. 204. His fleet anchored in the roadway of the town. He had two (perhaps three) strong legions, Roman and allied, — between thirty and thirty-five thousand foot and horse. Fifty war-galleys protected four hundred transports, on which the army was embarked. He had chosen those legions numbered five and six, which had been formed of the survivors of Cannæ, and had been on duty in Sicily as punishment for what had been deemed breach of their oaths in flying from that awful field. These troops were, in Scipio's eyes, guiltless of the charge, and they were veterans hardened by many years' campaigning in Sicily, and burning to wipe out the stigma attached to their names, and to regain the favor which they, as representatives of the defeated soldier, had under the austere Roman law been condemned to forfeit. Other Roman legionaries had survived defeats; Varro, the head and front of the disaster, had been pardoned, and had since been constantly in command; these men were merely the scape-goats, no worse than the others, but selected to be sent out into the wilderness. Scipio could not have better chosen. These legions were bound to him, body and soul, not only for this act of generosity, but from a soldier's appreciation of Scipio's brilliant and winning qualities. They, as well as the other legions, were strengthened up to sixty-five hundred men, of which three hundred were horse. The places of those who were no longer fitted for hard campaigning had been filled by volunteers. He carried with him none but the best material. It was probably the stanchest Roman army of the war.

Some generals would have declared these means insufficient; but Scipio possessed an abundance of self-confidence which supplemented material strength in all but severe tests. He was eager to command the expedition to Africa; he feared that some one might supplant him, and he sacrificed everything to this end. The number of his army has been stated from ten thousand to thirty-five thousand and upwards; Cælius inclines towards a still greater number. He says that

" birds fell to the ground for the shout of the soldiers, and that so great a multitude went on board the fleet that it seemed as if there was not a man left in Italy or Sicily." Paying small heed to such a highly-colored statement, the number was probably not far from thirty-five thousand men. This was a third more than Hannibal commanded when he attacked Rome in her strength; and in Carthage Scipio had an opponent ground down to extreme weakness by the attrition of the war, and lacking every quality and resource which made Rome powerful. There was embarked on the fleet forty-five days' rations, of which fifteen were cooked, and water for an equal period.

Scipio first proposed to besiege Utica. He deemed it wise to secure a foothold in some city. He moved his forces up from the fleet to a camp about five miles from the place, with this purpose in view.

Carthage was now as terror-stricken as Rome had been. There was at the moment no army, no general. She had

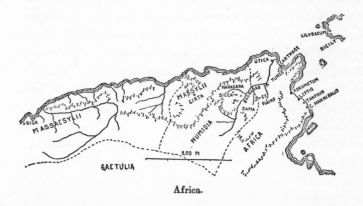

Africa.

known that a descent would be made on her coast, but with her usual improvidence she had failed to prepare for the event. She had for years frittered away her resources in short-sighted schemes instead of supporting her one captain on the true battle-ground for her cause, — Italy. We can imagine that she sadly deplored her neglect of Hannibal now that it was too late.

Mention has already been made of the two rival African kings who had already figured in the Spanish campaigns, Masinissa, the ruler of the Massylians, whose capital was Cirta, and Syphax, ruler of the Massæsylians, whose capital was Siga. Of these, the Carthaginians had succeeded in attaching to their cause the latter, by treaty and a marriage with the daughter of Hasdrubal. Masinissa, an old rival of Syphax for the hand of Sophronisbe, had succumbed to the new alliance, and was wandering in the desert with a few horsemen. In addition to what Syphax could bring, Carthage, by summary efforts, managed to raise twenty thousand foot, six thousand cavalry, and one hundred and forty elephants, — all of questionable quality. Hasdrubal, son of Gisgo, who was the general most fit for command, was for the moment on a mission to Syphax. A fair fleet lay in the harbor. A Macedonian corps was awaited, and some Celtiberian mercenaries. This force was in marked contrast to the nearly eight hundred thousand men Rome had been in a position to raise, when the Carthaginians descended from the Alps upon the Po, — to the two hundred thousand men she could have put in line at a week's notice. It well marks the difference in the task of Scipio and Hannibal.

As a first step, a small party of five hundred Numidians had been sent out. These had crossed swords with the Romans and been defeated. Then Hanno, whom Livy calls the son of Hamilcar, was dispatched with a body of four thousand horse to observe the Roman army. This general set out on his reconnoissance and camped some eight miles distant from Utica, in a town named Salera. Scipio, not liking the

threat of this corps, sent out Masinissa, who had joined him
with a Numidian body of horse, two thousand strong, to
skirmish with Hanno, and draw him back to a place where he
had stationed the bulk of his Roman cavalry in hiding behind

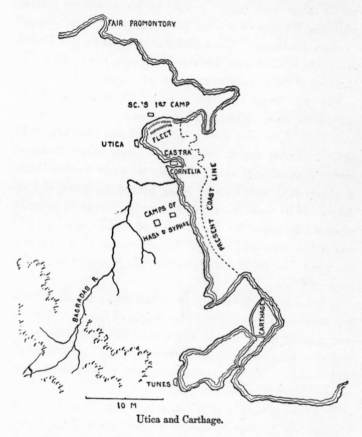

Utica and Carthage.

some hills. Masinissa accomplished his duty well. Hanno's
courage quite outran his discretion. He rightly gauged the
size of Masinissa's column as much smaller than his own, and
considering nothing more broke hastily out of camp, and fell
in careless order upon the Numidians, his ancient allies, now

all the more bitter enemies. Masinissa simulated retreat.
Hanno followed, eager for a first success. His expected triumph was short. Reaching the plain near which the Roman
horse lay in ambush, Masinissa turned again upon Hanno,
whose ranks were much broken by his overeager pursuit,
while the Romans debouched from their hiding and charged
in upon his flanks. The defeat was overwhelming. Hanno
fell at the head of some three thousand men, among them two
hundred of the most prominent sons of Carthage.

Now was Scipio's chance, if ever. Carthage was practically defenseless. She had all but no army to man her walls,
and while these were strong, they could not be readily held
against serious attack. Scipio had thirty-seven thousand
men. A small body could watch the fleet and observe Utica.
A strong day's march would bring him to the gates of Carthage. If he could not enter them at the first rush, he could
without effort shut the city in by land and by sea. And it
was at the gates of Carthage that Scipio could soonest end
the war. But he let his opportunity slip and returned to the
siege of Utica.

It is a common habit to place Scipio on a par with Hannibal, because he was victor in the battle of Zama. That the
best general is not always the winner in a battle, or at the
end of a long war, is abundantly proven by history, ancient
and modern. We Americans need not go beyond our own
recent history to prove this fact.

If it be assumed — as it often is — that Hannibal, after
Cannæ, was lacking in energy for not undertaking a two-
hundred-mile march upon Rome, well defended, and with
ample garrison, under the adverse conditions already pointed
out, what criticism shall be passed upon Scipio for neglecting
this exceptional chance of taking defenseless Carthage close
at hand? If Hannibal had failed in an attempt on Rome, the

consequences might have been disastrous, fatal to his entire scheme. But Scipio ran no danger whatsoever. He could retire from before Carthage to his base at Utica, if his anticipations should not be realized on reaching that city. Instead, then, of a vigorous course of action, he contented himself with foraging and collecting booty, which he sent by his fleet to Sicily and Rome, as if to show what he could do was more important than to accomplish results. It was safer and more like Scipio to content himself with the lesser problem. But this action helps to place him where he fairly belongs in the rank of generals.

But if Scipio lost time, not so Hasdrubal. During the forty days Scipio was wasting in siege‑preparations before Utica, this officer and his ally Syphax had been able to muster an overwhelming army, — stated by Livy at not less than eighty thousand foot and thirteen thousand horse, — and suddenly appeared in Scipio's front. It is probable that the bulk of this army was a mere rabble, all but worthless in pitched battle against Roman legions. But it put an end to any chance Scipio had of capturing Carthage out of hand. The vicinity of this force, indeed, obliged the Roman general to desist from the siege and go into defensive winter‑quarters. He was, in other words, driven back to his ships. He took up a strong position north of the Bagradas, near the coast, on a peninsula jutting out into the Gulf of Carthage, where he could take advantage of and protect his fleet, and wintered there, strongly fortifying his camp, at a place since known as Castra Cornelia. The contrast of Hannibal's early work on reaching Italy, and that of Scipio on reaching Africa, is answer enough to those who place Scipio on Hannibal's level.

The war in Italy had practically died out from sheer inanition. Hannibal was entirely shut in by surrounding armies — at least forty thousand men — to the neighborhood of Cro-

tona, without a possibility of undertaking anything, and relying solely upon the slender chance of Mago's accomplishing
some lucky stroke in Liguria. He was no longer able to force
his way towards the north; his army was of a quality quite
unequal to active operations. If he showed any military activity beyond the few recorded instances, we can only guess at
what it may have been in the light of the terror which undeniably still hung about his presence. A very few Roman generals, not to count the foolhardy ones, had dared to attack
Hannibal, — Marcellus, Fulvius, Nero, — when conditions
were well on their side. None of them, however, had been able
to inflict such a defeat on him as to compromise his safety, —
such a defeat as the Roman arms had often suffered at his
hands. The average Roman general was scrupulously careful not to burn his fingers. In Hannibal's case the vaunted
Roman fighting qualities were kept in the background.

The consul Sempronius was ambitious to see what impression he could make on Hannibal, whom he apparently encountered on the march not far from Crotona, his present base, —
probably foraging. We have no details of the combat, nor any
but Livy's account. It appears that Sempronius' attack was
a failure. He was beaten with a loss of twelve hundred men.
But what he could not do with twenty thousand men, the consul thought he might accomplish with forty thousand. Annoyed at his defeat, he retired and called on Licinius to join
him. This made four Roman and four allied legions. Hannibal could have had no more than half the number. The
Romans camped near Crotona and again offered Hannibal
battle. Feeling constrained to accept it, for he must keep
open his way for foraging, Hannibal emerged from the gates.
But the weight and quality of the Roman troops were too great
for him to win another victory. He was obliged to retire into
Crotona with a loss, as claimed by Livy, of four thousand

men. The Roman loss is not given. The consul had won a questionable victory; but Hannibal was still on Italian soil. Nor does it appear that this Livian defeat in any wise hampered his movements. The Roman army retired, and Hannibal, except for his loss in men, was uninjured. He was still free to move throughout Bruttium. Clampetia was taken by storm, and Consentia and Pandosia voluntarily submitted, but nothing else was accomplished by the Romans this year in Bruttium.

The consuls for B. C. 203, the sixteenth year of the war, were Cnæus Servilius Cæpio and C. Servilius Geminus. The former took Bruttium in charge, the latter Etruria. The prætors were P. Cornelius Lentulus in Sardinia, P. Quinctius Varus at Ariminum, P. Ælius Pætus in the city, and P. Villius Tappulus in Sicily. Scipio was confirmed in his office as proconsul till the ending of the war. There were this year twenty legions, somewhat over two hundred thousand men, and one hundred and sixty ships for duty.

Publius Sempronius was continued in command for a year and succeeded P. Licinius. Cæpio got Bruttium by lot, and commanded the army of Sempronius; Servilius Geminus got Etruria and took that of M. Cornelius. Lucretius was continued in command in order to rebuild Genoa, destroyed by Mago. Three thousand men were levied for Sicily, which had been depleted of troops by Scipio, and forty ships were on the Sicilian coast. The fleet was divided. Lentulus and Manlius retained command in Spain. Success in Africa was felt to be the great object in view, and everything bent to this one thing. Clothing and corn went thither from Sicily and Sardinia, and arms and all kinds of material from Sicily.

We left Scipio in his winter-camp at Castra Cornelia, near Utica, and his enemy, powerful in numbers if not of soldierly material, in his front, camped some six miles away. The

Carthaginians had utilized their fleet in raids on Scipio's supplies. Scipio, during all his period of delay, was endeavoring to gain Syphax to his cause; perhaps the Carthaginians were seeking to delay Scipio's operations by having Syphax keep up negotiations with Scipio looking towards peace, in the hope that either Mago might succeed in Italy, or that Hannibal might return to take command at Carthage. Nothing came of these negotiations, as it was scarcely expected there would; but Scipio was able to learn about the movements of the enemy, by means of his Roman emissaries who went to and fro between the camps. He sent with his negotiators centurions of ability and clad them as servants, whom, as not apparently soldiers, the enemy allowed to wander through the camp, where they could see and report all its details. On the whole, if the Carthaginians profited by delay, Scipio gained more than they could profit. The information thus derived, with "more artifice than honor," says Mommsen, for Scipio had not only no intention, but no right to negotiate for peace, enabled him to form a project for defeating the Carthaginian plans. His negotiators and their "servants," of whom he chose different ones on each occasion, so as to have as many points of view as possible, had reported that the discipline within the Punic lines was lax — the more so for the negotiations, very naturally — and the camps badly guarded.

When he had learned all he desired, Scipio broke off the negotiation. "Thus," says Livy, "he put an end to the truce, in order that he might be free to execute his designs without breaking his faith," — a wonderful instance of literal honesty. During the entire war there is no sample of "Punic Faith" which approaches Scipio's trickery in this matter, unless it be Hasdrubal's negotiations in Spain with Nero. Hannibal misled the Romans by every device, known and unknown; but he never violated a truce, nor is there an instance

of his deceit on record which the conditions do not fully justify. Scipio was perhaps warranted in playing what he understood to be the Carthaginian game; but the Romans
could not afford to throw stones.

Early in the year B. C. 203, Scipio dispatched a corps of
two thousand men to take up the same position near Utica
which he had previously occupied, and shipped engines and
siege-material to the place, in order to lead the enemy to believe that he was about to resume the siege, and at the same
time to forestall a sally while he should be absent. This ruse
succeeded absolutely. Hasdrubal and Syphax kept only this
movement in view, while Scipio had made his plans to attack
and burn their camps. Under cover of the diversion on
Utica, Scipio broke up one night, shortly after dark, he commanding one half his army, and his efficient legate the other.
To Lælius and Masinissa was assigned the task of setting
fire to the camp of Syphax, the huts in which were woven of
reeds and covered with mats; he himself undertook the Carthaginian matter, where the huts were of wood, equally in-
flammable. By the knowledge acquired of the enemy's can-
tonments, both parties so moved as to close all the debouches
to their camps by suitable bodies of troops; and from the fact
that there was no out-post service, nor any regularity in the
shape of the camps, the surprise was easy. Lælius and Masinissa first reached the camp of Syphax and set it on fire.
The frightened Africans, supposing the fire to be accidental,
rushed out unarmed, only to be met by another form of death.
The Carthaginian army, equally terrified at the fire, and
quite unaware of its origin, lest their own should fall also
a prey to the flames, deserted the camp in herds. They fell
in like manner upon Scipio's legions, which cut them down
without mercy. Having thus destroyed the bulk of the Carthaginian army and dispersed the rest, the camp of Hasdrubal

was also set on fire. Only twenty-five hundred men and the two generals are said to have escaped. No less than forty thousand men were killed and five thousand taken, with endless Carthaginian nobles, eleven senators, one hundred and seventy-four ensigns, twenty-seven hundred horses and six elephants. Scipio then actually set about resuming the siege of Utica, as well as moved out into the adjoining country, and captured several towns.

The Carthaginian senate behaved with courage and prudence; it "breathed the spirit of Roman constancy," says Livy. Hasdrubal and Syphax managed to collect new troops in a comparatively short time. These, with the fugitives who reassembled, amounted to thirty-five thousand men, including Celtiberians, of whom a fine body was enlisted in a town named Abba, and a few Macedonians who had come from Philip. This force they again brought to confront Scipio on the " Great Plains," five days' march from Utica.

But they accomplished nothing by their energy and diligence. Scipio again moved against them and took up a position on a hill five miles from the king's camp. For three days constant skirmishing occurred between the lines : on the fourth the lines met in battle. The Carthaginian line consisted of a miserable lot of rustics and vagabonds, whom nothing could constrain to face the Roman charge. Only the Celtiberians in the centre fought with any show of valor. These men fell where they stood; the rest decamped, but were largely overtaken and cut down. The slaughter ended, Scipio detailed Lælius and Masinissa, with a chosen body of horse sustained by some light infantry, to follow up the fugitives and to prevent their reassembling. Both leaders again escaped. Hasdrubal took refuge in Carthage and Syphax fled towards Cirta.

Scipio, who was bringing up his engines to the walls, then

left to the fleet the duty of blockading the port of Utica; and marched with the bulk of his army against Carthage, ravaging the country on the way, and capturing several towns which were necessary to holding his position. Their names are not given us.

Syphax was not readily abashed. His newly-wedded wife, the daughter of Hasdrubal, exerted great influence over him and prevailed on him to remain true to his alliance. He retired to Numidia, whither he was followed by Lælius and Masinissa, a march of fifteen days. He tempted fortune in still a third battle against Lælius and Masinissa, but was wounded and this time himself captured. On this occasion his then capital, Cirta, which he had taken from Masinissa, fell into the hands of the Romans. Scipio could congratulate himself on having able lieutenants.

The Carthaginians showed a worthy spirit of resistance; everything was done to fortify and victual the city for a siege. No mention was made of peace.

Advancing to Tunes, Scipio found this town abandoned by its garrison. He occupied it, in the hope that his near presence might oblige Carthage to surrender. The Carthaginians sent orders to Hannibal and Mago to return to Carthage. They then essayed to destroy the Roman fleet and relieve the blockade of Utica, but unsuccessfully: and the news of Syphax's defeat robbed them of any hope of continuing the war to any advantage. The peace party prevailed; Hasdrubal was condemned to death, though the sentence was afterwards revoked; overtures of peace were made in earnest. Later, when the patriot party again won the upperhand, the senate made a veil of continuing negotiations for peace, hoping that time might aid their cause. They begged for an armistice, made a show of agreeing to all the terms Scipio proposed, including the evacuation of Italy and Gaul; the cession of

Spain and all Mediterranean islands ; giving up all their war-
vessels except twenty ; and the payment of a heavy indem-
nity in wheat and money.   A truce was agreed to while the
treaty was sent to Rome for ratification.   Meanwhile the
Carthaginians were aiming to get Hannibal and Mago back
in season to forestall further disaster.

Mago had advanced into cisalpine Gaul as far as the territory of the Insubrians.   The proconsul M. Cornelius and the
prætor Quinctilius, with four legions, moved up to oppose
him.   It would have perhaps been wiser of Mago to avoid
battle, and make a push southwards to join fortunes with his
brother.   But he chose to fight and displayed all the family
skill and courage.   The Roman cavalry was defeated by
Mago's elephants, and the legions thrown into confusion.   Victory appeared certain for Mago.   But a Roman troop bravely
attacked the elephants, which, as usual, wheeled around on
their friends and turned the tide.   Serious wounds prevented
Mago's personal efforts to retrieve the disaster.   The loss of
the Carthaginians was five thousand ; of the Romans, twenty-
three hundred killed, figures which show heavy fighting.
Among the Romans were three military tribunes, twenty-
two distinguished knights, and several centurions.   The relics
of the Carthaginian army retired to the coast.   But a small
portion of his forces reached Africa, for which place they
sailed on receiving the senate's orders to return.   Mago died
on his voyage home.

Thus was extinguished the sole remaining hope of Hannibal.   He was now in every sense alone, for Mago was his last
brother.   Hanno had fallen the year before when Scipio first
landed in Africa.   Towards the end of the summer he too
received the orders of the senate to return to Carthage.   The
Fates were inexorable !   For years the smiles of Fortune had
ceased for him.   They now beamed warmly upon the young

Roman chieftain who was laying siege to the capital of his own dear land, as he had hoped, but despite heroic efforts had been unable, to lay siege to Rome. For years he had acted the manly part; he had sought in vain to win back the favor of the capricious nymph. Now the last hope had fled. He must return home to conquer the invader at his own doors, or see his country once more humbled to a greater degradation than before.

Hannibal accomplished a difficult military feat in saving his army in Bruttium. Curiously enough, he was not seriously interfered with during his operation, despite that the senate had ordered the Roman army in his front to attack him. If it did so, we have no record of it. Perchance Hannibal's measures were too well taken to warrant interference. Valerius Anteas states that the Romans fought a battle with Hannibal in which five thousand Carthaginians were slain. But there are no other records of such an action, and Livy doubts it. Hannibal embarked at Crotona and brought his army safely to Africa. He left a few small garrisons behind to protect his movement, which the consul later reduced; and on his own ships, for Carthage sent him no fleet, and not covered by the truce existing between Scipio and Carthage, but by his own skill and rapidity, he embarked for Castra Hannibalis.

Hannibal had been obliged to kill his horses for lack of transportation. That he killed those Italians in his army who refused to accompany him to Africa is not to be credited. He could persuade many and force the rest aboard, and did in fact do so. That many went against their will is an additional reason for his having such poor material in his ranks at Zama. Hannibal reached the African continent in safety, with some twenty-four thousand men, disembarked at Leptis towards the end of the year B. C. 203, and wintered at Hadrumetum.

Hannibal had set out from Carthage as a mere boy. He
had victoriously fought his way all around the Western Sea;
he now returned as an old man to seek to save a lost cause.
Emboldened by his return, the Carthaginians broke the truce,
made but for a purpose, by seizing some Roman vessels bearing victuals for Scipio, which had been driven into the port
of Carthage by a storm, and by attacking Scipio's messengers, who came to Carthage to demand satisfaction. Scipio,
perhaps expecting nothing less, began preparations to resume
hostilities.

" Meanwhile, hope and anxiety daily and simultaneously
increased; nor could the minds of men be brought to any
fixed conclusion, whether it was a fit subject for rejoicing, that
Hannibal had now at length, after the sixteenth year, departed
from Italy, and left the Romans in the unmolested possession
of it, or whether they had not greater cause to fear, from his
having transported his army in safety into Africa. They said
that the scene of action certainly was changed, but not the
danger.   That Quintus Fabius, lately deceased, who had fore-
told how arduous the contest would be, was used to predict,
not without good reason, that Hannibal would prove a more
formidable enemy in his own country than he had been in a
foreign one; and that Scipio would have to encounter not
Syphax, a king of undisciplined barbarians, whose armies
Statorius, a man little better than a soldier's drudge, was
used to lead; nor his father-in-law, Hasdrubal, that most
fugacious general; nor tumultuary armies hastily collected
out of a crowd of half-armed rustics, but Hannibal, born in a
manner in the pavilion of his father, that bravest of generals;
nurtured and educated in the midst of arms; who served as a
soldier formerly, when a boy, and became a general when he
had scarcely attained the age of manhood; who, having
grown old in victory, had filled Spain, Gaul and Italy, from

the Alps to the Strait, with monuments of his vast achievements; who commanded troops who had served as long as he had himself; troops hardened by the endurance of every species of suffering, such as it is scarcely credible that men could have supported; stained a thousand times with Roman blood, and bearing with them the spoils not only of soldiers but of generals. That many would meet the eyes of Scipio in battle who had with their own hands slain Roman prætors, generals, and consuls; many decorated with crowns in reward for having scaled walls and crossed ramparts; many who had traversed the captured camps and cities of the Romans. That the magistrates of the Roman people had not then so many fasces as Hannibal could have carried before him, having taken them from generals whom he had slain." — Livy.

While this is not quite true, it reflects the probable sentiment at Rome. So far as Hannibal's veterans were concerned, any old soldier can estimate for himself how many would be apt to be left out of twenty-six thousand men after sixteen years of constant campaigning without substantial reinforcements in an enemy's country, where, not to refer to the losses incurred in battle, every month's victual had to be gathered at the point of the sword. There are no historical data from which to figure; but Hannibal's "veterans" could have been but a handful.

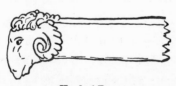

Head of Ram.

XLII.

ZAMA. SPRING 202 B. C.

THE last year of the war, B. C. 202, had no important incident but the battle of Zama. Carthage had made a truce with Scipio, but broke it. Hannibal essayed to negotiate a peace, but failed. Both generals drew up at Zama for a last struggle. Scipio had twenty thousand heavy foot and fourteen thousand light, twenty-seven hundred Roman and six thousand Numidian horse. All of this was of the best. Hannibal was very weak in cavalry. He had a small number of Carthaginian horse and two thousand Numidians. His total infantry was under fifty thousand, and he had eighty elephants. The quality of his army was low. Scipio drew up his cohorts as usual, and with cavalry on the flanks, but the maniples did not stand checkerwise. They were back of each other, making long lanes through which the elephants could be driven to the rear. The elephants were in Hannibal's front line. Then came the Gauls and Ligurians of Mago, unreliable to the last degree. The second infantry line was of Carthaginians, Africans and Macedonians, fairly good. The third had the Italians Hannibal had brought over with him from Bruttium, mostly against their will, with a very small leaven of his old soldiers. In the battle the elephants proved useless. Scipio's cavalry drove Hannibal's from the field, as Hannibal's had Varro's at Cannæ. The Carthaginian first and second lines made poor resistance to Scipio's hastati and principes. In the struggle of Hannibal's third line against Scipio's fresh formation, it seems that Hannibal came very close to victory ; but the Roman and Numidian horse returned from pursuit, and fell upon his flanks and rear. The battle was lost, and Rome imposed her own terms on Carthage. Hannibal lived nineteen years after Zama, partly in the service of his country, partly as a fugitive from Roman hate.

THE coming year, B. C. 202, the consuls were M. Servilius Geminus and Tiberius Claudius. Each desired Africa as his sole province, but neither received it; Scipio was retained, but Claudius was allowed to go to Africa with equal authority. There were sixteen legions in service, including the three on duty in Africa. Scipio was continued in his command.

Hannibal had joined to his own army of twenty-four thousand men the remains of Mago's forces, twelve thousand strong, which had returned from Liguria, and some new levies, —forty-eight thousand men in all. He had with much effort procured some two thousand Numidian cavalry from king Tychaos, but had not had time to discipline the body. His army numerically was strong enough. He had carried through his most successful campaigns, had won his most brilliant victories, with less. But he lacked now that famous cavalry which had always been his strongest arm, and the infantry was far from being reliable or such as he had in his palmy days been able to command. In this respect Scipio was vastly his superior. It may fairly be claimed that the legions about to face Hannibal were the best which had ever fought for the cause of Rome.

Scipio had taken his revenge for the Carthaginian breach of the truce by passing from Tunes into the rich valley of the Bagradas, devastating right and left and selling the inhabitants as slaves. He had got up the valley to the region of Sicca. His purpose was not only retaliation, but to isolate Carthage, cut it off from supplies from the interior, and strengthen his own position. His work was thorough, if not bold. The result of this work Hannibal foresaw must soon prove fatal. Urged by the Carthaginian senate and by this manifest fact, he left Hadrumetum and advanced to Zama, not far from Sicca, about five days' march southwest of Carthage, near which place the Roman army already lay.

The exact location of Zama is not known. It was probably on the west bank of the Bagradas. Hannibal was intent on either concluding a satisfactory peace, which he himself now saw was the wisest thing to do; or, if this was impossible, of appealing for the last time to the arbitrament of arms. Some of his spies, sent out to ascertain the position of Scipio, were captured. Instead of being given the treatment usual to spies, these men were by Scipio's orders conducted through the Roman camp, shown everything, and sent back to report what they had seen to Hannibal. Scipio was satisfied with his army, and what he could do with it.

Hannibal sought and obtained an interview with the Roman general. This took place near Naraggara, towards which place both armies moved, and camped four miles apart. The interview was held between the two camps on a hill in sight of all. The generals dismissed their suites, retaining each only an interpreter. There is not a more interesting picture in history than the encounter of these two men, who had never personally met, yet knew each other's character and ability so well. The greater was the representative of the losing cause; the servant of a senate and people which had ruined his country by their folly; the one man who had been right when his government had been wrong. The other was the servant of a republic whose stanchness and wisdom no disasters could defeat, whose cause was bound to win, not because it had greater generals, but because of the strength of its organization and the soundness of its body politic. The interview led to no results. Scipio insisted on the unconditional surrender of Carthage. This Hannibal would not grant. There remained but an appeal to battle.

It is altogether probable that Hannibal was acting under positive instructions from the Carthaginian senate. That body was unteachable and not apt to forego its right of dictation. Aware of his lack of strength, it would have been more like Hannibal, had he been unhampered, to manœuvre for a better chance for battle than in an open plain with the superiority in cavalry on the enemy's side. However this may be, the two armies next day drew up before each other in the open plain near Zama, for a last and bitter struggle. The

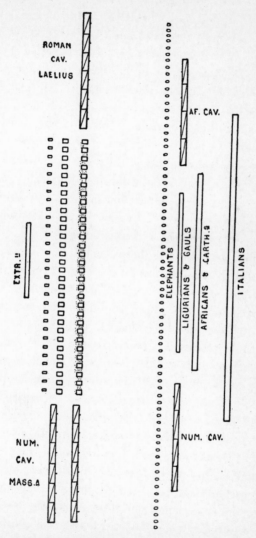

Troops in line at Zama.

date of October 19, fixed by a certain solar eclipse, is not correct. The time was probably the spring of 202 B. C.

Scipio had lately received reinforcements, brought by Masinissa, of six thousand infantry and six thousand Numidian cavalry. The cavalry was of the best; the foot would fight well in company with the Roman legions. He had his two Roman and two allied legions. That he had three, as stated by some authorities, is doubtful. His two counted eight thousand hastati, eight thousand principes and four thousand triarii, twenty thousand heavy foot. His light troops, including Masinissa's, were at least fourteen thousand strong, and he had twenty-seven hundred Roman and allied cavalry, and Masinissa's six thousand Numidian horse. His total force was thus nearly forty-three thousand men.

Hannibal had hitherto been superior in cavalry. This time it was the reverse, though the exact number Hannibal could dispose of is not known. There was some Carthaginian cavalry, but it was green, and there were only two thousand Numidians, usually Hannibal's chief reliance. He had been unable to bring his horses from Italy, so that his old cavalry, if any of it was left, was newly mounted and mixed with the Carthaginian. His infantry force, including twelve to eighteen thousand light troops, was somewhat short of fifty thousand men, and he had eighty elephants. Numerically he was stronger, in material far weaker, than his opponent.

Scipio's legions were formed in the usual three lines, but the maniples, instead of standing checkerwise, were placed behind each other, the intervals making long lanes right through the army from front to rear. In the first line the light troops filled the intervals, with orders to attack the elephants and drive them back on Hannibal's line, or failing this, to vacate the intervals by stepping behind the hastati or principes, and allow them to tramp through these lanes to the rear of the army, wounding them on the way. This arrangement, in view of Hannibal's large number of elephants, was admirable. Masinissa, with his Numidian cavalry, stood on the right flank; Lælius, now quæstor, with the Roman and allied cavalry, on the left.

Hannibal placed his elephants in front and his infantry in three lines. In the first were the mercenary light troops, — Ligurians and Gauls, whom Mago had enlisted in Italy, Balearians and Moors, twelve thousand strong. On these Hannibal was far from placing reliance. He posted them in front, hoping to tire the Roman hastati and blunt their weapons. In the second line, at the usual distance in rear of the first, were Africans, Carthaginians and Macedonians, also about twelve thousand in number. These were the troops which had been raised by Carthage after Hasdrubal's last defeat. They were of fairly good material, but fresh levies, not yet used to campaigning and unaccustomed to their surroundings. They were placed between the two lines, says Polybius, so that each one should be forced, according to the maxim of Homer, to show his bravery in spite of himself.

In the third line were the troops he had brought from Italy, commanded by Hannibal in person, about twenty-four thousand in number. We already know the composition of these troops. There was a small nucleus of old stock in them, in which the instinct of victory was still strong. But the bulk was made up of Bruttians enlisted in the past few years, most of whom would have preferred to remain behind in Italy to crossing to Africa to fight the battles of Carthage, — men pressed into the service, in fact. The whole body was the same which had, during the past few campaigns, barely held its own against the Roman legions in action, and this only by the ability of its chief. The one element in its favor was the personal devotion of the men to

Hannibal, despite the fact that he had thus forced them away from home.

The front of this third line was about equal to Scipio's, which being the case, the first and second lines must have been very thin or of much less front, probably the latter. The third line was, as it were, held in reserve farther back, over a stadium from the second line, so that, if beaten or called in, the two first lines could retire about its flanks without confusion. The infantry was all in phalangial order. The African cavalry was opposed to Lælius; the Numidians were on the left, opposite to Masinissa.

This formation was well conceived. Hannibal not only hoped that his cavalry would be able to prevent the Roman line from encompassing the flanks of his first and second lines, but that these lines would break, or at least seriously unsettle, the steadiness of the Roman centre, whereupon he might, with his reserves, complete their defeat before the triarii could reëstablish the fight. This patchwork body was appealed to by as many different motives as there were nationalities. The Gauls fought from native hatred of Rome; the Bruttians from fear of Roman vengeance, love of pay and hope of spoil; the Ligurians in the hope that they would return to the fertile plains of northern Italy; the Africans from fear of the tyranny of Masinissa, if they should not conquer; the Carthaginians alone from love of country. This was material in great contrast to Scipio's. There was defeat lurking in it, unless, perchance, Hannibal's personality should exert an exceptional influence, and things worked well.

There appears to have been no preliminary fighting of light troops between the lines. As the engagement opened, after the Numidians had indulged in some skirmishing, Hannibal's elephants were pushed sharply forward. But the Romans received them with the blast of many trumpets, usual at the beginning of a battle, and now employed for a double purpose, and with their battle-cry and a violent clashing of spear and sword on shield. This attempt to frighten these ill-trained monsters produced such good effect that, in lieu of trampling down the legionaries, they rushed wildly to right and left or through the Roman lanes, while many of them stampeded towards the Roman right wing, whence they were driven against the Numidian cavalry on the Carthaginian left, throwing it into great confusion.

This disorder was at once taken advantage of by Masinissa, who was a cavalry leader of no mean order. He dashed down with his own Numidian horse upon the Numidian allies of Hannibal to so good effect, that these squadrons were speedily broken and driven in utter disarray from off the field. Other elephants, wounded and chased by the velites, of whom, however, they had crushed many, fell back upon the Carthaginian cavalry and produced marked confusion in its ranks. Lælius, equally sharp-eyed as Masinissa, launched his own horse upon the Carthaginians at this instant, broke their ranks and sent them whirling backward, beyond usefulness for the day. The Roman and Numidian cavalry followed in pursuit. The elephants, as has so often been the case in war, had proved allies of the enemy. Thus at the outset Hannibal was deprived of his entire body of horse. His flanks were naked.

The same cavalry manœuvre threatened to lose Zama which had won Cannæ.

The elephants and cavalry thus disposed of, the infantry alone remained to contend for mastery. Scipio noticed that, while of less front, Hannibal's first two lines were heavier than his own. He remembered that the Gauls, more than once, with their fierce gallantry, had broken through the intervals and attacked the flanks of the Roman maniples, and he feared that his centre might be broken. Instead of filling the intervals of the hastati-maniples with the principes, he gave orders quickly to close the intervals of the maniples of the first line on the centre, while the second and third lines should keep their distances so as to overlap and protect its flanks, and ˙be ready to move up to sustain the first line. He thereupon sounded the charge.

The Gauls and Ligurians of the first Carthaginian line fought with consummate bravery, but proved no match for the tremendous shock of the veteran Roman legions.

" In addition to this there was one circumstance, trifling in itself, but at the same time producing important consequences in the action. On the part of the Romans the shout was uniform, and on that account louder and more terrific; while the voices of the enemy, consisting as they did of many nations of different languages, were dissonant. The Romans used the stationary kind of fight, pressing upon the enemy with their own weight and that of their arms; but on the other side there was more of skirmishing and rapid movement than force. Accordingly, in the first charge, the Romans immediately drove back the line of their opponents; then pushing them with their elbows and the bosses of their shields, and pressing forward into the places from which they had pushed them, they advanced a considerable space, as though there had been no one to resist them, those who formed the rear urging forward those in front, when they perceived the line of the enemy giving way, which circumstance itself gave great additional force in repelling them." — Livy.

Hannibal's second line, consisting of Carthaginian and African new levies, unlike their Roman antagonists failed to second the efforts of the first line, but moved up to its support in so undecided and sluggish a manner that the first-line

allies conceived the impression that the Carthaginians were
about to desert them. Maddened with fury at this idea, and
at the same time borne back by the Roman hastati, they
turned upon and attacked the Carthaginian second line, thus
for the moment emulating the elephants in giving succor to
the foe. The second line resisted the onset, however, better
than they had sustained the fighting of the first. In a brief
space the relics of the first line had disappeared around the
flanks of the second and practically dispersed, like the elephants and cavalry. Order was reëstablished by Hannibal,
and a temporary resistance to the onset of the hastati, who
were weary with fighting, was enough to throw the latter into
considerable confusion. Even the principes were somewhat
unnerved, which speaks well for the fighting done by the
Africans and Carthaginians. But the principes recovered
themselves and came up at the opportune moment to sustain
the flanks of the hastati, and, with a joint effort, Hannibal's
second line was definitely broken and hustled back. Its first
disorder was multiplied sevenfold. So wild was its flight
that only the protended lances of Hannibal's third line prevented its rushing upon and disorganizing this also.

The ground between the rival armies was littered with
dead and wounded, and with the weapons of those who had
lost them bravely, and those who had cast them away in flight.
Scipio sounded the recall to his hastati, and sent out his velites to collect the Roman wounded.

Hannibal still had his twenty-four thousand Italian troops.
Among these were the few remaining veterans of his Old
Guard, whose intense devotion to their chief made them all
but invincible. But they were a bare handful, which could
not leaven the lump. Scipio's velites and hastati had already
suffered great loss and were disorganized by the effects of the
struggle, but his principes had lost but few men, and his

triarii were fresh. The Romans had more and better men.
There was not apt to be manœuvring; the battle was to be
decided by the shock and by hand-to-hand fighting.

The Roman and Masinissa's cavalry had pursued the Carthaginians too far from the field, but Scipio was confident
that it would return in time to turn the tide in his favor.   He
could afford to wait.   Hannibal, on the contrary, proposed to
seize the period of their absence to advance upon the Roman
line, hoping to crush it before the horse could return to its
aid.

Some historians read Polybius and Livy to say that Scipio
took time to re-form his troops, and then attacked Hannibal;
but the time must have been short, — one of those half-hour
lulls which frequently occur in action.   It was unlike Hannibal to await an attack, or allow a loss of time under such conditions.   He must positively beat his enemy before the return
of the cavalry, or lose the battle and his country's cause.

Scipio, in order to deliver a final effective blow, found it
necessary to rearrange his troops.   This looks like change-
ableness, but shows his troops to have been well in hand.
Hannibal's reserve line was equal in front to Scipio's, and
there was always, with this crafty general, the danger of a
flank movement.   This Scipio desired to guard against, and
if possible overlap Hannibal's flanks.   Believing that the enemy's first and second lines had been so thoroughly beaten as
not to be available again for the day, and that he had only
the reserve to contend with, he determined to put in the triarii, leaving the extraordinarii and velites in reserve.   In the
short lull, while Hannibal was disposing of the scattered troops
so as to be able to advance his fresh line in perfect order, the
Roman principes were ordered quickly to close their intervals
from the centre towards each flank and move up on either
flank of the hastati; the triarii performed the same manœu-

vre, and moving right and left took place on the extreme flanks
of the legion. Scipio can have had barely time thus to extend
his main line when the Carthaginian reserves were seen advancing. Hannibal's front had been equal to Scipio's front
of principes, with regular intervals. It was thus equal to

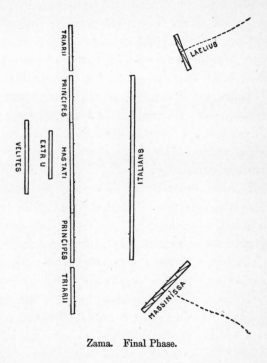

Zama.   Final Phase.

Scipio's present line of hastati and principes without intervals, and therefore the triarii extended beyond Hannibal's
flanks.

The depth of Hannibal's phalanx cannot be stated with accuracy. He had long ago assimilated his formation somewhat to the Roman, but the details we do not know. It is
probable that it was ten deep, the same as the file of a legionary maniple. It had not been the old Greek phalanx for

some years; it had been extended and the depth decreased to correspond more nearly to the Roman standard.

Scipio, by his last change, had now practically formed the Roman legions into phalangial order, though the space occupied by each man was somewhat greater with the Romans. Hannibal's troops, all through the Italian campaigns, had gradually taken to the Roman weapons, so that each was what might be called a phalanx of legionaries. Scipio had not lost many men; and though his hastati had been fighting hard, the rest and the ordering up of the principes and triarii on their flanks, and the presence of the reserves immediately behind them, would encourage them to one more effort. He still had twenty-eight thousand men in line, and the velites and extraordinarii in their rear. Hannibal had twenty-four thousand, with no reserves.

The shock was tremendous. The contention at once became desperate. Hannibal's veterans were fighting for their firesides as well as victory, and gave the example to the rest. The struggle was uncertain. Every manly effort was put forth. The battle, on the Roman side, was for the mastery of the world; on the Carthaginian, for the possession of Africa. Hannibal and Scipio each put his last ounce of moral strength into inciting the ardor of his troops. Each was omnipresent. To each this was the crowning act of the great drama. The lines met in hand-to-hand contest and held desperately to their ground. The event seemed to hang upon a hair.

It is said that Scipio was about to be overwhelmed. But Fortune, once the friend of Hannibal, but now on the side of his younger rival, turned from him in a pitched battle for the first time. Lælius and Masinissa, with such of their victorious squadrons as were not cutting down fugitives, returned from pursuit of the Carthaginian horse at

just this instant. Square against cavalry was of no avail
in the days when deadly weapons carried a bare fifty feet;
and Hannibal's line was struggling to overcome the Roman
legion. Lælius and Masinissa fell with the white weapon
upon Hannibal's line in flank and rear. There was not a
single mounted man to oppose their deadly onslaught. This
was the *coup de grâce.* No courage, no genius, on an open
plain, could turn the tide of victory. Surrounded and
crushed, Hannibal's phalanx, with the historic body which
had won at the Trebia, Trasimene, Cannæ, now but a small
group, sustained nobly its reputation. It held aloft its ensigns, and faced the foe till it was cut to pieces where it stood.
The vanquished of Cannæ were the victors of Zama.

The soldiers of the first and second Carthaginian lines had
most of them taken to flight; but in a flat country the cavalry allowed few to escape. Some twenty thousand of Hannibal's army remained on this bloody field; other twenty
thousand were made prisoners; one hundred and thirty-three
standards and eleven elephants were lost. The Romans had,
it is stated by Livy, but two thousand killed. Polybius gives
fifteen hundred. Both are manifestly in error. The loss
must have been greater.

Appian is frequently quoted as an authority on the Second
Punic War. But he is unreliable. Most prominent in his
account of the battle of Zama, which he treats at considerable length, is a duel between Scipio and Hannibal, and another one between Masinissa and Hannibal, much in the
Homeric strain. Out of his picturesque and interesting narrative we can doubtless glean a stray fact or two; but Appian can scarcely be used when in conflict with Polybius,
Livy, or even Plutarch.

When Hannibal saw that the battle was irretrievably lost,
knowing that his country now needed his counsel more than

ever, he displayed a greater moral courage than his brother Hasdrubal, and left the field with a small escort to return to Hadrumetum. Scipio plundered Hannibal's camp and then returned to Utica, proposing to lay siege to Carthage so soon as he had recuperated from the efforts of the battle.

The loss of the battle of Zama left the Carthaginians no means of further resisting Rome. They at once tendered submission, and were obliged to accept the terms offered by Scipio, namely: —

1. To make reparation for breaking the truce. 2. To deliver up all their war-ships but ten, and all their elephants. 3. To deliver up all Roman prisoners and deserters. 4. To undertake no war outside of Africa, nor in Africa without consent of Rome. 5. To restore Masinissa to the throne they had taken from him. 6. To provide for the Roman army three months. 7. To make an annual payment of two hundred talents for fifty years. 8. To deliver up one hundred hostages to be chosen by the Romans. Had Hannibal not been beyond reach at the moment, his surrender would have been demanded; and, as in the case of other brave soldiers who had fought against Rome, his life would have paid the forfeit. Generosity to a beaten enemy was not one of the Roman virtues.

This humiliation, at the end of a war of eighteen years, was but a prelude to the Third Punic War, which resulted in razing Carthage to the ground.

The constancy of Rome during the Second Punic War is best measured by the casualties. These have been stated at three hundred thousand men. They must have largely exceeded this amount. Although Livy's figures manifestly underrate the Roman and overrate the Punic losses, we find from this historian's figures, supplemented by an occasional estimate, that the Army of Italy (by which is meant the force which crossed the Alps, kept up by recruitment among Hannibal's Italian allies, and reinforced by the paltry squads which reached him from Carthage) lost in pitched battles in Italy and at Zama, about ninety thousand men. This includes no losses from the constant small-war, nor deaths from wounds or disease ; nor does it count any part of the enormous losses of the other armies in Italy or by Hannibal's allied cities, or by the operations in Spain or elsewhere. It is fair to assume that for every man killed in action two die in camp. This would make the losses of the Army of Italy during its sixteen years' campaigns, some two hundred and seventy thousand men, or nearly seven times its average strength of say forty thousand men.

Now, the Roman casualties in these same battles were over one hundred and fifty thousand men, taking the smaller figures given by the ancient authorities when a massacre ensued — *i. e.,* estimating lower losses than those given by Livy. The Romans may not have lost so large a percentage in camp, for the sum of their battle losses is high on account of these same massacres. But assuming their camp losses to be one hundred thousand men in the armies which fought Hannibal, the total would rise to a quarter of a million men. The armies on outside operations must have lost at least an equal number; making a sum of half a million men during the sixteen years. This seems to be a low estimate, but it was a terrible drain on the population of Rome.

Hannibal was later enabled to return to his native city. He lived nineteen years after the battle of Zama ; he devoted himself to the service of Carthage, and was elected chief magistrate; but, in endeavoring to check abuses, he raised against himself enemies in the government; and when, in B. C. 195, he was suspected by Rome of fostering an alliance against her with Syria, and his delivery as a hostage for the good behavior of Carthage was demanded, Hannibal was forced into flight. He took refuge with Antiochus, king of Syria, who not long after was at war with Rome. Had Antiochus been wise enough to follow Hannibal's advice, he might not have been beaten at Magnesia. In the treaty of peace which ensued, he was ordered to deliver up Hannibal to the Romans, but, learning of this clause, Hannibal again fled, this time to the court of Prusias, king of Bithynia. Rome never felt secure until his death. This occurred, some say by suicide, at the age of sixty-four, fearing that Prusias might be induced to deliver him up.

Outpost Blockhouse on River. (Antonine Column.)

XLIII.

THE MAN AND SOLDIER.

THE Barcas traced their lineage back to Dido. They were at this period the most distinguished of the noble families of Carthage. Hamilcar had four sons, Hannibal, Hasdrubal, Hanno and Mago. Three died in defense of their country. The greatest lived to aid Carthage in her sorest need. Hannibal's education was of the best. All that Carthage could teach, and Greece withal, was assimilated by him. He wrote several books in Greek. His military education he received from his father, and practically in Spain under his brother-in-law, Hasdrubal. When his father died, Hannibal became the head of the Barcas. The Phœnicians were no taller than the Romans, but the beauty of their women is often spoken of. Hannibal was tall for his race, strong, and of commanding presence. His features were noble, and his smile as friendly as his anger was terrible. He was peculiarly endeared to his army by his sharing all their dangers, as well as by his skill and strength in martial exploits. His character was pure and noble. All that his enemies have been able to say cannot besmirch it. What we know of him has been written by his enemies ; he is the sole great captain of whom we must thus judge. The Roman historians credit him with exemplary virtues ; they charge him with cruelty, perfidy, impiety, avarice. As regards cruelty, war was, at that era, cruel beyond anything we can imagine. That Hannibal was less cruel personally than the Romans appears conclusively from their own testimony. His perfidy consisted in the employment of stratagems in war, which even to-day are allowable, but which the Romans could not understand. His impiety lay largely in his believing in other gods than the Romans. He was wealthy, perhaps avaricious ; but he used his money, not for his own personal gratification, but to maintain his army and the war against Rome. Hannibal was deep, original, bold, secretive and self-reliant, persuasive as an orator and as a statesman. His power over men was extraordinary. No one ever held an army of such heterogeneous materials together under such trials as he. His career tells its own story best. No captain has so brilliant a record as he in the first three years in Italy, — but what he did in the dozen years after Cannæ is still more wonderful. He had taught the Romans how to wage war, and they waged it against him with ability. Abandoned by Carthage, he maintained himself in Italy by a series of bold and skillful campaigns against vast odds, which have no equal in history. He taught the Romans their trade, and is worthily named " The Father of Strategy."

In the galaxy of great captains the stars are equal. Many claim for Hannibal a lustre beyond the others. Measuring his task and resources by those of any soldier of history, he may be not untruthfully said to be *primus inter pares.* His character has already been drawn in his wonderful campaigns; but, at the risk of repetition, it is worth while to sum up the man and soldier.

The Barcas were an old race, on whose family-tree the names of Belus and Dido were written in letters of gold. Its pride was inborn; it held up its head from no upstart arrogance. Genius and patriotism stood at the service of every earnest project of the state, and ennobled the race more than its ancient lineage. While Hamilcar and his sons lived, the Barcas were distinctly the first family in Carthage.

Hamilcar had four sons and two daughters. Of the latter, one married a Massylian prince, the other Hasdrubal the Handsome; the sons were Hannibal, Hasdrubal, Hanno and Mago. Some authors exclude Hanno; but Livy mentions him as the son of Hamilcar when, in 204 B. C., he rode out at the head of his four thousand horse from the gates of Carthage never to return, and Valerius Maximus makes Hamilcar speak of " four lion's whelps which I have raised to exterminate the Roman name."

The earliest recollection of Hannibal was the sight of his father clad in mail; the first stories to which he listened were those of his father's wonderful defense of Ercte and Eryx against the Romans. His childhood's pleasures were in the camp; the keenest impulse on which he acted was hatred of the name of Rome. The Phœnicians were good haters. Hannibal proved no exception.

The most familiar story about the lad Hannibal is that of the oath taken by him at the instance of his father, before accompanying him to Spain. Silius Italicus places the scene in the sanctuary of Dido: " So soon as age will permit," the oath ran, " I will follow the Romans both at sea and on land. I will use fire and steel to arrest the destiny of Rome. Nei-ther the gods, nor the treaty which forbids us war, — nothing shall stop me. I will triumph over the Alps as over the Tar-peian Rock. I swear it by the god Mars who protects me! I swear it, great Queen, by thy august manes!"

The education given to Hannibal, and already referred to, was — though Hannibal was his father's favorite — no doubt equally partaken by the others, and took root according to the character of each lad. The sons, like the father, were all soldiers; each died a soldier's death, except Hannibal, who acted the part of a true patriot and lived to rehabilitate the fortunes of his native land.

Speaking of Hannibal's abilities, Dion Cassius observes that " he owed these advantages not only to nature, which had endowed him with her gifts, but also to a broad instruction. Initiated according to the custom of his country to the know-ledge spread among the Carthaginians, he added to them the light of the Greeks." And referring to his mental gifts, " This great man," says Cornelius Nepos, " though occupied in such vast military operations, devoted a portion of his time to literature, for there are some books of his written in the Greek language, and among them one addressed to the Rho-dians on the acts of Cnæus Manlius Vulso in Asia." Han-nibal's teacher in Greek was a Macedonian named Sosyles, who, with one Philenus, was much in the Punic camp and in Hannibal's company; and these two men contributed to the knowledge of Cornelius Nepos about the great Punic leader.

These facts, from Roman sources, abundantly prove Hannibal's mental equipment and culture. He was a "barbarian" among the Romans much in the same sense that we are barbarians to many of the peoples of the Orient.

On the death of his father, Hannibal formally succeeded him as the head of the Barca family. He perpetuated the teachings of Hamilcar.

The Carthaginians were not a tall race. Their average height did not probably exceed the Italian. But they were a handsome people. Many ancient authors refer to the beauty of the Phœnician women. Plautus tells us that they were straight as Grecian columns, of noble shape, and that they possessed the rare type of light hair with black lustrous eyes. The Carthaginian coins of the period show a distinguished cast of feature.

Hannibal was tall for a Phœnician. His figure indicated strength and agility; he carried his head high, and his face, which showed breadth and intelligence, was lighted up by an eye which beamed kindly on the friend, but which no one dared encounter when kindled by anger. His suit of hair was full, and he was wont to be much without head-gear.

It is immaterial for us to know whether Hannibal possessed beauty of feature; he certainly had stamped on his face that which is better. The only portrait of him which has any claim to authenticity, and this only because probably copied from some portrait existing at the time, — the Capuan bust given in the Frontispiece, — shows noble. lineaments; but these are marred by the Roman idea of the man, — by an attempt to express cruelty and passion.

The ideal Hannibal has been often described by Latin poets and authors, but in truth we know little of the man's person, except what we can judge from his life and his wonderful control over all who approached him. Nothing can improve upon Livy's pen-picture of the young general when he first joined Hasdrubal in Spain, which has been already quoted. It was his strength, vigor and courage which most strongly appealed to his soldiers. He excelled in all manly sports ; he was untiring in his performance of duty. He was skillful and daring beyond any officer or soldier in his command. He once swam alone a river which cut off his cavalry column, and from the other bank beckoned his men across. He was the comrade of the common soldier as he was the master of the whole army. He — as well as Alexander and Cæsar — was noted for horsemanship, and his chief pride lay in the beauty of his arms and steeds.

There are a few anecdotes which show us the human side of Hannibal. He seems to have had his love for a jest. When before the battle of Cannæ, Varro had hung out his purple cloak as a signal for battle, " this boldness of the consul," says Plutarch, " and the numerousness of his army, double theirs, startled the Carthaginians ; but Hannibal commanded them to their arms, and with a small train rode out to take a full prospect of the enemy as they were now forming in their ranks, from a rising ground not far distant. One of his followers, called Gisgo, a Carthaginian of equal rank with himself, told him that the numbers of the enemy were astonishing ; to which Hannibal replied with a serious countenance, ' There is one thing, Gisgo, yet more astonishing, which you take no notice of ; ' and when Gisgo inquired what, answered, that ' in all those great numbers before us, there is not one man called Gisgo.' This unexpected jest of their general made all the company laugh, and as they came down from the hill they told it to those whom they met, which caused a general laughter amongst them all, from which they were hardly able to recover themselves. The army, seeing Hannibal's attendants come back from viewing the enemy in such a laughing condition, concluded that it must be profound contempt of the enemy that made their general at this moment indulge in such hilarity."

Cicero tells us that when at Ephesus in exile, Hannibal attended a lecture by a philosopher named Phormio. Among other things, the lecturer expatiated upon the duties of a commander-in-chief, much to the admiration of the audience. Hannibal being asked his opinion, " I have seen," said he, " during my life many an old fool; but this one beats them all."

When Antiochus, proudly reviewing his enormous army, and quite ignorant of Roman courage and skill in war, pointed out his preponderance in force to Hannibal, and asked if these were not enough for the Romans, — " Yes," said Hannibal, " enough for the Romans, however greedy they may be."

We seize on these paltry stories with eagerness because of their scarcity. The personality of this great man is made up of mere shreds and patches from the Roman authors.

Hannibal's character was pure and elevated. His habits were simple. He drank little wine, and when chief magistrate of Carthage did not recline at his meals. He sometimes ate but once a day, rose at daybreak and retired late, says Frontinus. He faced the cold of the Alps and the scorching sun of Africa with equal unconcern. " Only a woman needs shade," quoth he. Scarcely a fault can be traced to him. Scipio's continence is a never-ending theme of praise; but no word is said of Hannibal's fidelity to Imilcea, his Spanish bride, from whom he was, almost in the honeymoon, separated for sixteen long years. " He is said to have exhibited so much pudicity among so many female captives that one would scarcely credit his having been born in Africa," testifies Justinus.

These facts are what his enemies tell us, and there is such

singular unanimity in their testimony, that we may well accept them as conclusive. Only by acknowledging Hannibal's great qualities could they mitigate the stigma of their inability to cope with him. Of all the great captains Hannibal stands alone in having not one word spoken of him by a friendly pen. This thing we must constantly bear in mind. Alexander had Ptolemy and Aristobulus beside him to record his glorious deeds; Cæsar wrote his own commentaries; but Hannibal's picture is drawn solely by his enemies. Polybius is the only even-handed historian he has; and as he was in the service of the Roman state, and gathered his materials from Roman sources, however fair he may have been, he could not but lean towards the bitter Roman prejudice. The few personal traits vouchsafed us, added to the earnest consistency of Hannibal's whole life, make up a character unsurpassed in its nobleness, which not all the venom of his foes has been able to besmirch.

Let us look at what these same enemies charge him with. Livy, after the pen-picture already quoted on page 150, adds: " Excessive vices counterbalanced these high virtues of the hero; inhuman cruelty, more than Punic perfidy, no truth, no reverence for things sacred, no fear of the gods, no respect for oaths, no sense of religion."

The impeachment may be summed up as cruelty, perfidy, impiety. To these is to be added avarice, of which it is stated by Roman and Greek authors that his own people accused him. "It is difficult," says Polybius, in summing up what ill may be said of him, " to decipher what was in truth the character of Hannibal, but one may say that with the Carthaginians he passed for avaricious, and as a cruel man among the Romans." Here, then, are four vices which it is well to examine. But this is the sum of all which is laid to Hannibal's charge, and we must judge him by the age in which he lived.

With regard to cruelty. It is only the cruelty exhibited in war to which the Romans referred. War has always been and is still cruel. It was peculiarly cruel in that era. Hannibal was herein no exception to his age. He punished for rebellion provinces which had once joined his standard. So did the Romans; what cruelty can exceed their treatment of Capua on its capture, or of Bruttium after Hannibal left the peninsula? Hannibal devastated provinces as a war measure or for subsistence; and no doubt his Numidians were guilty of much rapacity and many inhuman acts. But wherein were the Romans better? Did not Marcellus devastate the territory of Hannibal's Samnite and Lucanian allies with fire and sword, in revenge for their having given up the alliance of Rome when she failed to protect them from the Punic sword? Hannibal punished mutineers, deserters, faithless guides. There are fourfold as many cases on record during this war of the Romans doing the same thing.

In this connection the Romans speak with horror of the human sacrifices supposed to obtain in Carthage. These are not denied, but let us read Livy as to what was done in Rome, to propitiate the gods after the terrible disaster of Cannæ. "Meanwhile certain extraordinary sacrifices were performed, according to the directions of the books of the fates; among which a Gallic man and woman, and a Greek man and woman, were let down alive, in the cattle market, into a place fenced round with stone, which had been already polluted with human victims, a rite by no means Roman. The gods being, as they supposed, sufficiently appeased," etc. With what justice can the Romans denounce sacrifices to Baal? That it was only in the first century before the Christian era that Rome renounced publicly the habit of immolating prisoners to the gods, Pliny tells us. And that the Roman officers could be more brutal to conquered towns and provinces than the Carthaginians, is testified by Livy in his narration of what happened at Locri, and of the appeal of the Sicilians against Marcellus.

Cruelty was habitual with the Romans. " When Scipio," says Polybius, " believed that there had entered enough soldiers into Cartagena, he sent the most part against the inhabitants, as the Romans are accustomed to do when they capture a town by assault, with order to kill all they met, to give no quarter, . . . and thus to inspire terror of the Roman name." Scipio Æmilius cut off the hands of his captives — a common Roman punishment. Crassus hanged on crosses, erected on the road from Rome to Capua, six thousand gladiators. Cæsar exterminated in one day a tribe four hundred and thirty thousand in number, men, women and children, for fighting for their independence, — and by treachery at that. He cut the hands off thousands of Gallic prisoners, to cow their fellow-countrymen. All this is not palliative of Hannibal's cruelty, but it shows that the Romans cannot rightfully charge Hannibal with inhumanity, and that cruelty in war was not a personal vice.

Perhaps the most marked instance in which the Roman and Punic characters were contrasted was in the case of Nero. Hannibal, after the battle of Lake Trasimene, had scrupulously sought for the body of Flaminius, in the hope to give it honorable burial; he had paid the most devout rites to the bodies of Gracchus, Æmilius Paulus, Marcellus, all of whom had fallen in lawful warfare or in battle. How was he rewarded for this soldierly piety? When Nero had defeated Hasdrubal at the Metaurus, where this brave soldier had perished sword in hand, the consul cut off his head, and, transporting it a six days' journey, cast it, like the carcass of a dog, into the outposts of his brother's army. This incident is narrated by the Roman authors with the utmost unconcern.

Had Hannibal been guilty of such brutish conduct should we not have heard even more of his cruelty?

No instance of outrage or treachery alleged by the Romans against Hannibal but is more than matched by even gallant Marcellus' cutting down in cold blood the garrison of Casilinum, which had received from his colleague, Fabius, a promise of free exit to Capua; or by mild-mannered Fabius' punishment of Tarentum, or by cultured Scipio's devastation of the Bagradas Valley — or by scores of other instances. The Romans forgot their beam in gazing at Hannibal's mote. The Phœnician's cruelty was to Roman citizens. This the Romans could not forget. But when they punished Capua they forgot that the Capuans were men. So much for cruelty.

The matter of perfidy has been already spoken of in various places when Punic Faith has been the question. It is only in instances of this kind that Hannibal's perfidy is supposed to have been prominent. That ruses of war, allowable in all ages, but unknown to the Romans, should have been cleverly employed by the Phœnicians to entrap the Roman armies, sufficed to class all Hannibal's stratagems as instances of perfidy. The Romans learned the trick, and then " ce ne fût que la victoire qui décida s'il fallait dire *la foi punique* ou *la foi romaine.*" Craftiness was a Punic instinct. It was as natural for Hannibal to resort to rapid and secret marches, to employ strange ruses, to make use of unexpected schemes, to lie in ambush, as for the Romans to push straight for their objective and secure their end by stout fighting. However distasteful to the Romans, this habit was fully appreciated by the clear-sighted. "Hannibal appears to me a great captain under very many conditions," says Polybius, "but what especially makes his superiority is that, during the many years he made war and under all the caprices of fortune, he had the cleverness to mislead the enemy's generals, without his enemies ever being able to deceive him." And the Romans were not slow to pattern by his skill.

Impiety. Wherein this consisted it is hard to say, unless in the fact that the Punic gods and worship were not in all respects those sacred to the Romans. We are told by the Latin authors that Hannibal paid a vow at the temple of Hercules in Gades, in the presence of his entire army, and called on the gods to approve his march on Rome; that he sent Bostar to the temple of Jupiter Ammon to ask the oracle to pronounce on his Italian expedition; that he told his army of the dreams sent to him by Jupiter; that he took Jupiter to witness his promises to his soldiers on the Padus, — with numberless other instances of his reposing trust in his own peculiar deities. The caption of his treaty with Macedon shows that he observed the formalities of religion. "In presence of Jupiter, of Juno and of Apollo; in presence of the goddess of the Carthaginians, of Hercules and of Iolaus; in presence of Mars, of Triton, of Neptune; in presence of all the gods who protect our expedition, of the Sun, the Moon, and the Earth; in the presence of the rivers, the fields, the waters; in presence of all the gods honored in Macedonia and the rest of Greece, in presence of all the gods who preside over war, . . . Hannibal and his soldiers have said," etc., etc. That temples were sometimes profaned by his soldiers is a fact common to all warfare, — but very rarely alleged against them. The Romans were not above desecrating temples, and in all ages down to the present generation, heathen and Christian temples alike have been used for defensive purposes in war.

When Hannibal gave up a town because he feared that the inhabitants would massacre his garrison, this was a "violation of his treaties" with them which showed that he had "no respect for oaths." When he razed a town to the ground because it had massacred his garrison, this was " worse than inhuman cruelty." Half of what we hear told of Hannibal's vices comes not from historians, but from Roman poets and playwrights, who were writing to cater to the taste of the Roman plebs, and, oblivious of fact, were prolific of their gibes to raise a laugh or sneer.

Hannibal used his hatred to advantage. But he was scarcely behind the Romans in this quality. It seems to strike Livy as indefensible that Hannibal should exhibit " hatred of the Roman name." This he certainly did from boyhood to old age, consistently and heartily. He hated Rome, root and branch, and with good reason. But his hatred was manifest solely in acts warranted by the international law of that day; and that he was less barbarous than the Romans is abundantly shown by their own testimony. The Roman authors persistently misrepresent every large-hearted act of the Punic chieftain; but Hannibal's conduct towards Fabius, in sparing his farm from devastation; the respect paid to the remains of Gracchus, Marcellus, Æmilius, and many other facts, show a chivalrous spirit, which, when we remember the hatred ingrained in his very fibre, speaks the generous impulses of the true soldier. Can as much be said of Nero, bearing brave Hasdrubal's head, to cast it, brutally dishonored, at the feet of his brother? And yet history does not reproach Nero with the act, and Nero was one of the best of soldiers, who, with Marcellus, and perhaps Scipio and Fabius, stood at the head of the Roman generals. " Les reproches de l'historien " (Livy) " sont donc des louanges," says Thiers.

Avarice. The Barcas were wealthy. Their possessions in Africa were vast. When Hamilcar conquered Spain, he added largely to the family property. One mine in the neighborhood of Cartagena, Pliny tells us, is reported to have yielded them revenues amounting to nearly five thousand dollars a day, then a much larger sum than now. It is not unlikely that Hannibal hoarded his means with covetous care. But he was not miserly. He neither locked up his gold, nor did he use it for his own personal gratification. Every coin went to buy or equip or feed one more soldier. Every grain of gold dust sharpened the point of a missile which should slay a Roman legionary. If this was avarice, then Hannibal must be found guilty of the charge.

Hatred, malice and all uncharitableness have painted the picture of Hannibal. But, if we thrust aside such manifest fabrications as best furnish their own refutation, there remain but a few things which are claimed to have been done in Hannibal's name by one Monomachus and by Mago the Samnite, which can be laid at the door of this great man. This Monomachus advised Hannibal to teach the men to eat human food, as a means of rationing them on their way to Italy. "It is this Monomachus, they say, who is the author of whatever cruelty was practiced in Italy with which they charge Hannibal," says Polybius.

For generations, the naughty Roman child was frightened by "Hannibal at the gates," as the little Briton was by "Boney," and the hatred of the Punic race as exemplified in Hannibal was mixed with a sentiment of dread which Horace best sums up as "dirus Hannibal." But putting aside Roman hate and fear, there is not in history a figure more noble in its purity, more radiant in its patriotism, more heroic in its genius, more pathetic in its misfortunes, than that of Hannibal. "Ce que la posterité a dit, ce que les générations les plus reculées repéteront, c'est qu'il offrit le plus noble spectacle que puissent donner les hommes, celui du génie exempt de tout egoïsme, et n'ayant qu'une passion, le patriotisme, dont il est le glorieux martyr." — Thiers.

The depth and fecundity of Hannibal's conceptions, the originality of his system, were what made him so difficult to match. His strength of character was invincible, his will was adamant, his heart free from disturbing passions. He was intrepid, mentally and physically, and his presence of mind never forsook him. His penetration, his ability to read the enemy's purpose, to gauge his opponent's character, enabled him to lead him astray and save himself from deception. He was singularly fertile in expedients. We do not know just how he eluded his enemies on his wonderful marches through territory held by their armies, but he did so constantly during his fifteen years in Italy.

Hannibal was equal as a statesman to what he was as a soldier. This is well shown by his conduct in Italy, and especially by what he did for Carthage after Zama. No man ever united more varied qualities in their highest expression than he.

Hannibal's control over men was singular. He had the genuine orator's power of convincing his audience, of charming his hearers. He was a true leader of peoples. His soldiers followed him blindly from equal affection for and confidence in him. He never saw a mutiny in his camp, which, when we consider the piece-meal construction of his army, is remarkable. " It is," says Polybius, " a singular thing that this Carthaginian general should have been seventeen years at war at the head of an army composed of different nations, countries and languages, that he should have conducted astonishing expeditions, and such that one could scarcely hope for success in them, without one of his soldiers even undertaking to betray him."

Hannibal's organizing ability was unmatched. Out of the most ragged material he could speedily produce a disciplined army. This power was bred of his knowledge of men, his steadfast purpose, his never-ending capacity for labor. He outweighed all men who came under his sway. Dion Cassius says he governed people by their interests; that he saw the real value of things and cared naught for the looks; that he was arrogant, but could bend to those he wished to honor or seduce; that those who were not devoted to him feared him. " He could lower the superb, elevate the humble, inspire here terror, there confidence; all this in a moment whenever he chose."

" Gifted," continues the same author, " with the liveliest power of conception, Hannibal could aim at his end by wise caution; and yet his sudden resolutions required a prompt spirit because they were instantaneous. . . . He profited by the present without making mistakes and strongly dominated the future. Of a consummate prudence in ordinary conjunctions, he divined with sagacity what was the best part to take in unseen cases. Thus he drew himself with fortune and at once from the difficulties of the moment, at the same time that his reason showed him the necessities of the morrow. Appreciating with equal justice what was and was apt to be, he always adapted his speech and actions with ability to the existing circumstances."

His power over men accomplished remarkable results. Reaching cisalpine Gaul, it was but a few weeks before the tribes of the whole province became his sworn allies. They remained faithful to his cause, and bore their heavy burden with cheerful alacrity, though notably the most unstable of peoples. Hannibal possessed a keen insight into human nature, as well as boundless personal magnetism. However little we are told of his appearance, we know that he carried that in his face and manner which lent wonderful force to what he said or did.

Hannibal's victories were as brilliant as any ever won: but

on these does not rest his chief glory. When he wrested
from the arrogant Romans the victories of the Trebia, Lake
Trasimene, Cannæ, he had opposed to him generals ignorant
of the art of war, which art his own genius, the instruction he
had received from his father, and his experience in many
hard-fought campaigns enabled him to use after a fashion beyond what the Romans had ever dreamed of. But Hannibal
instructed these same Romans in this very art of his, and his
later opponents fought him on his own system, and with the
wonderful Roman aptness at learning what he taught them at
so high a cost. These scholars of his, however, strong as they
became, in no sense grew to their master's stature. They
surrounded him on all sides, they cut off his reinforcements
and victuals, they harassed his outposts and foragers, they
embarrassed his marches, — all in the style he had shown
them how to use. For all that, though outnumbering him
many times, not one or many of them could ever prevent his
coming or going at his own good time or pleasure whitherso-
ever he listed, and never was a decisive advantage gained
over him in a pitched battle till the fatal day of Zama. Even
after Hasdrubal's death, his aggressors dared not attack him.
Like a pack of bloodhounds around the lion at bay, none
cared to close with him in a death-struggle. When, depleted
by the toils and losses of half a generation, he embarked for
Carthage, — the most dangerous of proceedings possible for
an army, — though the Roman generals had been ordered by
the senate to attack him, they did not attempt to embarass his
operation. The Carthaginian had laid his plans with too
much skill. Even Scipio, the most self-confident of the
Roman generals, seemed by no means anxious to encounter
him, except at a disadvantage.

Like all great captains, Hannibal not infrequently violated
the maxims of war. It is doubted by some able writers

whether there are such maxims. " It would be difficult to say what these rules are or in what code they are embodied," says a distinguished soldier, the author of one of the best of existing books on military science. The answer is, that these maxims are found in this very author's work, and in the history of every captain whose campaigns or battles he uses as illustrations. " Don't manœuvre so as to be obliged to form front to a flank," might stand for a good maxim of this author's. "It is dangerous to turn an equal adversary with one wing, unless you refuse or protect the other," is a crisp rewording by him of a maxim we owe to Epaminondas. "Never do what the enemy wishes you to do," which is given as one of Napoleon's maxims, but which is as old as Xenophon, probably older, may stand as another. Referring to phrases similar to the one which stands at the head of this paragraph, " Such criticisms have only very vague ideas for their foundation," says this author. Too many soldiers of repute, from Napoleon down, whose ideas are usually credited with being far from vague, have used the phrase " maxims of war " to make it worth while to discard it. It has a settled meaning, like many aphorisms of the Common Law. It or any other axiom or proverb may be vaguely used. But if to employ the phrase " to violate the maxims of war " argues opacity of thought, we must condemn many admirable critics, beginning with Jomini. We may call these rules or maxims by any other name, or hide them in the ablest or clearest exposition, such guiding principles there are and always must be. Napoleon enunciated a few which are not inapt. Frederick did the like. Alexander and Hannibal and Cæsar showed what they were in their wars. The " Commentaries " give us as many excellent maxims as the " Anabasis," and Onosander fairly bristles with maxims. War has been likened to a game of chance; strategy to the thimble-rigger's skill in deceit.

Both similes are apt; but there is more in war than chance; strategy is broader than the ablest gambling. So long as military schools teach, so long as text-books treat of a science of war, so long will there be maxims. A change in nomenclature will neither expunge them from existence, nor destroy their usefulness.

Hannibal, like Alexander, was educated under certain rules, well known to the Greeks. These in later life he observed or disregarded, as the circumstances warranted, when a lesser captain would have been uniformly bound by them. The reason why he defeated the Romans so constantly in the first three years, and thereafter marched so boldly through and through their lines and in and out among their armies, was primarily owing to the fact that they were hide-bound in their principles and theories, and he was not. Whenever they expected him to do or refrain from a certain thing, he was sure to act as they least expected. When Hannibal disregarded what were at that day accepted as the rules of war, he did so with that admirable calculation of the power or weakness of the men and force opposed to him, which of itself is the excuse for the act by him who is able to take advantage of as well as to make circumstances. All great captains are cousins-german in this respect.

Napoleon aptly says : " The principles of Cæsar were the same as those of Alexander and Hannibal : to hold his forces in hand; to be vulnerable on several points only where it is unavoidable; to march rapidly upon the important points; to make use to a great extent of all moral means, such as the reputation of his arms, the fear he inspires, the political measures calculated to preserve the attachment of allies and the submission of conquered provinces."

Great captains use the maxims of war only so far as they fit into their plans and aid their combinations. Success justifies them. The failure of the lesser lights who infringe these maxims, or who are blindly subservient to them, only proves them to be maxims indeed.

To some modern writers, the *dicta* of Frederick and Napoleon, the charts and diagrams of Jomini, are pedantic, antiquated, useless. No doubt there is a material advance in military criticism, which keeps pace with the growing comprehension of the art of war; but is it time to discard what these masters have said within not much more than a century? While "maxims" alone will not equip the general or make a well-read military critic, they are none the less a handy note-book, to remind him of what, with its kaleidoscopic modifications, he has more deeply studied. And, adding materially to our vocabulary, they subserve the purposes of clearness.

A familiar American instance will illustrate the matter. It is an ancient and well-accepted rule or "maxim" not to divide your army on the eve of battle, especially when in the presence of superior forces. Yet Lee did this thing at Chancellorsville, was justified by the circumstances in doing it, and won, considering the great disparity of forces, perhaps the most brilliant victory of the war. Another man, had he decided on such action, or perhaps Lee under other conditions, might have failed. It is a convenient expression to say that Lee "violated a maxim of war," and won when another would have lost. Lee knew Hooker's character, and risked his all on Hooker's keeping quiet during the second of May. At the same time, it was in defiance of a well-known rule of modern, as well as ancient, war, that he acted. If for no other reason than convenience and meaning settled by long usage, the phrase is acceptable until some one produces a more apt one which can be equally well and generally understood. If not satisfactory to English-speaking critics, it is yet in constant use among the Continental nations, who, it must be allowed, have carried war and its nomenclature to a higher degree than has been done in England or America.

When Hannibal reached Italy he began his campaigns with a bold offensive. Rome had been used to no system other than taking the offensive herself. To be driven to the defensive was so much of a novelty to her that it required the lesson of three or four bitter defeats to teach her that there was something greater than even her military audacity in the genius of Hannibal. These defeats, however, did teach Rome the necessary lesson. She went diligently to school to Hannibal, and first under Fabius, but more intelligently under Marcellus, began a system of what is called offensive-defensive, which was her only safety. From the time she did this, and put her ablest men to the front, the scale began to turn in her favor, because her body-politic was sound and her system right, and because the system of Carthage was blind in not sustaining Hannibal, and her political structure feeble from the corner-stone up. While Rome was acting the patriotic part, and with military sense, Carthage was intent on nothing but the holding of Spain as a mere mart for trade.

Apart from the fact that for the future of the world it was essential that Rome should be the winner in the struggle against Punic institutions, it was a predetermined fact that Rome must succeed, owing to her military soundness as against the military rottenness of Carthage. If Rome did not succeed in this war, she would in the next. It is all the more wonderful that Hannibal held himself for fifteen years in the Italian peninsula. It has already been pointed out how, after Cannæ, there were opposed to Carthage at all times twenty to twenty-five legions, of which four to twelve were in Hannibal's immediate front. The Roman armies always outnumbered him, as the allies did Frederick; at any time forces could be concentrated against him which to all appearance could not fail to overwhelm him. And yet, though under favorable conditions the bolder of the Roman generals were able to snatch minor successes from Hannibal, none ever had the hardihood to risk a battle to the bitter end, however great the odds. Nor was it the Roman army which finally drove Hannibal out of Italy. It was the military necessity and the call of Carthage to resist Scipio at her gates which rid Rome of this incubus of half a generation.

What makes Hannibal's military accomplishment so noteworthy is his skill as a strategist. As the Romans learned their trade from him, and what they learned has been perpetuated, Hannibal has been well called the Father of Strategy. Excepting in the case of Alexander, and some few isolated instances, all wars up to the Second Punic War had been decided largely, if not entirely, by battle-tactics. Strategic ability had been comprehended only on a minor scale. Armies had marched towards each other, had fought in parallel order, and the conqueror had imposed terms on his opponent. Any variation from this rule consisted in ambuscades or other stratagems. That war could be waged by avoiding in lieu of seeking battle; that the results of a victory could be earned by attacks upon the enemy's communications, by flank manœuvres, by seizing positions from which safely to threaten him in case he moved, and by other devices of strategy, was not understood. This came into play after Cannæ, when Rome adopted her new policy and Hannibal was compelled by poverty of resources to pursue the same course. For the first time in the history of war, we see two contending generals avoiding each other, occupying impregnable camps on heights, marching about each other's flanks to seize cities or supplies in their rear, harassing each other with small-war, and rarely venturing on a battle which might prove a fatal disaster, — all with a well-conceived and definite purpose of placing the opponent at a disadvantage. During this period, for the first time, the brain on both sides did better work than the sword. That it did so was due to the teaching of Hannibal.

The Romans, after Cannæ, waged war on a systematic plan and with their best men. Fabius was abler in the closet; Marcellus and Nero were stronger at the front. Each year the Romans devised a general scheme with special details, and carried these out with firm but elastic measures. They always covered Rome and the most important provinces; they kept Hannibal in view, and cut down his power of doing harm as fast as circumstances warranted. Each army had a definite and well - considered duty to perform, and was based on a province or city which enabled it to do this duty well. It was no longer a mere march to seek and fight the enemy; there was a far greater degree of intelligence and skill in what the Romans did. Though we cannot admire the hyper-caution, to call it by a mild term, which the Romans exhibited in their unwillingness to fight Hannibal *à outrance*, we must recognize the sound practical methods they pursued in other respects. They imitated Hannibal in his stratagems. They sought to divine his purpose and to conceal their own. They would fight only when everything was in their favor. They endeavored to starve him out rather than destroy him in battle. The finest piece of Roman strategy of the war, the march of Nero to the Metaurus and back, would never have been thought of by a Roman general, but for the study of Hannibal's methods.

The season of operations began as a rule so soon as there was forage growing for the beasts, and ceased with the crops. Compared with Hannibal, Rome had abundance of men, money, material. These were often hard to raise, but they were raised. The twenty-three legions which for several years were put afoot contained between two hundred thousand and two hundred and thirty thousand men, a remarkable number for the population sustaining the army. Nothing better illustrates the elasticity of the Roman military system. The methods pursued in collecting victuals, storing them, protecting the magazines and convoys, and generally in conducting the quartermaster's and commissary departments, were faulty at the start, but grew in excellence as the necessity grew. The same observation applies to the marching of troops with suitable van- and rear-guards and flankers.

The narration of their campaigns has demonstrated how much the Romans profited in their battle-tactics. By this is not meant the mere matter of fighting; this was always admirable; but the several battles of Marcellus, Nero and Scipio show a material advance in breadth of management. This would not have come about had not the intelligence of the Roman commanders been taxed to the utmost to meet Hannibal's remarkable dispositions; had they not been willing to imitate what he did. The fighting traditions of Rome, as well as the method of ranking troops for battle, militated against such mobility on the field as is common to-day. The Romans only knew the battle-order in the three lines of maniples of hastati, principes, triarii, with cavalry on the flanks and skirmish line in front. This was excellently adapted to the requirements of the majority of cases. The successive acts of the battle-drama — the opening by the velites and their withdrawal through the intervals; the advance of the hastati, sustained, when needed, by the principes; the holding back of the triarii and extraordinarii until called on to decide the conflict; and the endeavor of the cavalry to rout its opposing cavalry and surround the enemy's flanks and rear — were apt to be much the same. Variations in these successive acts were called out by coping with or imitating the originality of the Punic methods; and each variation was a gain.

Hannibal, though he copied the legionary system to a certain extent, retained the phalangial formation as a basis; but his dispositions varied as the circumstances varied. No doubt the legion — as it afterwards proved itself — was even then superior to the phalanx, except in the hands of a Hannibal; but for his raw levies, interspersed with his older troops, the phalanx was the steadier formation. That Hannibal should so long have kept his elephants, which Alexander discarded as more dangerous to friend than foe, is curious. We do not hear much about these creatures in most of the battles. They were generally kept well in hand, but were of doubtful value after the Romans became used to them.

Whatever the gain in battle-tactics, it cannot be compared to the growth of what among the Romans was the new science of strategy; for though the soundest strategy was exhibited by Alexander and by one or two other generals previous to this time, the Romans at the beginning of the Second Punic War had no conception of what such a science could teach them. After this struggle they proved themselves to be consummate masters of war.

In pursuit after battles neither party showed the abnormal energy and persistency of Alexander, whose sleuth-hound sticking to the heels of his beaten foe will ever remain the pattern of patterns. A battle won was not always put to use in the way the Macedonian did it. The conditions under which Hannibal fought made it impossible for him to produce the gigantic results which other captains have shown. He alone of all the leaders of history fought against a power and against armies which were unequivocally his superiors in intelligence, breadth, discipline, military training,—in every quality except only his individual genius.

In sieges and fortification the Second Punic War shows limited skill; but the Romans were superior to Hannibal. As with Frederick, siege-work was Hannibal's weak side, and he probably recognized the fact. The sieges of Capua and Syracuse show what Roman engineering methods were. They blockaded rather than besieged. The remarkable defense of Syracuse by Archimedes exhibits in a high grade the art of the time. As in most celebrated sieges the work was that of an individual.

Among the Roman generals, first in time came Fabius, great in his conceptions of the necessities of the moment, great in persistent execution of his conception, but often weak in active war. He was the father of the Roman sys- tem of defensive war, which turned the tide of fortune in favor of the republic. Next came Marcellus, who first put a period to Hannibal's successes and won so great credit in the capture of Syracuse. Marcellus combined the caution of Fabius with boldness equal to any task. It was he who best learned what Hannibal had to teach, and from him his brother generals caught their inspiration. " Hannibal himself confessed that he feared Fabius as a schoolmaster, Marcellus as an adversary ; the former lest he should be hindered from doing mischief ; the latter lest he should himself receive harm," says Plutarch. Then came Nero, with equal bold- ness and intelligence, whose Metaurus campaign is the finest Roman feat of arms in the Second Punic War. Last, and by many considered the greatest, Scipio. But to rank Scipio beside Marcellus and Nero is praise enough. He was more brilliant than either, less solid ; and had not Nero come to his rescue and at the Metaurus rectified his error in allowing Hasdrubal to escape him in Spain, he would scarcely have earned the reputation history has given him.

Excepting Hannibal, the Carthaginians were far inferior in armies and army commanders to the Romans. Even Hasdrubal, who came next to Hannibal, — with a long interval, — was not beyond Marcellus or Nero in ability. He occasionally showed a touch of the family genius, but not often. In junior officers and in rank and file, the Romans were far superior to Hannibal from the third year on.

As the Second Punic War furnishes one of the most interesting of military studies, so the origin and progression of all which makes this interest centre in Hannibal, with but a reflected light upon some of his antagonists. From beginning to end Hannibal is the pivot about which all else revolves. Every manœuvre in these seventeen years is traceable directly to what Hannibal willed or did. He was not only pivot but main-spring of the whole movement; to study him is to study the Second Punic War. The Romans properly called it The War against Hannibal.

The project of crossing the Alps, as we have already seen, was not Hannibal's, but his father's. It was Hannibal, however, who executed in all its details what was with Hamilcar a bare conception, even if a great one. He prepared his base by completing the conquest of Spain, and left in the hands of Hasdrubal and Hanno a territory which he calculated on their holding, and which they ought to have held. He had, with the utmost care, made himself familiar with the route he must follow, its peoples, its climate, its topography, and had won friends along his proposed path. The energy, skill, intelligence and determination with which he carried out his plan would have made him one of the greatest of leaders if he had never advanced beyond the Po.

But this was only a first step in Hannibal's military career. He had only begun to tax his resources. The self-reliant courage which prompted him, after he reached the Po, to undertake the conquest of Italy at the head of twenty thousand foot and six thousand horse, with only the promised support of fickle barbarian allies to base upon, is marvelous. It is the mark which stamps the genius — or the fool. Without the iron will and intellectual grasp to do just such a thing, no great captain ever accomplished his aim. Upon such a rock have been shattered many reputations.

That Hannibal should begin with a distinctly offensive campaign was in accordance with his enterprising nature, his youthful ardor, his active temperament, his plan and his existing resources. Four brilliant victories rewarded this enterprise, which, joined to the bold flank-march through the morasses of the Arnus, and preceded by the march from Spain and the crossing of the Alps, illustrate a page which has not its equal in the history of war.

However brilliant his success, we must remember that Hannibal depended on diplomatic rather than military gain. His political aspirations centred in the hope that some members of the Italian confederacy would forsake Rome. When, after Cannæ, these aspirations began to pale, so also did his military fortunes. Without the resources such seceders could contribute, or constant reinforcements from Carthage, Hannibal could not expect to gain further ground or even hold his own. While in history the first three years lend greater lustre to the name of Hannibal, to one familiar with war the period which follows far outshines it. From now on, the Romans opposed Hannibal with their best men and arms, and, as in those days they could do, declined to fight him while he was still equipped for fighting. His own government forsook him. He became the play of the winds of fortune. Daily growing weak beyond the point where he was a match for the able enemy who was daily growing stronger in numbers and experience, he carried on a series of campaigns the like of which the world has never seen. They are only approached in defensive skill and grit by those of Frederick. The ability so shown is beyond all praise. Unable to compass victory, Hannibal still remained master of the field. Never yielding an inch which he could occupy, he kept his enemy at arms' length by sheer command of intellect. Too weak to attack, he remained too terrible to his adversaries to be attacked. His utmost means sufficed to hold important points or keep the enemy from seizing them; to tire him by unexpected marches or surprise him so as to avoid attack; to strike a series of partial blows when he could not strike a heavy one; to avoid every blow intended for him or prevent its being decisive, — all this in the hope that Carthage would lay aside her quarrels and support him. With what consummate skill was all this done! Before Hannibal grew so weak as to be driven back to Bruttium, his work was full of brilliant resources, prolific in instances of clever management, a pattern of the highest art.

Hannibal has been the subject of close study by every great general; he has been the admiration of the soldiers of every age. Even the great Condé paid him a curiously Gallic compliment. "Messieurs," said he one day to a group of his officers, "si Annibal pouvait revenir, il battrait tous les généraux de Louis XIV.!"

That the campaigns of Hannibal cannot be so readily used to illustrate the operations of modern war as those of Napoleon is due to the difference in armament, the conditions of battle and the system of supplies. As a study in strategy, and in some instances in tactics, nothing exceeds in value the Second Punic War.

It is almost beyond a peradventure certain that had Carthage sustained Hannibal instead of wasting her resources on doubtful ventures in Spain, he would have dictated a peace on the Capitoline Hill.

Carthage was lost long before Zama. When Hannibal was ordered back to Africa, every chance of saving Carthage or of redeeming the fortunes of the war had already been forfeited. Had he won Zama, he must speedily have gone down in another battle fraught with the same results. Carthage had lost the game years before. It was but the genius of Hannibal which prolonged the struggle.

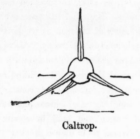

Caltrop.

XLIV.

HANNIBAL AND ALEXANDER.

HANNIBAL, as a young general, showed the same bodily strength, enthusiasm and gallantry as Alexander. Later in life, while never lacking boldness of conception and execution, he was not reckless. His moral bearing was higher; his passions well under control. Each had abundant will-power; each had remarkable intellectual qualities. Hannibal was probably a man of greater culture. Alexander, as king, commanded the fealty of his army, as well as won its love as leader. Hannibal had but his character to rely on; but he held the affection and duty of his men as no general in history has done. Both were keen and longheaded in diplomacy. Alexander always had success to aid him; Hannibal did his greatest diplomatic work under difficulties. The king was a prime favorite of Fortune. She smiled on Hannibal until after Cannæ; thereafter no man ever faced luck so contrary. Each conducted war with method, and a wise weighing of resources and work to be done. Hannibal was crafty, Alexander open and bold, in conducting a campaign; but both kept with equal clearness their object in view. Each was a master of logistics; each was careful in rationing, arming and equipping his army. As tacticians it is hard to choose between them. Arbela and Cannæ stand on the same level. Each inherited an army; each used it with extraordinary ability, and kept it in the best condition. Alexander got larger results from his victories; but this was owing to the conditions under which he wrought. Hannibal could not make his battles decisive; the Roman Republic was like a cyclopean wall. In pursuit and in sieges, the Macedonian was the bolder and greater. Gauged by the work he had to do, the resistance he encountered, and the means at his command, Hannibal outranks any general of history.

IT may not be amiss to draw a comparison between Alexander and Hannibal, or rather to point out certain salient and contrasting features in the life of either. Both were alike in the quality of their gifts and powers, but the factors governing the work of each varied widely.

We know so little about Hannibal's personal appearance that

we cannot assert that he possessed the charm of beauty which
exercised so marked a sway in the person of Alexander. But
in his other bodily qualities, endurance, strength, activity, as
well as in his mental equipment, Hannibal was fully the peer
of the monarch; in moral bearing by far his superior. His
appetites were always curbed; they never overrode him as
they did the conqueror of the Great King. His life was simple, abstemious, full of active employment, never given to
indulgence. So far as character is concerned, — judged exclusively by his enemies, — there is shown to us by history
no more perfect man, among those who have wrought on so
gigantic a scale, than Hannibal.

Alexander was of a different temperament. Kindly by
nature, he was hot-headed where Hannibal was measured.
Both were tireless in activity of mind and body. Both had
noble impulses. Both were guilty of cruelty, according to our
standard; but the laws of war of their era called this forth
rather than their individual character, and Hannibal's hatred
of Rome was inspired by more grievous cruelties inflicted
upon his own country by Rome. Hannibal was never guilty
of an act of ruffianism, as was Alexander in the case of Clitus
or of Batis, or of cruel injustice as in the case of Parmenio.
Neither Hannibal nor Alexander permitted contradiction, but
Hannibal was far beyond Alexander in self-restraint. It is
said that from his face it could not be guessed what was passing within his soul. This self-control was possessed by Hannibal in so marvelous a degree that Livy accuses him of being
naturally perfidious. Hannibal had no confidant or adviser.
Alexander had Hephæstion, Parmenio, Craterus.

Will-power in each was strongly developed. But Hannibal at all times had his will under control. Alexander's fiery
impulses not infrequently ran away with his discretion. The
difference was primarily one of character; partly one of years.

Hannibal's great work was done in the thirties and forties; Alexander's in the twenties.

Hannibal's mind was as broad, delicate and clear as Alexander's, and he was less tainted with what may be called Macedonian roughness. His Greek training made him intellectually the superior of any of his opponents, for Greek learning and culture had not yet made their way among the naturally self-sufficient Romans. This training showed in the intelligent conception and execution of his projects and in the nicety of his discrimination. It was no doubt apparent in his personal bearing; but of this we have no record. The charge of cruelty against Hannibal is more than met by his chivalrous conduct to his fallen enemies, which distinctly proves that he had a gentle trait which was stronger than even his hatred. So much cannot be said of Alexander.

Hannibal's natural courage was great. The execution of his projects was not only bold but obstinate. In his youth he gave his men the same example of individual bravery as the king. His personal conduct is testified to by his bitterest enemies, but he did not, like Alexander, in his bursts of enthusiasm forget that the life of the general is necessary to his army and his country.

Hannibal's influence over his men was perhaps his most remarkable quality. He managed to preserve the strictest discipline without the cruel measures which were often, in ancient times, resorted to as a means of compelling subordination. He won the love and confidence of his men to an extraordinary degree. He was able to hold their affection in adversity as markedly as in prosperity. He could win from his soldiers the greatest efforts with cheerfulness. This control was obtained by the same means Alexander used, — never-ceasing personal care for the comfort and well-being of his army, his friendly bearing, his own example, and perfect justice in awarding punishments and rewards.

Hannibal, like the Macedonian, was gifted with the truest eloquence — not that eloquence of which mere grace is the chief ornament, but the power of saying those things which stir men's souls and shape their deeds. But few of his words are preserved by tradition.

Hannibal and Alexander won their standing among their men under different conditions. Equal in the personality which attracts the soldier, Hannibal kept his influence, not because he was king as well as general, not because he had in his army a leaven of men bound to him by allegiance as well as affection, but among a patchwork crowd of all nationalities, from African to Gallic and Bruttian, each with his own fealty, sentiments, habits and methods. And yet, during the fifteen years he campaigned in Italy, as is testified by all the Roman authors, but especially by Polybius and Nepos, there was never a mutiny in Hannibal's camp; nor (excepting what was shown in the desertion of the twelve hundred Spanish and Numidian horse and of a few isolated individuals) was there even dissension. We remember how much, on more than one occasion, Alexander had to contend against.

Hannibal was ambitious, as was Alexander. But the personal element was less prominent in Hannibal. His intense hatred of Rome was really at the bottom of his ambition to abate the arrogance of Rome. Nothing in Hannibal's life shows that he labored to create a name. Probably Gustavus, Frederick and he were more unselfish patriots than either Alexander, Cæsar or Napoleon. The latter were kings in their ambitions; not so Hannibal.

In his political management Hannibal was, as all soldiers who enact so great a part must be, sagacious and clear-headed, able and successful. No one could have gone so far to unsettle the very foundations of the power of Rome, the fealty of the confederates, unless he had been a very master of diplomacy. The manner in which he held the allegiance of the Gallic peoples, the most like weather-vanes of any of the tribes on Italian soil, was a *chef d'œuvre.* He knew just when to mix force with persuasion, just how far he could rely on what was told him, just how much he could get from any given alliance. He distributed gifts with a liberal hand; he used threats; he remorselessly punished those cities which deserted him. The result was that more than half the area of the peninsula was at one time or other subject to his will, and contributory to his arms. But the structure of the Latin confederacy remained sound, despite Hannibal's successes in war and diplomacy. When we consider how readily the Eastern peoples accepted the yoke of the new and conquering lord, and how strong the hold of Rome on her allies uniformly was throughout her history, we are tempted to believe that what Hannibal accomplished was beyond even Alexander's gigantic performance.

The marvel in the life of Hannibal is the amount he effected with the small means at his command against the vast resources of his opponents, and the length of time he maintained the struggle. Starting from New Carthage with one hundred thousand men, he had but twenty-six thousand left when he reached Italy. This force rarely grew beyond forty to fifty thousand men for field duty, while the Romans had from sixty to ninety thousand men immediately arrayed against him, not to count huge armies elsewhere. Without fleet or home support, relying solely on his own exertions, he was forced to resort to every diplomatic means to keep his allies in heart and induce them to furnish him with troops. This part of his work was difficult beyond anything which Alexander had to contend with.

Alexander always had luck running in his favor. This was a marked feature of his life. Hannibal's luck ran but a

brief career, and after Cannæ no man ever had fortune's
back more persistently turned upon him. Alexander was always victorious, and he and his men had the cheering effect
of success to encourage them; Hannibal was rarely so, in the
last dozen years, and was forced to hold his men up to their
work against constantly blackening prospects. Alexander,
after Arbela, commanded unlimited resources; loss of men
was easily reparable. Hannibal's supplies of men and means
came by the hardest, were in fact generally self-created; he
could not fill the gaps rent in his line by battle. Alexander's campaigns were against a huge but unwieldy and rotten
empire. Hannibal's were against the most compact and able
nation of the world, at its sturdiest period, a nation which
was the best type of a fighting machine. Alexander had no
brilliant general, excepting Memnon, to contend against, and
Memnon was so hampered by the jealousy of his Persian col-
leagues that his opinion could not prevail. Hannibal, during all but the first three years, had strong generals opposed
to him. Alexander's enemies fought on a senseless method;
Hannibal's on the method they learned from him. All this
does not prove Hannibal greater than Alexander. Such
giants override comparison. Alexander was the most brilliant in fortune; Hannibal was undeniably the most stanch
and uncompromising and admirable in misfortune of all captains of whom we have any record.

Hannibal's art was based on the same appreciation of intellectual war as Alexander's. Each, as Napoleon expresses it,
carried on war by a method, that is, by a well-conceived and
intelligent plan, suited to the conditions and to the obstacles
to be overcome. Hannibal always had a well-defined base,
and never forsook it, unless for another which at the time
was a better one for his purposes. He never so manœuvred as
that he could not return to his base to victual or recruit. His

communications were never compromised. This base was successively Spain, cisalpine Gaul, Apulia, Campania, Lucania, Calabria, Bruttium. Hannibal was bold in cutting away from his communications when necessary, but he always kept the road open, and always got back.

Up to Cannæ, Hannibal acted in a single body well concentrated. After Cannæ, he was compelled to divide his forces; but he was wont to concentrate and divide again as circumstances demanded. This, and the selection of the important points on which to concentrate, is a marked feature in his conduct. His movements were generally quick and decided, but prudent, secret and craftily thought out. He not only kept the enemy from a knowledge of what he was about to do, but led him to expect some other thing. His self-reliance and natural secretiveness and craft, as much as his want of material strength, led him naturally to resort to night-marches, surprises, ambushes, stratagems of all kinds. Such victories as the Trebia and Lake Trasimene, such a retreat as that over Mt. Callicula, are distinctly in Hannibal's vein. In this particular he is unlike Alexander, who not only did not as a rule do such things, but is said to have looked upon them as unworthy. But though Alexander declined to "steal a victory" at Arbela, he was more than once, as at the Persian Gates or among the Uxians, driven to stratagem to save himself.

Hannibal took none into his confidence. He knew his own plans and how he proposed to execute them, but he sought no advice. If his schemes failed it was solely for reasons within his own knowledge or circumstances beyond his own control. He had, like Alexander, the peculiar capacity of reading his opponent's character, of guessing his weaknesses, and of acting promptly and energetically on this knowledge.

After Cannæ, Hannibal was obliged to confine his natural

activity within narrower boundaries, was often compelled to periods of long inaction. His habit was to campaign only in summer, but if anything was to be gained no season was too hard, no obstacle too great, no difficulty such as to daunt him. Witness his passage of the Alps and the Arnus marshes. Alexander was more restless, and allowed no season to arrest or delay his movements. This is well shown by the extraordinary campaigns beyond the Parapamisus.

Hannibal's victualing of his men was ably done. He foraged in summer and collected rations in strong camps or towns for the winter season. That he never saw the time when his men lacked bread is a remarkable fact; for he had not Alexander's unlimited resources. His own personal means went to feed his army. This was miserliness to be highly commended, if indeed it be true that Hannibal was a miser.

Of Hannibal's tactical dispositions much has already been said. In logistics he was especially strong. His marches were always carefully made, with proper van-, rear-guard and flankers, at a time when such precautions were unknown. This art he taught the Romans by bitter experience. He suited the order of march of his troops to the existing conditions with great ability. Witness the columns up the Little St. Bernard and through the Arnus marshes. The Macedonian habit was equally ahead of its age, except in such cases as Xenophon.

In battle Hannibal adhered to the phalangial order to which he had been habituated. Alexander maintained his army on the footing Philip had given it. He could make no changes to advantage. Hannibal was not slow to see the superiority of the Roman organization and armament, and in the second year in Italy had already armed some of his troops with Roman weapons. He altered the Greek phalangial disposition to a certain extent, leaning towards the legionary in what he did; but we do not know the details of his changes. They are only referred to in general terms by the ancient authors. The effort was apparently to make the phalanx cover more ground.

As was the habit with Alexander, Hannibal was apt to choose open flat ground for battles, as best suited for his evolutions, but he utilized every kind of accident in the ground for stratagem. Both were able mountain fighters. Hannibal was not unapt to invite attack and meet it halfway. Alexander always attacked. Both personally manœuvred as well as commanded their armies. Their troops fought well in hand and sustained each other admirably. Both got the best work of which their men were capable. Hannibal was singularly apt at making raw levies available. Cavalry was the particular arm of each. Both gave it the best of care and demanded great things of it.

Some historians, by dint of repeating the words supposed to have been uttered by Maharbal, after Cannæ, have convinced themselves that Hannibal did not follow up or get results from his victories. This is an error. Few generals have ever got better results, so far as they could be had. The circumstances under which Alexander fought enabled him to secure enormous remuneration from his victories. This was not possible to Hannibal. But to count his allies after Cannæ shows that he made the best of use of his gain. Alexander pursued the broken enemy with a ferocity and determination never equaled. Hannibal did not allow himself, in the ardor of victory, to be led in pursuit beyond what the circumstances warranted. He was equally cautious after a victory as after a defeat. He had a different enemy in his front.

As a besieger Hannibal was not the equal of Alexander or

of some other generals. This was not his forte. The siege of Saguntum is his only noteworthy success, and this does not compare to the siege of Tyre. In Italy he was not accompanied by siege-material. He felt that sieges did not fall in with his plans. They were costly in time, men and material, and he often got hold of cities more easily by stratagem or by storm. Even at Saguntum, after a long and exhaustive siege, he lost patience and took the place by storm; and as he assaulted it too soon, so the storming operations lasted five days and cost heavily in men.

It is a common thing to compare Hannibal and Scipio. This has already been commented upon. Scipio was a brilliant general, a fine diplomat. He was equipped with some of the best qualities of man and soldier. His character was blameless except that he lacked the sense of subordination. He was a fine tactician. His influence over men was considerable. But he was fortunate in never, till Zama, having an opponent who was his equal, in never meeting a force which in any sense matched his own, taking all qualities into consideration. Except Hasdrubal, Scipio met no great general in Spain or Italy. At Zama it was the Roman army and its excess in cavalry which won; not Scipio. His capacity as a captain should not be underrated, but he can in no wise be placed beside Hannibal. The similes and anecdotes of the Roman historians cannot be accepted for more than they are worth. We must remember the violence of their prejudices, which of necessity warped their judgment. Here is one of Livy's stories.

"Claudius," says Livy, "following the history written in Greek by Acilius, says that Publius Africanus was employed in this embassy, and that it was he who conversed with Hannibal at Ephesus. He even relates one of their conversations in which Scipio asked Hannibal ' whom he thought the greatest captain?' and that he answered, 'Alexander, king of Macedonia; because with a small band he defeated armies whose numbers were beyond reckoning; and because he had overrun the remotest regions, the merely visiting of which was a thing above human aspiration.' Scipio then asked 'to whom he gave the second place?' and he replied, 'To Pyrrhus; for he first taught the method of encamping; and, besides, no one ever showed more exquisite judgment in choosing his ground and disposing his posts; while he also possessed the art of conciliating mankind to himself to such a degree, that the nations of Italy wished him, though a foreign prince, to hold the sovereignty among them, rather than the Roman people, who had so long possessed the dominion of that part of the world.' On his proceeding to ask 'whom he esteemed the third?' Hannibal replied, 'Myself, beyond doubt.' On this Scipio laughed, and added, 'What would you have said if you had conquered me?' 'Then,' replied the other, 'I would have placed Hannibal, not only before Alexander and Pyrrhus, but before all other commanders.' This answer, turned with Punic dexterity, and conveying an unexpected kind of flattery, was highly grateful to Scipio, as it set him apart from the crowd of commanders, as one of incomparable eminence." Whether true or not of Hannibal, this anecdote is characteristic of Scipio.

Hannibal excelled as a tactician. No battle in history is a finer sample of tactics than Cannæ. But he was yet greater in logistics and strategy. No captain ever marched to and fro among so many armies of troops superior to his in numbers and material as fearlessly and skillfully as he. No man ever held his own so long or so ably against such odds. Constantly overmatched by better soldiers led by generals always respectable, often of great ability, he yet defied all their efforts to drive him from Italy for half a generation. Not even Frederick was outweighed as was Hannibal, for though Frederick's army was smaller, it was better than that of any of the allies.

As a soldier, in the countenance he presented to the stoutest of foes and in the constancy he exhibited under the bitterest adversity, Hannibal stands alone and unequaled. As a man, no character in history exhibits a purer life or nobler patriotism.

Cap of Velite.

XLV.

LEGION VERSUS PHALANX. 197–168 B. C.

ROME soon stretched her arms abroad and grasped at foreign conquest. In so doing, legion was again pitted against phalanx. The first conflict was at Cynocephalæ. Here, on ground which was hilly and rough, the legionary proved easily superior to the phalangite with his long sarissa; and the Roman consul, though coming close to defeat, by tactical boldness and prompt action, aided by an able lieutenant, won a handsome victory. In the war against Antiochus, at the battle of Magnesia, the phalanx was sustained on right and left by other troops. In the course of the battle these were driven away, and the legionary cohorts, attacking the phalanx in flank and rear, easily cut it to pieces. The Macedonian phalanx could no longer manœuvre like Philip's and Alexander's. In a third test at Pydna, the Romans were at first driven in; but the pursuit of the phalanx opened gaps in its formation. Rallying his men, Æmilius pushed small groups into these gaps. The legionary with his gladius, when he got at his man, was easily superior to the unwieldy phalangite. The Macedonian formation was broken, and the phalanx annihilated. In all these battles, however, the best phalanx never met the best legion, under equal leaders and conditions. The value of the legion lay more largely in the character of the Roman citizen of that era than in its tactical formation. A hundred years later, when the Roman army consisted of material less good, the quincuncial formation disappeared, and the legion again became a phalanx, as it had originally been. But, for intelligent rank and file, the legion was indisputably better than the phalanx.

ROME was no longer satisfied with her dominion in Italy. She had got a taste of foreign conquest, and the appetite grew with what it fed on. The senate, throughout the Second Punic War, had displayed rare wisdom, and entire ability to manage the affairs of Rome on a larger basis; and the aristocracy had, by its services, not only earned a title to recognition, but had imbibed an ambition which threatened to lead it beyond its purely patriotic impulses. The Romans showed

a marked gain in military boldness and skill. They played
the rôle of conquerors well. The army habit of nightly fortifying the camp, the limited baggage, and the fact that the
men carried ten or fifteen days' rations, made them indepen-
dent and adventurous in their campaigns. Among the Greeks
and in Asia Minor, these advantages gave to the Romans a
strength beyond their numbers. They had Hannibal's instruction to profit by, and did not have Hannibal for an opponent. Their operations exhibited a much higher grade of
skill; and while they resumed the old habit of initiative which
Hannibal had compelled them to lay one side, they used this
in so discreet a manner that the victories they won were apt
to be followed by marked gain, and as a rule to give them
control of the enemy's cities. In fact, sieges became uncommon events, and assault, treachery or ruse were resorted to
for their capture, when the cities did not surrender. The
Romans had recovered all their ancient offensive instincts,
and the feeling of superiority which for half a generation
Hannibal had checked.

In narrating the campaigns of Pyrrhus in Italy, the relative value of legion and phalanx as military formations was
enlarged on. The Roman campaigns in Greece brought the
two methods once more into conflict.

Rome could not forgive Philip for the aid which he had
yielded to Hannibal during the Second Punic War, nor was
it long before the turn of Macedon came for retribution.
The Second Macedonian War lasted from 200 to 197 B. C.
It was terminated by the battle of Cynocephalæ.

Quinctius Flaminius, the Roman consul, and Philip, king
of Macedon, were near Pheræ in Thessaly. Each had moved
his army into close proximity to the other without intimate
knowledge of his enemy's whereabouts,· though there had
been some outpost combats between the two. The Pheræ

territory, being much cut up by trees, hedges and garden-walls, did not afford a suitable battle-ground, and both generals concluded to make for the grain-fields of Scotussa, which lay across a range of hills from Pheræ. Two days' marches were made. On the third, rainy, lowering weather kept the Romans in camp ; the king set out, but, owing to the difficulty in keeping his column from straggling in the fog, soon camped. He took the precaution to send a detachment to occupy the hills known as Cynocephalæ, somewhere on the farther side of which he divined the Roman army to be located.

The consul from his camp likewise sent out a detachment of one thousand light foot and ten turmæ of horse to beat the country and discover the location of the Macedonian army, warning the leaders against ambuscades, particularly dangerous under the curtain of fog, even in an open country, and ordering them to ravage the land by the way. This party happened to ascend the Cynocephalæ hills, and struck the Macedonians posted there by Philip. Each party, somewhat abashed by the sudden encounter, sent back word for succor, but indulged meanwhile in active skirmishing. The Romans were considerably outnumbered, but Flaminius sent up two thousand Ætolian foot and five hundred horse, which restored a fight already failing, and began to crowd back the Macedonians, whose heavy armor and weapons made them poor skirmishers, and gradually to drive them up to the summit of the hill.

Expecting nothing less than a general engagement, Philip had sent out a large part of his troops to forage. The fog had fallen from the summit of the hills so as to allow him to see that his troops had been pushed back, and the messengers from the front were urgent. Philip determined to sustain his advanced body at the risk of a battle. He dispatched

the bulk of his mercenary troops and the Macedonian and
Thessalian cavalry to the support of his hard-pressed men,
and recalled his foragers. The reinforcement was opportune,
and by its aid the tide was turned and the Romans hustled
down nearly to the level plain, where lay their camp. Only
the Ætolian horse, then ranking as the best in Greece, by its
able resistance, kept the Romans from a *sauve qui peut.*

This slight success, the urging of his lieutenants and the
general desire of the army to continue the fight, prevailed
upon Philip, against his better judgment, to order up from
the camp the entire Macedonian army with a view to battle.

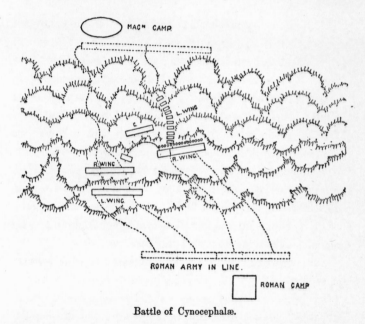

Battle of Cynocephalæ.

The ground was peculiarly unsuited to the manœuvres of a
phalanx. The Cynocephalæ hills are rough and broken with
sharp and ragged slopes. It was only a place for light troops.
The Macedonian phalanx was no longer that of Alexander,

which could fight on any ground. The conditions were much better suited to the legion, for the legionary was a skirmisher by no means to be despised. Flaminius ordered the Roman army into line, lest his men should be discouraged by the loss of even a partial engagement.

The king had a grand phalanx of sixteen thousand hoplites; two thousand peltasts; of allies and mercenaries, each two thousand, and two thousand horse, somewhat over twenty-four thousand men in all. The Roman force was about the same, and the consul had a superiority in cavalry, numerically and in quality.

The Roman detachment had fallen back to the valley not far from their camp, where the men had rallied. The arrival of the consul and reinforcements gave back their vigor to the troops. Flaminius ordered the Roman right to remain in place, and covered it with some elephants, and then advanced the left to sustain the skirmishers who had been driven back. With a stanch onset they once again began to force the Macedonians up the slope. This driving of the enemy uphill demonstrates excellent work on the Roman side. With the ancient weapons, to fight downhill was a distinct advantage. Missiles carried farther, and the men had a better footing, not to count the moral advantage of looking at your opponent literally *de haut en bas*.

Philip, with the right wing of the phalanx and the peltasts, was soonest on the field; the left, under Nicanor, was delayed by the difficulty of the ascent from the Macedonian camp. The king had got his right in line before the Macedonian mercenaries again began to fall back; he speedily rallied the flying men, and placed them on the right of the peltasts and phalanx.

Livy states that Philip ordered the phalangites to lay aside their sarissas, as less serviceable on the rough field than their swords. This would have made the contest, not one between legion and phalanx, but between Macedonians armed with a weapon they were not peculiarly skillful in wielding, and a poor one at that, and Romans armed with their terrible gladius. Polybius does not mention the fact, and the rest of Livy's account disagrees with this statement. But Philip did commit an almost equal blunder. He ployed his sixteen-deep phalanx into files thirty-two men deep, and directed it to take close order on the right, that is, with the men occupying each but one and one half feet space. On the rough ground, the king should have sought to give his line mobility rather than stability; but he transformed it into a body quite unwieldy on any but a plain, and if deprived of the sarissa, its chief weapon for close order, it would be helpless. The sword was the weapon of open order, when used at all.

Polybius states that the king advanced on the Romans with sarissas couched. Flaminius had again to advance uphill. But his men were in good spirits, and raised their battle-cry, on the signal for advance being given by the trumpet, with uncommon good-will, which augured good results for the outcome of the affair. The king had got his line well in hand on his own right, and the favorable ground, the heavy arms of the men, and his own personal exertions enabled him to check, and then to thrust back, the Roman left in marked confusion.

The Macedonian centre, which had already reached the field, did not join in the advance, but stood in place as mere lookers-on. Of what forces it was composed is not stated; probably part of the phalanx. Nicanor, whose men had been much disordered by the bad ascent from the camp, was leading the Macedonian left on the field in decidedly poor order for battle.

Philip's work had been sharp and decisive. The consul's

left wing, though under his own conduct, had been badly broken and was gone beyond rescue. But Flaminius had the eye of a soldier. He saw at a glance that he could best retrieve the battle by prompt action with his right, and he acted with the courage of his convictions. Leaving the left to hold its own as best it might, he immediately joined the right wing, threw it sharply forward, reached the summit of the hill and formed in good order before Nicanor's phalanx emerged upon the open slopes where the battle was engaged. Giving Nicanor no time to deploy, Flaminius struck his head of column a mighty blow. He drove his elephants at the half-formed phalanx, and followed these up with the sword. The result was not a minute doubtful. The Macedonian left, not ready for battle, was at once demoralized by the onset of the Romans and dissolved in confusion before it had fairly begun to form. The Macedonian centre appears to have been carried away at the same time. The Roman right followed in pursuit.

At this moment, a military tribune of the Roman right, whose name is not disclosed to us, seeing that his wing was victorious and that he could no longer be of use at this point, took quickly in hand his small detachment of twenty centuries of the legion and hurried by a circuit over to the rear of the Macedonian right, whose success had advanced it far beyond the general alignment and thus rendered it liable to just this manœuvre. Here he fell lustily upon the rear ranks of the unwieldy thirty-two-deep body of the phalanx. Unable to face about to meet this new assault, the phalanx began to waver. The Romans who fronted this body, encouraged by the diversion, plucked up a new heart and fell to again with reviving courage. It is a pity that the name of the intelligent Roman tribune has been lost. He deserves honorable mention.

The Roman right had won a complete victory; the left was

on the point of doing the same. Philip, startled beyond measure at the new turn of affairs when he had supposed he was winning the fight, galloped to an adjoining eminence to overlook the battle as a whole, and seeing from thence the irretrievable loss of the field, made haste to leave it. His army was wiped out. No less than eight thousand men were killed; five thousand were taken. The Roman loss was but seven hundred killed.

The result of the battle was to obliterate the power of Macedon. But the relative value of legion and phalanx was as little determined as ever. Extrinsic circumstances had decided the battle.

Another instance of legion versus phalanx occurred in the war against Antiochus, king of Syria. Antiochus had got mixed up in Grecian affairs and had landed in Greece to free it from Roman influence; but by injudicious proceedings and for lack of native support had been driven back to Asia Minor. In 190 B. C. the Romans, under the consul Lucius Cornelius Scipio, for the first time crossed the Hellespont and trod the soil of another continent. Lucius had taken with him as legate his brother Publius, victor of Zama. It was he who really directed the campaign. The Romans gave battle to Antiochus at Magnesia, on the Hermus, near the Sipylus mountains. Livy gives a full and clear account of the battle.

The Romans were confident and strong, though fewer in numbers. They "never despised any enemy so much." After a thorough reconnoissance, Scipio advanced his camp to the immediate vicinity of Antiochus, and on the third day battle was offered. Antiochus, relying on numbers, did not decline it. Scipio had two Roman and two allied legions each of fifty-four hundred men. The former were in the centre. The army stood as usual in three lines, hastati, principes and triarii. The left of the line was not far from the river and had but four turmæ of cavalry to protect it. On the right of the Roman army stood Eumenes' foot, and the Achæans, three thousand in number, and on their right the rest of the cavalry of the legions, which, with about eight hundred of Eumenes', made nearly three thousand men. On the extreme flank were

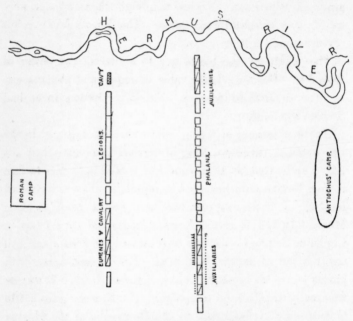

Battle of Magnesia.   First Phase.

one thousand light troops. Scipio's total force was thus nearly thirty thousand men, of excellent material throughout, well disposed and in good heart.

The king's line presented a splendid but motley aspect when compared to the consul's, which exhibited little of the pomp and circumstance of war. In the centre was a grand phalanx of sixteen thousand men, armed with the sarissa and standing thirty-two deep. This gave it too little front and such depth as to make it unwieldy rather than able. This trick of doubling the depth of the phalanx, which seems to have crept into use about this time, was a step backward to the ponderous but useless masses of the Orientals. The phalanx of Antiochus was placed in ten divisions each of fifty men front, and between each two was an interval held by two Indian war elephants of great size and courage, their towers holding each four men, with a large supply of javelins and other missiles. On the right of the phalanx was a body of nine thousand horse, among them the agema with sixteen elephants in reserve. Next the horse were the Argyraspides, or silver shield-bearers, the agema of foot; then twelve hundred Daän horse-bowmen and fifty-five hundred light troops, with four thousand archers and slingers to cover the wing. On the left of the phalanx were alternate bodies of horse and foot, with elephants in reserve, much like and equal in numbers to those on the right. But the cavalry was covered by a number of scythed chariots and war-dromedaries. The king commanded the right, his son the left wing.

The morning was wet and foggy. The king's line was longer than the Roman, and could not well be seen from end to end. The moisture unstrung the archers' bows and made unserviceable the slings and javelin thongs. The Roman soldiers, mostly heavy-armed, did not suffer this inconvenience. The scythed chariots were opposite Eumenes, a general who had learned how to deal with this arm. Before the battle opened, he sent out the archers, darters and slingers to skirmish in their front, and by shouts and wounds to frighten the chariot-horses and the dromedaries. This they readily accomplished, and not only drove the chariots away from their post, but these, wheeling, some to the rear, others to right and left, so unsteadied the auxiliaries of the enemy's left wing that they mostly took to flight before even coming into action. The Roman cavalry was then sharply pushed

forward, and, owing to the confusion made by the flying
chariots, dromedaries, elephants and auxiliaries, it made
short work of the mailed horse which protected the flank of
the phalanx. With scarcely any loss to the Romans, Antiochus' whole left wing had been dispersed.

The legions now advanced on the front and swung round
on the flank of the phalanx, while the horse rode round to its
rear. The elephants gave them no trouble, for they had long

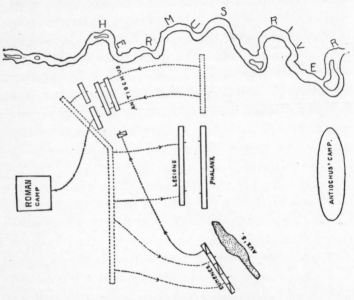

Battle of Magnesia.   Second Phase.

ago learned how to avoid the danger of these monsters by
wounding them in the sides and cutting their hamstrings.
The flight of the left wing had already unstrung the phalanx, which needed to have its flanks protected, and the sudden onset of the Romans had allowed them to use their
sarissas to but poor advantage. This was not the quick manœuvring phalanx of Philip and Alexander, which could face

at command to any front. The battle seemed already lost, when the Romans were themselves unsettled by bad fortune on the left.

Antiochus, who commanded the right of his army, had observed that the Roman left, which was close to the river but still not leaning on it, had no reserve and little cavalry. About the time Eumenes had succeeded in disorganizing the enemy's left, the king, heading a choice body of auxiliaries and mailed horsemen, drove in the four turmæ of Roman horse, and, attacking the legion in flank, forced back a considerable section of it towards the camp. The military tribune, M. Æmilius, who had command of the camp, was fortunately equal to the occasion. Issuing from the gates with his entire force of extraordinarii, two thousand strong, by dint of entreaties and threats, and by cutting down some of the runaways in their flight, he brought them to a standstill, faced them about, and sustaining them with his own fresh forces, checked the king's further advance. A force of two hundred horse galloped over from the victorious right to aid in rallying the left, and took Antiochus in flank, and a part of the legion wheeled on the king's left. He was forced back and the line reëstablished.

Meanwhile the phalanx, taken fully in flank and rear by the Roman right, and pressed stoutly in front as well, began to waver. No sooner had Antiochus been driven back from his promised victory on the Roman left, than his centre failed him. The Romans were winners at all points, and the king's army was cut to pieces. Some fifty thousand foot and three thousand horse perished, according to Livy, while but three hundred foot and twenty-four horse were killed in the Roman army, and twenty-five of Eumenes' men. The Romans had won a noble victory. The legion had shown itself markedly superior to Antiochus' phalanx.

The battle of Pydna (168 B. C.), in the Third Macedonian War, is so illy described by both Livy and Plutarch, that, Polybius' books containing the account of the battle having been lost, we know next to nothing of its tactical manœuvres. Æmilius Paulus, son of the Roman hero of Cannæ, commanded the Romans, who were about twenty - six thousand strong, to forty thousand men under Perseus, king of Macedon. The Macedonians apparently surprised the Romans, or at least the action began before Æmilius had his legions in line. The result was that the Romans were, at the opening of the battle, sharply thrust back, and, to judge from the accounts, in much confusion, to the very walls of their camp. The Roman legionaries had in vain sought to break the bristling array of sarissas, to push through them with their bucklers, to cut the lances with their swords, or, indeed, to tear them asunder with their hands. Even the hurling of a Roman standard into the midst of the phalanx could not bring the legionaries to break the Macedonian formation. They finally fled from before it. It seemed as if the tables were to be turned on the legion.

But the overardent pursuit by the phalanx on ground which was somewhat uneven, and the fact that they assumed the victory won, gradually opened a few gaps in the body. Rallying his scattered legionaries as best he could, and disposing his cohorts in small bands under stout leaders, Æmilius ordered these parties to break through into these gaps and fall on the phalangites with the gladius. This method of attack succeeded admirably. So soon as the Roman could get at his man he was far his superior. The gladius was a fearful weapon in expert hands, and the Roman scutum a full defense against the small weak sword of the Macedonians, whose shield, moreover, was far less good than the legionary's. Encumbered with the long and awkward sarissa, the phalangite was at the legionary's mercy.

Recovering themselves, and encouraged by the first show of success, the Romans, used to open-order fighting, quickly rallied to a man, fell upon the dissolving phalanx in front, flank and rear, and cut it to pieces. Plutarch says the battle lasted but an hour. This scarcely agrees with what is told about the course of the action. Both Polybius and Livy give the Macedonian loss as twenty-five thousand men killed, twelve thousand captured; the Roman as only one hundred, illy as the figures accord. Either this or the initial defeat of the Romans would appear to be an error, — unless, indeed, the Romans ran before they fairly got into action.

The legion had clearly won the superiority. No doubt its mobility, its reliance on the individuality of each man, the subordination of the soldier, and its suitability to the character of the Roman people, made the formation better than any phalanx of that day. But in reading the struggle of the two methods, it becomes plain that the best phalanx never met the best legion under equal circumstances and leadership. Pyrrhus was the only great general who ever led the phalanx against the Romans. Though his phalanx was not of good material, being largely Tarentines unused to the long spear, he nevertheless came close to success in a merely military sense. It was Roman discipline and character which won, rather than the Roman formation, though the legion had unquestionably a higher tactical value. The legion succeeded as the Romans succeeded. In the conflict between legion and phalanx the latter was never organized, drilled, manœuvred or led as it was under Philip or Alexander.

We shall see, in the succeeding century, when the material of the legion degenerated from the citizen whose service was a privilege rather than a burden, to the proletariat who enlisted as a means of a better livelihood, and the individuality of the soldier could no longer be depended on, that the mobility of the legion disappeared. The men were no more to be relied upon unless held close in hand by the general commanding, and unless they were massed for mutual support. The intervals between maniples became dangerous; they were gradually decreased and finally given up; the legion reverted to a body resembling the old Dorian phalanx from which it had sprung. The period of its elastic structure was coincident with the service privilege of the Roman citizen. So long as the terms citizen and soldier were equivalents, so long lasted the best period of the legion. The great victories it later won, the splendid work of which it was capable, were no longer due to the rank and file, to the Roman burgess, that perfect type of the citizen-soldier, but distinctly to the skill of the leader, to the talent of such men as Marius, Sulla, Pompey, to the genius of Cæsar.

Casting Javelin with a Twist.

APPENDIX A.

CASUALTIES IN SOME ANCIENT BATTLES.

Battle of	Date. B. C.	Number Engaged.	Nationality.	Number Killed.	Percentage.	Usual %.†	Loss of Enemy.	Remarks.
Marathon.	490	11,000	Greeks.	192	1¾	5	6,400	*Hoplites, who alone fought.
Platæa.	479	38,700*	"	1,360	3½	4	257,000	
Chæronea.	338	50,000	"	2,000	4	4	6,000	
Thebes.	335	33,000	Macedonians.	500	1¾	4	19,000*	{*Mostly massacre of Greek Phalanx —1,000 Persian horsemen fell.
Granicus.	334	3,000	" Cavalry.	85	3	2		
Issus.	333	30,000	Macedonians.	450	1½	4½	100,000*	*The usual massacre.
Arbela.	331	47,000	"	500	1	4	40,000	{*The usual massacre. Diodorus says 90,-000, Arrian says 300,000.
Megalopolis.	330	40,000	Spartans.	3,500	8¾	4½		
"	"	20,000	Macedonians.	5,300	26½	5		
Jaxartes.	329	6,000	"	160	2½	7	1,000	
Hydaspes.	326	14,000	"	930	6¾	5	12,000*	*Arrian says 23,000.
Heraclea.	280	25,000	Epirots.	4,000*	16	5		*Dionysius says 13,000 loss.
"	"	20,000	Romans.	7,000*	35	5		* " " 15,000 "
Asculum.	279	70,000	Greeks and Italians.	3,550*	5	4		* " " " "
"	"	70,000	Romans and Ital'ns.	6,000*	8½	4		* " " " "
At Rhone.	218	500	Numidian Cavalry.	200	40	2		
"	"	300	Roman Cavalry.	140	46½	2		
Geronium.	217	50,000	Carthaginians.	6,000	12	4		
"	"	50,000	Romans.	5,000	10	4		
Cannæ.	216	42,000	Carth. and Gauls.	6,000	14¼	4½	40,000*	*Some authors say 70,000.
" (Camp).	"	11,000	Romans.	2,000	18	5		
Nola, 2d.	215	20,000	"	1,000	5	5	5,000	
Beneventum.	214	20,000	"	2,000	10	5	15,000	
Nola, 3d.	214	20,000	"	400	2	5	2,000	
Asculum, 2d.	214	20,000	"	2,700	13½	5		
" 2d day.	"	17,000	"	3,000	17¼	5		
Grumentum.		40,000	"	500	1¼	4½	8,000	
Metaurus.	204	40,000	"	8,000	20	4½	8,000	
Crotona.	204	20,000	"	1,200	6	4½	35,000	
Mago's Battle.	203	20,000	Carthaginians.	5,000	25	5		
"	"	40,000	Romans.	2,300	5¾	4½		
Zama.	202	43,000	Romans.	2,000*	4½	4½	20,000	*Clearly understated.

† For armies of this size in a very stubbornly contested battle. The discrepancies are no greater than can be found in histories of our own civil war. The figures are given without comment.

From the difficulty of determining the wounded, only the killed are given in the above table. A discussion on losses in ancient battles will be appended to the table in the volume on Cæsar.

APPENDIX B.

SOME ROMAN MARCHES.

THE Romans marched about 15 miles a day. The Consul Sempronius, in 218 B. C., marched his army of 20,000 men from Lilybæum to Ariminum, about 650 miles, in 40 days, or 16 miles a day. The only march worth adding to the table in Appendix A, of Alexander, is that of the Consul Nero, who, in 207 B. C., with 7,000 men, marched from the vicinity of Canusium to the Sena, 250 miles, in seven days, and back again in six, meanwhile, with the Consul Livius, winning the victory of the Metaurus. Wagons were furnished for the tired infantrymen by the country people along the route. This was 38½ miles a day, counting the battle-day as the full equivalent of a march. It is one of the most noteworthy marches in history. Mention of rapid marches is not often made by Polybius or Livy.

INDEX.

LIST OF DATES.

LIST OF DATES.